American Literature Readings in the 21st Century

Series Editor: Linda Wagner-Martin

American Literature Readings in the 21st Century publishes works by contemporary critics that help shape critical opinion regarding literature of the nineteenth and twentieth century in the United States.

Published by Palgrave Macmillan:

Freak Shows in Modern American Imagination: Constructing the Damaged Body from Willa Cather to Truman Capote
By Thomas Fahy

Arab American Literary Fictions, Cultures, and Politics
By Steven Salaita

Women & Race in Contemporary U.S. Writing: From Faulkner to Morrison
By Kelly Lynch Reames

American Political Poetry in the 21st Century
By Michael Dowdy

Science and Technology in the Age of Hawthorne, Melville, Twain, and James: Thinking and Writing Electricity
By Sam Halliday

F. Scott Fitzgerald's Racial Angles and the Business of Literary Greatness
By Michael Nowlin

Sex, Race, and Family in Contemporary American Short Stories
By Melissa Bostrom

Democracy in Contemporary U.S. Women's Poetry
By Nicky Marsh

James Merrill and W.H. Auden: Homosexuality and Poetic Influence
By Piotr K. Gwiazda

Contemporary U.S. Latino/a Literary Criticism
Edited by Lyn Di Iorio Sandín and Richard Perez

The Hero in Contemporary American Fiction: The Works of Saul Bellow and Don DeLillo
By Stephanie S. Halldorson

Race and Identity in Hemingway's Fiction
By Amy L. Strong

Edith Wharton and the Conversations of Literary Modernism
By Jennifer Haytock

The Anti-Hero in the American Novel: From Joseph Heller to Kurt Vonnegut
By David Simmons

Indians, Environment, and Identity on the Borders of American Literature: From Faulkner and Morrison to Walker and Silko
By Lindsey Claire Smith

The American Landscape in the Poetry of Frost, Bishop, and Ashbery: The House Abandoned
By Marit J. MacArthur

The American Landscape in the Poetry of Frost, Bishop, and Ashbery

The House Abandoned

Marit J. MacArthur

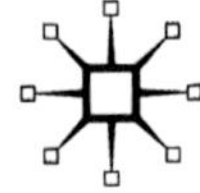

THE AMERICAN LANDSCAPE IN THE POETRY OF FROST, BISHOP, AND ASHBERY

First published in 2008 by
PALGRAVE MACMILLAN®
in the US—a division of St. Martin's Press LLC,
175 Fifth Avenue, New York, NY 10010.

Where this book is distributed in the UK, Europe and the rest of the world, this is by Palgrave Macmillan, a division of Macmillan Publishers Limited, registered in England, company number 785998, of Houndmills, Basingstoke, Hampshire RG21 6XS.

Palgrave Macmillan is the global academic imprint of the above companies and has companies and representatives throughout the world.

Palgrave® and Macmillan® are registered trademarks in the United States, the United Kingdom, Europe and other countries.

ISBN-13: 978–0–230–60322–6
ISBN-10: 0–230–60322–X

Library of Congress Cataloging-in-Publication Data

MacArthur, Marit J.
The American landscape in the poetry of Frost, Bishop, and Ashbery : the house abandoned / Marit J. MacArthur.
p. cm.—(American literature readings in the 21st century)
Includes bibliographical references (p.).
ISBN 0–230–60322–X (alk. paper)
1. American poetry—20th century—History and criticism. 2. Landscape in literature. 3. Abandoned houses in literature. 4. Rural conditions in literature. 5. Country life in literature. 6. Nostalgia in literature. 7. Frost, Robert, 1874–1963—Criticism and interpretation. 8. Bishop, Elizabeth, 1911–1979—Criticism and interpretation. 9. Ashbery, John, 1927—Criticism and interpretation. I. Title.

PS310.L3M33 2008
811′.540936—dc22 2007047161

A catalogue record of the book is available from the British Library.

Design by Newgen Imaging Systems (P) Ltd., Chennai, India.

First edition: August 2008

10 9 8 7 6 5 4 3 2 1

Transferred to Digital Printing in 2013

For my mother, Marit Sheldon Taylor

Without your love, resilience, and wisdom,
I would never have learned to flourish far from home.

Contents

Abbreviations

AW	John Ashbery, *A Wave*
AWK	John Ashbery, *As We Know*
ATSWS	John Ashbery, *And the Stars Were Shining*
CPPP	Robert Frost, *The Collected Poems, Prose & Plays*
CP	Elizabeth Bishop, *The Complete Poems: 1927–1979*
CPr	Elizabeth Bishop, *The Complete Prose*
CW	John Ashbery, *Chinese Whispers*
CYHB	John Ashbery, *Can You Hear, Bird*
EAP	Elizabeth Bishop, *Edgar Allan Poe & the Juke-Box. Uncollected Poems, Drafts and Fragments*
FC	John Ashbery, *Flow Chart*
HD	John Ashbery, *Houseboat Days*
HL	John Ashbery, *Hotel Lautréamont*
LRFLU	*The Letters of Robert Frost to Louis Untermeyer*
MSO	John Ashbery, *The Mooring of Starting Out*
NBRF	*The Notebooks of Robert Frost*
OA	*One Art. Letters. Elizabeth Bishop*
OT	John Ashbery, *Other Traditions*
SL	*Selected Letters of Robert Frost*
SPCM	*Self-Portrait in a Convex Mirror*
TP	John Ashbery, *Three Poems*
WSIW	John Ashbery, *Where Shall I Wander*
YNH	*Your Name Here*

Introduction

One might enumerate the items of high civilization, as it exists in other countries, which are absent from the texture of American life.... No country gentlemen, no palaces, no castles, nor manors, nor old country-houses, nor parsonages, nor thatched cottages, nor ivied ruins....

the effect...upon an English or French imagination, would probably, as a general thing, be appalling.... The American knows that a good deal remains; what it is that remains—that is his secret, his joke, as one may say.

—Henry James, *Nathaniel Hawthorne* (1879)

One sees in an ironic light, the flat matter-of-fact light of the American landscape, James's remark that America "has no ruins." America is full of ruins, ruins of hopes.

—Randall Jarrell, "An Introduction to the *Selected Poems of William Carlos Williams*" (1949)

In a land which is fully settled, most men must accept their local environment or try to change it by political means; only the exceptionally gifted or adventurous can leave to seek his fortune elsewhere. In America, on the other hand, to move on and make a fresh start somewhere else is still the normal reaction to dissatisfaction or failure....

Pluralist and experimental: in place of verfallen Schloesser *America has ghost towns and the relics of New Jerusalems which failed.*

—W.H. Auden, "American Poetry" (1960)[1]

The House Abandoned

In the view from my bedroom window, in the house where I grew up, an abandoned farmhouse stood in a nearby field, in the foreground of the foothills and the Front Range of the Rocky Mountains. My childhood in Lafayette, Colorado, east of Boulder and north of Denver, was more suburban than rural, but our house, joined in a row of others with small back patios and narrow unfenced front yards, skirted the countryside. Beyond the last row of houses, there was Coal Creek, bordered by cottonwoods, and open fields lay to the south, west, and east. Not far from the abandoned farmhouse, a family still lived on a functioning sheep ranch. (Now the ranch is gone, and new subdivisions and shopping centers have erased many of the open fields.) As a child in the 1980s, I often explored this rural landscape, and at the other end of the continent, I spent several weeks every summer on a horse farm in Pattersonville, New York, which my grandfather, a former business executive, had bought when he retired in 1974. On his land too I discovered an abandoned house—once owned by a Polish-American family by the name of Surin—pictured on the cover of this book.

My father died in 1988, my mother sold the house in Lafayette in 1993, and since then, like the statistically average American, I have moved often, living in Illinois, England, Colorado again, California, Poland, and California again. As it turned out, I finished the manuscript for this book while I was a visiting scholar at the University of Łódź, living in a Communist-era block apartment building, located in the neighborhood of the former Jewish ghetto. Aside from the repetition of the phrase, "LITZMANNSTADT GETTO 1940–44," which is stamped in white capitals at intervals along the sidewalks and along the route to the former ghetto quarter from the city center, there is little visible memorialization in the cityscape. These fading letters are left over from the city's ceremonies of 2004, marking the sixtieth anniversary of the liquidation of the ghetto. Small brown signs mark the buildings associated with the ghetto, numbered on a pamphlet for a self-guided tour, available from the tourist office. Since Łódź escaped the bombings that destroyed other Polish cities, many of these buildings still stand, some empty and dilapidated, many in disrepair.

Compared to the total displacement and systematic murder of Poland's Jewish citizenry by the Nazis, the subject of my study here—the poetic evocation of American experiences of displacement, loss and abandonment of houses and landscapes, and complicated nostalgia for these in the twentieth century—may seem inconsequential or myopic. Discussing my research inside and outside the United States, however, I have found that many people share an intuitive, personal sense of the pathos of the abandoned house in our time, and share stories about it from many different cultures and in various art forms. For example, in his 1962 collection *In a Green Night*, Nobel laureate

Derek Walcott wrote a remarkable meditation on an abandoned colonial plantation house, "Ruins of a Great House." In the early 1990s, the Columbian artist Doris Salcedo created a work called "La Casa Viuda" ("The Widowed House"), which memorializes houses left behind by the victims of political violence in her country, and echoes global experiences of displacement, including the Holocaust. In 1993 in London, the artist Rachel Whiteread created "House," a whole interior cast of a London row house marked for demolition. The film scholar Hamid Naficy, an Iranian who has lived in the United States since the 1970s, has written poignantly about the image of the lost house in the work of the Russian director Andrei Tarkovsky—particularly in the 1983 film *Nostalgia*—in *An Accented Cinema: Exilic and Diasporic Cinema* (2001). Evidently the abandoned house is a salient scene in the twentieth and twenty-first centuries all over the world, because of the widespread effects of colonialism, war, postwar and postcolonial restructuring of states, exile, and massive population shifts, still underway, from rural to urban areas.[2]

Experiences of displacement have become routine. Many would agree with Martin Heidegger that in modern life, it has become fundamentally difficult to dwell, which he defines as "to remain, to stay in a place." Insisting that "the real plight of dwelling is indeed older than the world wars with their destruction, older also than the increase of the earth's population and the condition of industrial workers," Heidegger also wonders pointedly, "what is the state of dwelling in our precarious age?" (Heidegger 146, 161). Robert Pogue Harrison argues that, for Heidegger, "modernity and homelessness are at some level necessary correlates" (Harrison 37). For Giorgo Agamben, too, control of dwelling and displacement define modernity: "[T]he politicization of bare life as such—constitutes the decisive event of modernity" (4). He sees the ultimate realization of biopolitics, or the political control of "bare life," as the rigid organization of human life everywhere in the mode of a concentration camp, breaking traditional ties to particular places and homes, preventing the formation of new ties, and creating large numbers of refugees (131). For a number of European thinkers deeply influenced by the Holocaust, "Dwelling, in the proper sense, is now impossible." Theodor Adorno makes this assertion forcefully in "Refuge for the Homeless," a section from *Minima Moralia: Reflections from Damaged Life* written in Los Angeles in 1944, during his exile from Nazi Germany:

> The traditional residences we grew up in have grown intolerable: each trait of comfort in them is paid for with a betrayal of knowledge, each

> vestige of shelter with the musty compact of family interests. The functional modern habitations designed from a *tabula rasa* are living-cases manufactured by experts for philistines, or factory sites that have strayed into the consumption sphere, devoid of all relation to the occupant: in them even the nostalgia for independent existence, defunct in any case, is sent packing.... Anyone seeking refuge in a genuine, but purchased, period-style house, embalms himself alive. The attempt to evade responsibility for one's residence by moving into a hotel or furnished rooms, makes the enforced conditions of emigration a wisely-chosen norm. The hardest hit, as everywhere, are those who have no choice. They live, if not in slums, in bungalows that by tomorrow may be leaf-huts, trailers, cars, camps, or the open air. *The house is past* [my italics]. The bombings of European cities, as well as the labour and concentration camps, merely proceed as executors, with what the immanent development of technology had long decided was to be the fate of houses. These are now good only to be thrown away like old food cans. The possibility of residence is annihilated by that of socialist society, which, once missed, saps the foundation of bourgeois life.... "It is even part of my good fortune not to be a house-owner," Nietzsche already wrote in the *Gay Science*. Today we should have to add: it is part of morality not to be at home in one's home. (38–39)

Inside a Communist block apartment on the site of the Łódź ghetto, this argument is particularly compelling, and in the aftermath of WWII, Marxist theorists were not alone in affirming, with reluctant conviction, that "the house is past." But for many Europeans eager to buy "period-style house[s]," and for middle- and upper-class Americans especially—some of the most autonomous, mobile, and unsettled people in the world—the question of dwelling now seems rather different. For Americans, the house may well signify the past, yet "the nostalgia for independent existence," for "traditional residences," is undergoing a long revival in a global era of displacement, the twentieth and early twenty-first centuries. Longing for home, of course, is the original sense of "nostalgia." Modern and contemporary Americans still ascribe considerable pathos to traditional rural dwellings and the ruins of them, not least, perhaps, because many of the vernacular ruins in the U.S.—abandoned houses—often were not the result of the destruction of war, but were more freely created by patterns of restless internal migration, in response to economic pressures and opportunities. Perhaps, also, Americans have often successfully resisted "the musty compact of family interests," embodied in family homes owned for generations, so that they are especially prone to idealize traditional dwelling. Recent studies of domestic tourism confirm the obvious: among the affluent, owning a second, frequently rural home is seen as a way to "'divorce' from the urban environment[,]" to live a "more 'authentic' and . . . 'real' life[,]" and to sustain "familial connections" (*Tourism, Mobility and Second Homes* 12–13).

Before Americans became nostalgic for settled rural life, however, they first had to reject it. There are unique reasons for the ubiquity of the abandoned house in the American rural landscape, and for its presence as a central image in American poetry of the twentieth century. Henry James, in the essay quoted at the outset, famously lamented the lack of "ivied ruins" in America. (He made this comment, of course, in marveling at Nathaniel Hawthorne's imagination, which found rich material—and decaying ancestral houses—in the relatively brief history of European-American civilization.) James's complaint about the American landscape may have been fairly accurate once, though only if we accept the oversight of Native American ruins, such as the cliff dwellings of southwestern Colorado. Yet in the twentieth and twenty-first centuries, the United States obviously does have its ruins. Some of them are no more than cellar holes, which Henry David Thoreau described as early as 1854 in *Walden*, and which Robert Frost evoked in his great elegy for the abandoned New England farmhouse, "Directive," in 1946. Often, our vernacular ruins are not made of stone, like the European "ivied ruin," but of wood, the "universal structural material" of North American buildings, especially in New England, in the early history of the United States and Canada (Kniffen and Glassie 40).

In his essay "American Poetry," W.H. Auden, with the insight of an immigrant, accounts for the different ruins that characterize Europe and America. In the densely populated and "fully settled" Europe, continuous societies have dwelt in and cultivated the same landscape for centuries, if not millennia. Many European ruins have been consciously preserved, restored, or torn down and built over, partly for lack of space. But in a much larger and less densely settled landscape, rich with natural resources, Americans have had the comparative freedom to move often, to begin new lives and found new settlements, and thus have left the "ghost towns" of failed hopes behind them, precisely because the land was not at a premium; for long periods, such landscapes remain in their abandoned state. The ubiquitous presence of abandoned buildings in the national landscape, Auden argues, is evidence that, in the United States, "mov[ing] on [to] make a fresh start somewhere else is still the normal reaction to dissatisfaction or failure." Studies of the U.S. Census corroborate Auden's observations about internal migration, revealing especially "[h]igh rates of geographic mobility.... In the twentieth century, Americans were twice as likely to relocate during their lives as the British or Japanese" and, in the eighteenth and nineteenth centuries, "The possibility of migration to cheaper western lands may have also overturned long-standing family support patterns" (Carter et al. 489).

Auden centers his discussion of modern American poetry on the work of Frost, who, he notes, particularly favors "the image of the abandoned house" (360). Indeed, abandoned houses are more common in the American landscape than the ghost towns Auden mentions. Americans have often abandoned houses, migrating rapidly from east to west, and from the country to the city, always claiming more land for lateral expansion, following what we may call, after Frederick Jackson Turner, the frontier mentality. In *Civilization and Its Discontents*, Freud famously used the city of Rome, with its historical layers of the ruins of successive civilizations beneath the modern city, as a metaphor for the psyche. We can infer something about the American psyche in the fact that signs of our abandonment of rural life are still fresh, compared to the landscape of Europe.

As the Industrial Revolution began in England, the transition from rural to urban life also began earliest there, not to mention the displacement of rural populations under a hundred years of Enclosure Acts, beginning around 1750. In the United States, on the other hand, the massive shift of rural populations to urban areas did not occur until well into the twentieth century. In the U.S. Census of 1880 (six years after the birth of Frost), 71.8 percent of Americans still lived in rural areas. It was not until 1920 that the majority of Americans living in urban areas overtook those living in rural areas (51.2 to 48.8 percent), and as of 1990, 24.8 percent of Americans were still living in rural areas (U.S. Census). In migrating westward and to cities, Americans left houses behind all over the country—Eastern farmhouses, Midwestern family farms, sharecropper shacks and plantation mansions in the South, frontier homesteads in the Midwest and the West. One infamous episode of large-scale abandonment of rural dwellings—due in part to environmentally disastrous land use policy and the growth of corporate agriculture—occurred during the Dust Bowl and the Great Depression of the 1930s, as documented by a number of photographs of abandoned farmhouses from this era in Richard and Maisie Conrat's history of the *American Farm* (1977).[3] The Conrats intended to show "the American farm in all its diverse aspects," concluding with "the human tragedy embodied in the image of a deserted farmhouse" (6). They include images of abandoned houses in Alabama, Kansas, Texas, Oklahoma, and Montana, ending with a photograph entitled, "Abandoned farmhouse. Nebraska, 1938."

It is in the twentieth century that a complicated nostalgia for America's vernacular ruin—the abandoned house—takes hold in poetry. Belated appreciation of these ruins may correspond to the later Romantic appreciation of wilderness in America as compared with Europe, as historian Roderick Frazier Nash argues in his landmark study, *Wilderness and the American Mind* (1982). Until early colonists had mastered and cultivated the American wilderness—frequently destroying it in the process—it was often seen, in Nash's words, as an "adversary" rather than an "asset." By contrast, the experience of confronting wilderness was remote in European culture, which developed the Romantic conception of sublime wilderness, and projected it upon the American landscape, before Americans were prepared to do so. "Living on the edge of what they took to be a vast wilderness, [the early Americans] re-experienced the insecurities of the first farmers and town builders." Simply put, the American "wilderness had no counterpart in the Old World" because Europeans had long directed their energies "at conquering wildness in nature and eliminating it in human nature," and then became nostalgic for it, as exemplified by the Romantic movement, which in turn sparked the environmental movement (Nash xii–xiii).

Probably the most famous abandoned house in British poetry is William Wordsworth's "The Ruined Cottage," a narrative within the long poem "The Excursion" (1814), which honors a lonely widow's enduring attachment to her cottage. After Thomas Hardy and William Butler Yeats, few major modern or contemporary poets from the United Kingdom or Ireland have meditated on abandoned or ruined houses in their work. Yet in twentieth-century America, the widespread phenomenon of abandoned houses and buildings has drawn the attention of major modern and contemporary poets. In 1949, Randall Jarrell countered James's comment, pointing out, in an essay on William Carlos Williams, that "America is full of ruins, ruins of hopes." We also find meditations on the scene of the abandoned house in Frost, Wallace Stevens, Elizabeth Bishop, Allen Ginsberg, W.S. Merwin, and John Ashbery, among other poets, and in the work of visual artists as well, notably Edward Hopper.

In this study, I consider poems about abandoned houses and rural landscapes in the work of just three distinctive poets—Frost, Bishop, and Ashbery—for a number of reasons. These three poets display affinities with Romanticism generally and, to a remarkable degree, with Wordsworth in particular. Unexplored lineages of influence and nostalgic affinities also run from Frost through Bishop to Ashbery. Further, the scene of the abandoned or neglected house is especially significant in these poets' lives and work. My study is firmly grounded in their biographies, which in some ways typify the unsettled patterns of American life. As we continue to move away from the decontextualized New Critical and deconstructionist approaches to poetry, it seems to me that biography is the beginning of cultural history, and in my analysis of the poetry of Frost, Bishop, and Ashbery, I also provide some context for their imaginative evocations of abandoned houses within relevant cultural trends, including patterns of rural desettlement, the problem of homelessness during the Great Depression, global fears of and the actual destruction and abandonment of dwellings during the buildup to WWII and the war itself, the rise of rural tourism, and contemporary Americans' enthusiasm for second homes and historical restoration. Ultimately, this book explores the ways that the abandoned house is reimagined, throughout the poetic oeuvre of each poet, as a trope of personal and cultural loss and consolation, which resonates with peculiarly American experiences, even as their poems speak to larger global audiences grimly familiar with displacement.

I have avoided the idea of "poetry of place" here, because these poetic meditations about abandoned houses and rural landscapes are fundamentally concerned with displacement and abandonment. Although I often trace poems' connections to particular landscapes, these are rarely places where the poets have chosen to or been able to dwell, in the Heideggerian sense, and such meditations can shift, encompassing and referring to new places, real and imagined, over time. In this regard, phenomenological theory seems more apt: in *The Poetics of Space*, Gaston Bachelard makes two observations that justly complicate the notion of poetry of place, especially for Americans who move often. He writes, "An entire past comes to dwell in a new house," and, "we cover the universe with drawings we have lived" (Bachelard 5, 12). These observations certainly illuminate the work of these poets. Bishop, for example, wrote intensively about her Nova Scotia childhood in her home in Brazil (the first stable home she found as an adult), where the slow pace of rural life recalled her childhood home.

Robert Frost

Frost is an obvious subject for this study. In American poetry, culture and landscape, the Romantic scene of the abandoned New England farmhouse or cellar hole has become an emblematic Frostian landscape. It appears throughout his work, from "Ghost House," the second poem in his first book, *A Boy's Will* (1913), to "Directive," from *Steeple Bush* (1947). As Harold Bloom notes, "Directive" "was the poem [Frost] always wrote and rewrote, in a revisionary process present already in *A Boy's Will*" (*Robert Frost* 5). Abandoned farmhouses and grave-like cellar holes appear in central poems from "The Need of Being Versed in Country Things" to "The Black Cottage," in the less-read poems "The Generations of Men," "The Census-Taker," "A Fountain, a Bottle, a Donkey's Ears and Some Books" and in the posthumously published "On the Sale of My Farm." Many other Frost poems concern the isolated farmhouse and its lonely inhabitants, who are threatened by the weather, strangers, abandonment, failure, and, at times, insanity.[4]

Frost himself led a decidedly unsettled existence—a fact that still startles some readers—moving often throughout his life and buying and selling a number of farms and houses. Among these, four houses—one in Vermont, two in New Hampshire, and one in Key West—claim the title of Frost's homes, functioning as tourist attractions that idealize the poet's life as settled.[5] The farm that meant the most to Frost (which, in some sense, he abandoned in 1911 for the sake of his poetic career) is in Derry, New Hampshire. He lived there as a young husband and father from 1900 to 1909, from the ages of twenty-six to thirty-five, and most of the poems just cited can be traced to the Derry landscape. Frost's Derry years were not entirely idyllic, but they were intense, poetically formative years. In Derry, for the first time, Frost could arrange his daily life around the reading and writing of poetry. Three of Frost's five children were born in Derry, and it was there that Frost made his only significant attempt at farming, from 1900 to 1905.[6] The nine years he spent on the Derry farm were the longest continuous residence of Frost's life, giving the lie to his popular reputation as a deeply rooted New Englander.

As a farmer, Frost failed after not trying very hard, as his notorious biographer Lawrance Thompson revealed.[7] But importantly, the effort drew him, at first as an outsider, into intimate terms with the New England rural landscape and its inhabitants, which would become his hallmark subject matter. From the Derry years, Frost reaped a rich poetic harvest. As he said more than once, in different ways, "the core of all my writing was probably the five free years I had there" (*Selected Letters* 552). No Frost scholar disputes the importance of Derry, yet what John Evangelist Walsh wrote in

1988, about the lack of critical attention to the Derry years, still holds true:

> It is remarkable that...all of his best and best-known work can be traced, directly or indirectly, to some experience of that memorable, long-ago decade [in Derry]....From then on,...he consciously hoarded his memories....This calculated use of his farm past—remote past...has not been given its due weight in studies on the development of his art. (129–130)

Frank Lentricchia made a beginning in *Robert Frost: Modern Poetics and the Landscapes of the Self* (1975), taking a psychological and phenomenological approach to Frost's poetry and employing the useful concept of "landscape," which fuses inhuman nature with humanity's shaping and perception of the land, to analyze recurrent objects in the landscape of Frost's poetry, such as the house. He also noted that, "[m]ore than most modern poets Frost needs to have some sort of historical context deliberately constructed for him" (19).[8]

In the first chapter of this study, I explore a series of interrelated questions, drawing together Frost's biography and poetry within a historical context: Why were the Derry years so significant for Frost's work? How did Frost first come to rural New England as an outsider and a tourist? How did he transform himself into a poetic guide to the region, whom many readers now take to be a native, though he was born and raised in California? Why does Frost return to the abandoned farmhouse throughout his career, and in many of his greatest poems? How should the tradition of Romantic landscape meditation, exemplified by Wordsworth's "The Ruined Cottage," inform our readings of those poems? And why does the Frostian scene of the abandoned farmhouse have considerable cultural resonance in the United States in the twentieth century?

Today Frost's Derry farmhouse, on Route 28 about forty miles north of Boston, attracts tourists as The Robert Frost Farm, a state Historic Site maintained by the New Hampshire Division of Parks and Recreation and the Frost Farm Trustees. It is in better condition than when the Frosts lived there. In 1900 Frost's grandfather had purchased the Derry farm for his grandson's use, and in 1911, when Frost sold it, he had to accept a low price: "Unfortunately, he had neglected the farm...and the place had begun to crumble" (Parini 104). Putting a good face on it, Frost boasted later that he had spent no money at all on the maintenance of the farm (Mertins 102).

The uninhabited farmhouse and barn now have the haunting, melancholy quality of an Andrew Wyeth or Edward Hopper house, as

Margaret H. Floyd observed in her "Architectural-Historical Analysis" for the state of New Hampshire (2). This quality is apparent in the back view of the house: three rooftops recede to the right, with a small, two-over-two window set high in each white clapboard wall, like three eyes staring out at the woods behind the house. The Robert Frost Farm, however, is too well kept to be an apt symbol of the Frostian scene of the abandoned farmhouse; to find that, we need only step across Route 28.

A literal ghost house—the one that inspired "Ghost House" and to which other poems refer—can be found not fifty feet from the Derry farm, but it is not part of the Historic Site. During Frost's years in Derry, it was an "old cellar hole with a broken chimney standing in it—what remained of a nearby farmhouse after a fire had destroyed it in 1867" (Parini 91). When I visited the Frost Farm in the summer of 2002, I asked the attendant where I might find the cellar hole. She said it was just across the road somewhere; the Frost Farm trustees had visited it twenty years ago. No one had looked for it since, and she herself had never seen it. She warned me of poison ivy. The cellar hole might be almost overgrown by now.

Indeed I stumbled around for half an hour before I found it. More than a century after Frost first wrote about it, the cellar hole is still "slowly closing like a dent in dough" (*CPPP* 342). Stone-walled, four feet deep at the lowest point, it has two adjoining holes, clearly marked as rooms that meet at one corner.[9] This cellar hole, just across the road from Frost's Derry farm, imbedded itself as deeply in Frost's memory as the poet's own farmhouse. Its proximity to the farm suggests the historical and personal immediacy of such scenes for Frost. Referring to "The Black Cottage," Lawrence Buell writes that

> the poem's central image, the ruined cottage, is obviously not New England-specific but transatlantic, indebted whether directly or indirectly to the dialogue at Margaret's cottage in Book I of Wordsworth's *The Excursion* (1814), the long poem by which America's favorite British Romantic was best known in the nineteenth century. (107)

Wordsworth's "The Ruined Cottage" is indeed an important model for "The Black Cottage" and "Ghost House." However, Frost could locate the "transatlantic image" of the ruined cottage in New England because he also found it there. Cellar holes or ruined cottages were not, for an American poet writing in New England in the early twentieth century, remote ruins associated solely with Romantic poetry. They were ubiquitous in the local landscape, reminders of a fading agricultural life and, increasingly, nostalgic sites for the rural tourist. "The Black Cottage" is based on a real cottage that stood "between RF's farm and Derry Village... weather-beaten, unpainted, and therefore almost 'black'—[once] inhabited by Mrs. Sarah J. Upton, [a Civil War] widow[.]" Frost began the poem, which features a minister-guide and an outsider-tourist figure, in 1905 or 1906 in Derry, and it was published in *North of Boston* (Thompson, *Early Years* 592).

By the late nineteenth century, in fact, when Frost first explored rural New England, the landscape was littered with abandoned farmhouses—perhaps the one Romantic ruin that Americans could find, and memorialize, in the national landscape. As historian Dona Brown recounts, abandoned farms reflected a widely perceived cultural and economic crisis of rural depopulation in New England, especially in Vermont and New Hampshire, in the late nineteenth century: "the specter of the 'abandoned farm' arose to haunt, first the politicians and planners of the northern states themselves, and later the reform writers of the national magazine circuit" (137). Frost's explorations of rural New England and his move as a young man to the Derry farm coincided with this growing concern about abandoned farms.

Bringing summer tourists to these farms was one proposed solution to the problem of their abandonment. In 1899, a holiday was invented for this purpose by New Hampshire governor Frank Rollins. During "Old Home Week," nonresident natives of rural New Hampshire were invited to "go home" for a reunion of sorts. (Ashbery mentions the same holiday, which caught on in other states, in *Flow Chart* [173].[10]) Persuading summer vacationers to "buy a summer home there, perhaps the 'old home' itself" was an express goal of Vermont's Board of Agriculture in these years (Brown 141, 143). Frost himself would eventually buy two farms in Vermont. His poem "The Generations of Men," originally titled "The Cellar Hole" (Cramer 39), directly refers to this holiday, bearing out "An often-repeated joke at the time... that at least one local industry had been given a tremendous boost by Old Home Week: poetry-writing" (Brown 143). Brown, who does not mention Frost in her study, makes a simple point that applies to his work: "Romantic artists and romantic scenery... depend on one another" (46–47). In his long title poem for *New Hampshire*, Frost would comment on the state's economy: "Do you know, / Considering the market, there are more / Poems produced than any other thing?" (ll. 169–171, *CPPP* 155).

In this pattern of rural tourism in New England and Frost's poetic evocation of the abandonment of the region's farms,[11] a parallel arises with literary landscape tourism in England. In a new appendix to his classic study, *The Tourist. A New Theory of the Leisure Class*, Dean MacCannell wrote in 1999 that "we are all tourists" and, "when we travel with others to a place we have been and they have not, *we are tour guides* [his italics]" (191). For poets writing about landscape after Romanticism, negotiating these dual subject positions seems unavoidable. The poet, composing nostalgic poems about the countryside, acts first as a rural tourist, then as a tour guide to his readers. In discussing Wordsworth's "local poetry" of landscape, Geoffrey Hartman notes that the guide figure in eighteenth-century English poetry illustrates the cultural expectation that "the poetical genius should reflect the genius loci, the spirit of England's religion, history, and countryside" (Hartman, *Beyond Formalism* 317). He notes elsewhere that "Frost's 'Directive' is a latter-day echo of the genre of [poems that] guide the stranger to suitable watering or resting places," a genre originating in Greek poetry which Wordsworth extends (Hartman, *The Unremarkable Wordsworth* 41).[12] The poet as guide then popularizes the site for his readers, as Frost did rural New England, and as Wordsworth popularized the Lake District, Dove Cottage, and Tintern Abbey, among other places.[13] As Marjorie Levinson observes, tourists and artists had long visited the ruins of abbeys in England, "celebrated since the middle of the eighteenth century for their picturesque qualities—their value enhanced by the increasing scarcity of unimproved areas," well before Wordsworth visited Tintern Abbey. In turn, the popularity of Wordsworth's poem measurably increased visits to the site by literary tourists (Levinson 35). With the increasing "scarcity of unimproved areas," the country cottage would also benefit economically from its literary associations with Wordsworth's "The Ruined Cottage," becoming a rural tourist attraction earlier in the United Kingdom than in the United States.[14]

For all his success at evoking rural New England, Frost was not immediately accepted as its legitimate representative. When he was named Vermont's poet laureate in 1922, some still perceived him as an outsider, even a summer tourist, as illustrated by a *New York Times* editorial:

> "[T]he natural expectation is that [a state poet laureate] would be a native or at the very least a long-time resident of that State.... But Mr. Frost was born in California, and his college days were spent partly at Dartmouth and partly at Harvard. He was a farmer for a while, or

> *Who's Who* says so, though one wonders, and then, after teaching in several New Hampshire schools he finally landed a post as Professor of English Literature at Amherst. His home is set down as Franconia, N.H., but he does have a summer place in South Shaftesbury, Vt., and that seems to be his only connection with the Green Mountain State." (qtd. in Thompson, *Years of Triumph* 202–203)

(Perhaps registering such accusations, Frost impudently concludes the poem "New Hampshire": "At present I am living in Vermont" [*CPPP* 162].) This roughly accurate description of Frost's movements up to 1922—the crucial years in England are omitted—begins to suggest the peripatetic nature of the poet's life, which Frost effectively disguised later.

In the mid-nineteenth century, Frost's own family had given up on farming. When the poet's father was born in 1850, his father, William Prescott Frost, Sr., was farming in Kingston, New Hampshire. But he soon found he could make a better living in the textile industry, and moved his family to Lawrence, Massachusetts, where he became foreman, and later overseer, of the Pacific Mill (Thompson, *Early Years* 3, 2). Frost's father, in turn, left New England for San Francisco, where the poet was born and raised to the age of eleven. In these patterns of migration, the Frosts were part of "the flight of young people [from rural New England] to the cities and the West . . . [which] writers in the agricultural press bemoaned" (Brown 135). The shift from the country to the city within Frost's own family corresponds to the larger shift from rural to urban areas throughout the country, which coincides rather neatly with the poet's lifetime, 1874–1963. As early as "the 1850s, . . . New England lost one tenth of its native-born male population" to migration to other states, while "it [has] experienced very little in-migration" ever since (Carter et al. 1–493). In his poem "The Census-Taker," from *New Hampshire* (1924), Frost registers the role of the U.S. Census in tracking this rural depopulation.

These biographical facts and historical trends, as well as the persistence of the abandoned farmhouse as an image in and subject of Frost's poetry, serve to remind us that Frost's poetry arises in response to the relative failure and abandonment of farms in New England. Frost took the title *North of Boston* from "a Boston newspaper advertisement which [he] remembered while he was living in England. It mentioned properties for sale in a geographical area referred to simply as 'north of Boston'" (Cramer 28–29). Frost may have placed such an ad for his own Derry farm, before selling it in 1911.

By 1931, Frost had gained acceptance as a legitimate poetic representative of rural New England, as evidenced by an interview for *Rural America*, "Poetry and Rural Life: An Interview with Robert Frost." The interviewer expressed a desire to "enlist the poets in our efforts to build a worthy country life in America," thus implying its decay or absence. Frost told him what he wanted to hear:

> Poetry is more often of the country than of the city. Poetry is very, very rural—rustic. It stands as a reminder of rural life.... Just so the race lives best to itself—first to itself—storing a strength in the more individual life of the country—of the farm—then going to market and socializing in the industrial city....We are now at a moment when we are getting too far out into the social-industrial, and are at the point of drawing back—drawing in to renew ourselves.... I think a person has to be withdrawn into himself to gather inspiration so that he is somebody when he "comes to market" with himself. (*Interviews* 75–76)

Emphasizing the nation's increasingly urban life, Frost here impersonally narrates the trajectory of his own poetic career, omitting details such as his urban beginnings in San Francisco and Lawrence, and his initiation into rural life as an outsider. Frost himself came to the country from cities, stayed there for a decade, and sold his Derry farm to take his poetry "to market" in the city of London.

In part, Frost came to feel so strongly that "poetry is rural" because the rural isolation of Derry brought him so much poetic inspiration, which he often lacked in his less rooted, and less remotely rural, later years. As he remarked privately in 1916, "'The poet in me died nearly ten years ago.... The calf I was in the nineties I merely take to market'" (qtd. in Thompson, *Years of Triumph*, 80). He made a career of "remind[ing readers] of rural life" in his poetry, though he often evokes and laments its failures and abandonment rather than its persistence; reminding implies forgetting. The rural tourist—Frost was one at the start of his career—longs to remember and recover rural life. Throughout his poetic career, he bought several more farms, but Frost never lived as long (without interruption) in the country as he had in Derry. Instead he moved often and ran himself ragged as a traveling poet-lecturer—Allen Ginsberg credited him with creating the poetry-reading circuit (Parini 319). Ironically, Frost's promotion of himself as a farmer-poet worked so well that some critics patronized him as a simple rustic talent. (In England, Thomas Hardy was similarly patronized for his success at evoking rural Dorset in his novels and poetry, with the significant difference that he was a deeply rooted native—though not a peasant, which English class snobbery sometimes failed to grant.)

In retrospect, Frost's story seems a distinctively American one, which Herman Melville would appreciate in the spirit of *The Confidence-Man*: a poet who never farmed much and rarely stayed put becomes closely identified, in the popular imagination, with a stable, enduring rural life in New England, and indeed convinces readers that he is a native of the region. (Invariably, undergraduates in Frost's native state, not to mention further afield in Poland, are surprised to learn he grew up in California and was not really a farmer.) Perhaps we have yet to appreciate fully that Frost's poetry of isolated and abandoned farmhouses points toward, and that his life exemplified, a different mythic American experience: a restless, deracinated life, marked by frequent displacement, dramatic reversals of fortune, and a lack of community and familial stability.[15] Frost's persistent reputation as an iconic New England farmer-poet belies these facts of his life and these themes in his poetry, distracting us from the fact that the Romantically salient scene of the abandoned farmhouse—the cellar hole that is only the ghost of a farm—may be more central to his work than the heroically surviving farmer. The idealized rural life that Frost represents in the nostalgic popular imagination is, in his poetry, threatened and disappearing from the start.

Elizabeth Bishop

In the second and third chapters, I consider how the scene of the abandoned house, and some of Frost's poems evoking it, engage later major American poets as different from Frost as Bishop and Ashbery. Although readers of Bishop notice her preoccupation with neglected, rural houses, there has been no sustained analysis of the image of the house in her work,[16] and few critics have placed Bishop in a direct lineage with Frost.[17] In this preoccupation especially, however, Bishop seemed to feel affinities with his work. In my research I found new evidence of Frost's influence on Bishop, as she furthered the revision of Romantic landscape meditation, especially Wordsworth's "The Ruined Cottage," which Frost began. When Bishop taught creative writing in the late 1960s and the 1970s, she often assigned Frost's poems, asking students to memorize, recite, or analyze "An Old Man's Winter Night," "The Hill Wife," "A Servant to Servants," "Home Burial," and "Directive," among others (Bishop 71.6). Although Bishop sometimes privately criticized Frost,[18] she was pleased to cross paths with him in Key West and Washington, DC, and made a special effort to see him when he gave a reading in Brazil in 1954. Bishop attempted to explain her esteem for Frost's poetry to Jarrell in 1965, favorably comparing Jarrell's *The Lost World* to Frost, valuing the "sorrowful," "beautiful," and "sympath[etic]" Frost against his seeming, false idealization of a lost rural life—which in my view arises from Frost's public persona, particularly prominent in mid-century, not from the best of his poetry (*OA* 432). She wrote to Anne Stevenson in 1964, "Frost is a complicated case—a lot of what he wrote about was just homely to me, after my Nova Scotia days, but the kind of thing I have tried to avoid sentimentalizing. I hate his philosophy, what I understand of it—I find it *mean*—while admiring his technique enormously" ("Answers to Your Questions of March 6th," Washington University Libraries). Admitting that she does not understand Frost's philosophy entirely, Bishop invokes the sense of "homely" as associated with home, suggesting that familiar scenes in Frost's poetry appealed to her because of her rural childhood, and that she felt the danger of sentimentalizing the rural in her own work. Late in life, Bishop attempted an explicit response to Frost's poetry about rural New England in a draft of an unfinished poem, "Just North of Boston," which obviously refers to Frost's second book. The draft describes the passing scenery on a drive back to Boston after a weekend in the country, juxtaposing glaring roadside advertisements with an abandoned farmhouse and its ghosts (*Edgar Allan Poe & the Juke-Box* 166–167).[19]

Bishop also shared with Frost a habit of imaginative and actual property speculation. For Bishop, as for Frost, the appeal of abandoned farmhouses and rural dwellings had much to do with an idealized lost home and her own rootlessness and lack of family connections. And, like Frost and Thoreau, she idealized such places for thinking and writing. Ranging from Canada to Europe to South America, Bishop often traveled farther than Frost. Even among American poets of her generation and privileged class, who traveled widely,[20] Bishop's wanderings are idiosyncratic. Arguably, one thing she was looking for in her travels was a home.

At 624 White Street in Key West, Florida, on the gate of a white picket fence, a plaque is inscribed with the closing lines of the title poem from *Questions of Travel*, Bishop's third book: "*Should we have stayed at home, / wherever that may be?*" (*CP* 94). This first house that Bishop bought, with Louise Crane in 1938, was designated a national literary landmark in 1993; it is the first of the "three loved houses" whose loss Bishop recounts in her late villanelle and *ars poetica* "One Art" (*CP* 178). The Key West house—wooden and painted white, with dark shutters—resembles the two white clapboard houses of Bishop's early childhood in Great Village, Nova Scotia, and Worcester, Massachusetts. It was one of many indefinite homes where, over the course of her life, Bishop did not stay long. The second loved house—Sítio da Alcobaçinha, Fazenda Samambaia, in Petrópolis, Brazil, evoked in "Song for the Rainy Season"[21]—belonged to Lota de Macedo Soares, Bishop's partner from 1952 to 1967, and Bishop lost it when their relationship ended with the death (an apparent suicide) of Soares. The third house, which Bishop had advertised for sale by the time she wrote "One Art," was a seventeenth-century colonial house in Ouro Prêto, Brazil. She had purchased it in a state of near ruin in 1965, to restore it as a second home (*OA* 435, 558).

Like the New England farmhouses that Frost acquired, lived in intermittently, then sold, what these three lost houses had in common was their relative rural isolation in or near a small town, a close community of neighbors, and a slow pace of life. To some degree, the houses in Key West, Petrópolis, and Ouro Prêto, and similar resorts and retreats Bishop found throughout her life (from a wooden shack outside Provincetown, Massachusetts, in the 1930s, to Sabine Farm on the island of North Haven, Maine, in the 1970s) recall Bishop's maternal grandparents' home in the tiny community of Great Village, where she lived for most of her first six years and spent summers later in childhood. These houses, including the two that Bishop sold rather than lost outright, represent attempts to make a home, which, for various reasons, she eventually abandoned.

As many readers have noticed, Bishop recalled her childhood in Nova Scotia in Brazil, writing many of her best poems and stories about Nova Scotia during her years in Brazil.[22] She wrote from Ouro Prêto in 1970 to Robert Lowell, "Probably what I'm really up to is re-creating a sort of de luxe Nova Scotia all over again, in Brazil. And now I'm my own grandmother" (June 15, 1970, Harry Ransom Humanities Research Center, University of Texas, Austin). Bishop's imaginative attachment to her three houses is akin to Frost's reverence for memories of the Derry farm and his willingness to sell it to advance his poetic career.[23]

Rather than focusing on the image of the house in her poetry, however, many readers think of Bishop as a poet deeply concerned with travel, and of course she is. But the strong appeal of a settled life and attendant skepticism about its viability, embodied in old and fragile rural dwellings, form the obverse of her preoccupation with travel. A virtual orphan from the age of five, Bishop might be described, for long stretches of her childhood and adult life, as homeless—though not in the impoverished sense, as she lived partly on inheritances for much of her life. All tourists are, at least temporarily, homeless; this was especially true for Bishop, who traveled and moved frequently, finding her first real home as an adult only at the age of forty-one.

In 1951, looking through poems for her second collection, *A Cold Spring* (1955), Bishop wrote self-deprecatingly to Lowell, "On reading over what I've got on hand I find I'm really a minor, female Wordsworth—at least, I don't know anyone else who seems to be such a Nature Lover" (*OA* 222). Like Wordsworth, Bishop often exerts her descriptive powers on landscapes, in meditations that express the poet's inner life as much as they evoke the physical landscape. She also shares with Wordsworth a persistent, tender regard for the experience of childhood, and a complicated nostalgia for the isolated, often neglected rural dwelling, exemplified by "The Ruined Cottage."

That Bishop appreciated Wordsworth is evident in accounts of her reading. At work in 1936 on several autobiographical stories and poems concerned with her childhood, which feature isolated and neglected houses, she wrote to Marianne Moore that she was reading "The Prelude" with a sense that "this heaped-up autobiography is having extreme results, maybe fortunate" (*OA* 45). In her respect and esteem for children and the childlike, who in their naïveté and innocence are bewildered by the cruelties of the adult world, she is also Wordsworthian (see Stevenson 33).

As Susan McCabe observes so perceptively, "Bishop rejects the house as a symbol of permanence and wholeness, of the integrated self; we must keep inscribing homes, the intimacy and loss they imply, while the memory of them changes over time" (195). As with Frost's cellar holes and abandoned farmhouses, often the fragile "crypto-dream-house[s]" in Bishop's poetry could not really be inhabited even if they were real houses, not poetic images (*CP* 179). They evoke and withdraw the possibility of dwelling at once. In "The End of March," the fantasy of living in the boarded-up dune shack is sadly dismissed as "perfect! But—impossible" (*CP* 180). Throughout Bishop's poetry and prose, dreamlike images of and meditations on neglected, fragile houses appear, constituting an imaginative reality that parallels her search for a stable home, as she sought to recreate something of the atmosphere of her Nova Scotia childhood. In this pattern, Bishop's life and work again echo Frost, who sold his Derry farm only to search endlessly for another just like it, and tried to buy it back, all the while evoking the image of the abandoned farmhouse in his poetry. The neglected, fragile, old rural houses where Bishop was a guest, and which she admired, rented, bought, and entertained fantasies of renting or buying—"dreaming about real estate," she called it in a letter to her aunt Grace—are found in rural Nova Scotia and Newfoundland, New England, North Carolina, the Florida Keys, Haiti, and Brazil (Bishop 25.11). Her rootlessness suggests an exaggerated version of the lives of many restless, peripatetic Americans, rich and poor, who often move in hope of finding a better life elsewhere, continually making new homes and abandoning old ones, which they sometimes leave, as Auden noted, as characteristic traces on the American landscape. The appearance in Bishop's work of such houses from North and South America also remind us that the neglected rural dwelling, as an emblem of both the abandonment and the loss of rural life, is a global phenomenon in the twentieth and twenty-first centuries.

Because of the distinctive and inherent interest of Bishop's biography, and the "predominant psychoanalytic paradigms for reading lyric poetry," readings of her work can seem rather narrowly biographical—though some psychoanalytic readings, such as Joanne Feit Deihl's, are extremely astute (Erkkila 285). Though I have aimed to integrate relevant cultural history with my reading of Bishop's career, I also rely on her biography, because of its inarguable relevance to her work. For Bishop, unique characteristics complicated her attempts to establish a home and a stable life: her status as an orphan, and, to some degree, her sexual identity as a lesbian. Of course, committed same-sex relationships, which involved living together, were not uncommon in Bishop's social circles. The Boston Marriage—the colloquial term for such a partnership in the late nineteenth century—had long been socially tolerated in the middle and upper classes (D'Emilio and Freedman 192). But the lack of an official blessing of such relationships could have destabilizing effects. In 1966, when her relationship with Soares began to fall apart, Bishop feared losing the only real home she had known since she left Great Village at the age of six. And she resented her lack of a legal claim to the home they shared because their long-term relationship was not legally recognized (Millier 384).

Dwellings in Bishop's work can signify the childhood trauma of being orphaned, and the recurring memory of that trauma; the memory of being taken away from Nova Scotia by her paternal grandparents; the guilt attached to feeling homeless and aimless as a young woman of leisure during the Great Depression; a place of illicit or secret, excessive, solitary drinking during and after Prohibition; the foreboding Bishop felt as a tourist in Europe in the thirties, as grim childhood memories, loosely associated with WWI and exile, resurfaced amid the build-up to WWII; deep gratitude at finding a home with Soares in Brazil; the gap between rich and poor in Brazil; the loss of a home and the lover who shared it; and finally, the retreats Bishop found in the 1970s in Duxbury, Massachusetts, and North Haven, Maine, which recalled earlier homes. My aim throughout is not to portray Bishop as a writer who is always explicitly concerned with larger cultural anxieties about dwelling, but to show that her poetry and prose often obliquely reflect, and are informed by, these concerns, as well as by her personal circumstances.

John Ashbery

Bishop's most distinguished poetic heir, Ashbery demonstrates an affinity not only with the surrealist elements of Bishop's early poems, but with her measured nostalgia for rural landscapes, old houses, and the loss of familial intimacy associated with them. In early childhood, Ashbery experienced a dislocation that was traumatic for him, moving at the age of seven from his maternal grandparents' house in Rochester to his father's fruit farm outside Sodus, near Lake Ontario in upstate New York. That landscape would later become associated with terrible losses as well—when his brother Richard died of leukemia at the age of eight on July 5, 1940, shortly before Ashbery's thirteenth birthday, and when, in 1964, his father Chester Ashbery died suddenly and unexpectedly at the age of seventy-three, leading Ashbery to return home from France for good in 1965, to look after his devastated mother.

In the 1970s, Ashbery and Bishop met and established a friendship, initiated by Ashbery, based on admiration for each other's work. He wrote to her in 1976:

> I have always considered you one of the greatest modern poets (much more so than my dumb review of *The Complete Poems* in the *Times* may have led you to believe), and your work has been a great inspiration to me (though I fear my own work doesn't, alas, show it). I'm sure you don't remember, but I wrote you a fan letter (the one and only time I've done such a thing), in 1948 when "Over 2,000 Illustrations" came out in *Partisan Review*; you replied on a postcard from Maine. (Bishop 1.6)

In 1948, when he read this poem for the first time, Ashbery was an undergraduate at Harvard. Enamored of Bishop's poetry, he was writing some of the earliest poems that refer to his childhood landscape, which would appear in *Turandot and Other Poems* (1953) and

Some Trees (1956). Writing about Bishop for the *New York Times*, Ashbery rhapsodized about this poem, which, he said

> form[s] a substance that is indescribable and a continuing joy, and one returns to it again and again, ravished and unsatisfied. After twenty years...I am unable to exhaust the meaning and mysteries of its concluding line: "And looked and looked our infant sight away," and I suspect that its secret has much to do with the nature of Miss Bishop's poetry. Looking, or attention, will absorb the object with its meaning. The power of vision, "our infant sight," is both our torment and our salvation. (*Selected Prose* 121–122)

Of course, the visual is equally important in the work of Ashbery. In Bishop's poem, the look of longing is directed at a lost, domesticated Nativity that also figures as a scene of lost childhood—following the juxtaposition, in the first two stanzas, of the ordered scenes of the Bible with the disordered, disturbing vignettes of travel—that may help account for Ashbery's intense admiration for the poem. David Lehman reports that, "In March 1997, at a group reading from Jorie Graham's 'Golden Ecco' anthology of great poems of the English language, Ashbery read 'Over 2,000 Illustrations and a Complete Concordance.' When he reached the last stanza, he cried" (Lehman 134).

When Ashbery won the Pulitzer Prize for *Self-Portrait in a Convex Mirror* in 1976, Bishop threw a party for him in Boston. The same year, he accompanied her to Oklahoma City when she received the *Books Abroad*/Neustadt International Prize for Literature, and to Rotterdam for the International Poetry Conference. Ashbery also provided Bishop with the long epigraph, and possibly inspiration for the title, for *Geography III*:

> As soon as I got back to New York [from Oklahoma] I left it to go upstate to visit my mother for Easter, which wasn't very pleasant since she has failed a lot since the last time I saw her three months ago. While I was up there I picked up the enclosed little book in an antique shop–I got it to send to you because it reminded me of your poetry (except for the rather pedestrian diatribe against "heathens")—though, since you are about to publish *Geography III*, this geography will probably seem like ancient history to you. Sorry it's so grubby—a condition of survival no doubt. By the way, the previous owner lived in Sodus, N.Y., the little dump where I grew up. (Bishop 1.6)

The book was *First Lessons in Geography* (1884), from which Bishop quotes Lessons VI and X. And the landscape that encompasses "the little dump" of Sodus, his father's farm just outside of town, and the surrounding region of upstate New York, has preoccupied Ashbery throughout his career.

The chagrined avowal of his origins is typical of the Ashbery who, when he first arrived at Harvard and in New York City, felt self-conscious about his upstate rural accent, and remade himself, with a little help from the art critic John Meyers and his friends, into the leader of The New York School of Poets.[24] This is the Ashbery whose standard book-jacket bio, for many years, simply said he was born in Rochester and now lived in New York City. But this private comment to Bishop hints at the fact that, growing up on his father's fruit farm outside Sodus, Ashbery had a childhood that was far more rural than Robert Frost's.

The simple fact that John Ashbery had a rural childhood still surprises some readers. And the argument that it constitutes an important theme in his poetry is still rather novel, despite the pervasive presence of this rural landscape in Ashbery's poetry, with its cherry and apple orchards, farmhouses, and the sweet tedium of the countryside, from the start of his long career through his recent work of the early twenty-first century. It is, however, understandable that we have often overlooked the significance of this landscape, because of our assumption that Ashbery is an urban poet, which derives partly from the anti-biographical stance of most Ashbery criticism.

Assuming a close association between New York City and the New York poets,[25] some readers conclude that Ashbery must be, first and foremost, a poet of urban sensibilities. And obviously, cosmopolitan interests are very important to his poetry. A self-declared "cinema maniac," with the varied reading interests of "a magpie," Ashbery seems to touch on the whole history of art, film, and classical and experimental music; his poems refer to newspapers, tabloids, overheard comments of strangers, cartoons, and telephone conversations ("Letter to Fairfield Porter," March 2, 1956, AM 6.25, Houghton Library; Gangel 14).[26] At this point, however, the cosmopolitan in Ashbery has been overemphasized at the expense of equally important themes in his work: rural and small town America, and the poet's evolving meditations on his childhood landscape.

One reason for such oversight is Ashbery's status as the leading (and now the only living) figure of the New York School. As such, we assume, he resides in his Chelsea apartment in Manhattan—although, since 1979, he has spent more and more time in the small town of Hudson, New York, famed for its antique shops, two hours north of the city by train. And, from 1965 until his mother's death in 1987, Ashbery visited his mother often, frequently once a month, in the village of Pultneyville on Lake Ontario, constantly refreshing his memories of "the patchwork landscape of childhood, north of here" (*AW* 76).[27] Ashbery's attachment to these rural landscapes is not just part of a typical New Yorker's country weekend lifestyle, but manifests as a thematic preoccupation in his poetry. Ashbery, of course, has helped create his urban reputation, just as Frost convinced readers that he was a New England farmer-poet. Frost was briefly among Ashbery's favorite poets in high school (Lehman 128), but in a college notebook he scribbled, "(Something there is that doesn't love Robert Frost) / me," and similarly disparaged Whitman ("[English] Tutorial Bibliography," "English 278," AM 6.31, Houghton Library). However, I do not argue that Frost had a marked influence on Ashbery, only that their poetry is sometimes, surprisingly, preoccupied with similar rural landscapes.

In fact, Ashbery is distant kin to earlier American authors with rural roots, such as Willa Cather and Sherwood Anderson, who fled the country for the city with a sense of having barely escaped—only to turn their attention, in the city, back to the rural world they had fled, expressing frank nostalgia and affectionate contempt for it in their writing. Somewhat like Bishop's early childhood in Nova Scotia, Ashbery's childhood was defined by a close extended family and a quiet rural lifestyle, almost Victorian in its staidness and security—a world he had in mind, he told me in an interview in 2003, when he wrote "Pyrography," as a character does in Cather's *O Pioneers!* as a place where people used to take up quaint hobbies like pyrography (MacArthur 194). As a child, teenager, and college student, Ashbery also reluctantly helped to harvest, preserve, and sell the fruit from his father's orchards. In his adult life and career as a poet and art critic, Ashbery has made drastic departures from this childhood world, but turning back to it in his poetry seems to him quite natural: "Auden says something like, 'Our childhood is all we have.' And the first experiences in one's life tend to be the strongest ones really, and I think it's just a sort of natural way for a poet to develop. Take 'The Prelude' for instance" (MacArthur 193).

As he cites Auden here, it may be relevant that the homosexual Auden, Bishop, and Ashbery are childless themselves, and thus may attach especial importance to their own childhoods in their poetry. Ashbery also suggests here and in his Charles Eliot Norton lectures, published as *Other Traditions*, his affinities with the British tradition of Romantic and rural poetry and the cult of childhood.

Describing the sources of his poetic inspiration, he can sound like Wordsworth or John Clare: "Much of my poetry comes out of memories of childhood, the feeling of some lost world that can't be recovered. At the same time, I think the present daily world in which I happen to be is what's writing the poem, what's dealing with these experiences of loss" (Poulin 253). Indeed, much of Ashbery's most moving poetry is often closely connected with his rural childhood.

Critics who are quite comfortable discussing irony and indeterminacy in Ashbery, however, rarely account for the emotional seriousness, intensity and occasionally touching sentimentality in his work, partly because of a disinclination to draw links between the poems and the life of Ashbery himself, the man who writes it. Avoiding the facts of Ashbery's life seems reasonable because his poetry evades autobiography on the surface, and, in several early, frequently cited interviews, the poet himself urged critics not to look for it. One of Ashbery's most astute readers, David Herd, may speak for many when he argues that "the facts of Ashbery's biography... do not, on the whole, enable one to read [his poetry]" (Herd, *John Ashbery* 20). But when we focus on Ashbery's urban associations and lack awareness of the poet's rural childhood, we may assume that the rural landscapes in Ashbery's poetry lack personal significance, and thus perceive them as pastoral parody. Ashbery's anti-autobiographical stance can be traced not only to T.S. Eliot's influential doctrine of impersonality in poetry, challenged by Confessional poets during the earlier period of Ashbery's poetic development, but to his rather conservative rural upbringing, as he suggested in an interview in 1984:

> I don't know that it is so much a sense of privacy as a feeling that to talk about myself would be immodest. Probably as a result of my upbringing: I was always told not to put myself forward, that children were better seen and not heard, and all that sort of thing which, for better or probably for worse, rubbed off on me so that it seems to me that the circumstances of my own life are of no compelling interest to other people... [I] try to write about paradigms of common experience which I hope other people can share. (Labrie 29)

In interviews, Ashbery often emphasizes the importance of his childhood and rural landscapes to his work, yet critical studies of his poetry have rarely focused on these themes as biographical. However impersonal Ashbery's writing may seem, his urban, cosmopolitan reputation has led us to make narrow assumptions about his biography and his poetry. If many readers miss the persistence of rural landscapes in Ashbery, they do so partly because they do not expect them from an urban poet. One of the "paradigms of common experience [that Ashbery] write[s] about" is rural childhood, and a widespread American nostalgia for the country and abandoned houses.[28] Harold Bloom and Angus Fletcher certainly perceive the importance of the pastoral in Ashbery, and the poet's debt to Romanticism, yet they see this as a result of Ashbery's reading more than of his biography. A few critics, such as Andrew Ross and especially Bonnie Costello, have noted Ashbery's strong interest in landscape, but have not pursued connections to his own life very far, perhaps for lack of biographical information (see Ross 174–175, 185 and Costello, "John Ashbery's Landscapes" 60, 70).

While we are swept up in the momentum, in the linguistic dazzle and shifting tones and tropes of an Ashbery poem, it is sometimes hard to notice personal subject matter or credit it as such. Although Helen Vendler pronounced in 1981, "It seems time to write about John Ashbery's subject matter," critical emphasis on his style, which she noted then, has persisted (Vendler, "Understanding Ashbery" 179). Like all of the raw material of Ashbery's poetry, his childhood landscape passes through the signal scrambler of his poetic consciousness; meditations on and references to that landscape manifest among disparate elements and scenes. Perhaps Ashbery has dazzled and amused us so much that we have often failed to see that he is writing about anything literal or referential at all, or that we should sometimes take sentiment in his poetry seriously.[29] Or if we do see consistent themes, what we tend to expect and therefore notice is Ashbery's parodic response to contemporary American culture, rather than anything so personal and (in terms of poetic subject matter) conventional as his own childhood and a peculiarly American nostalgia for rural landscape—the sweet, safe boredom of rural life, and the sudden, utter loss of it. Robert Crawford's characterization of Ashbery is typical:

> Where Whitman sang of the open road, Ashbery constructs a poetry for and of the age of the multi-lane highway.... a spy-satellite view of the freeway traffic as well as an account of the flux and unending spool of the self which delights in the continuous linguistic play of novelization.... a poetry of later twentieth-century media-saturated America, particularly metropolitan New York. (102–103)

There are few freeways or satellites, if any, in Ashbery's poetry. To his credit, however, Crawford also offers a partly biographical argument that the poet draws on "nineteenth-century British literature in order to construct his own particularly American idiom" (115, 104, 103).

Many critics have followed the example set by Marjorie Perloff's *Poetics of Indeterminancy*, offering rather abstract, philosophical accounts of Ashbery's apparent project of deconstructing perception and the capacity of language to communicate at all. I would never advocate biographical reading as the most important approach to Ashbery, but integrating it with other approaches does reveal some of our critical blind spots, and extends a critical trend of taking his poetry more seriously. Charles Altieri was among the first to qualify Perloff's insights, arguing in 1984 that

> for Ashbery the problematics of relation are not primarily of sign to signified but of act to other acts as the mind tries to identify secure resting places.... We are certainly caught up here in problems of indeterminacy, but these are means, not ends. Ashbery's purpose is probably not simply to present indeterminate discourse or even to show the inherent duplicities of language. (140–141)

What is Ashbery's purpose, then? Alan Williamson describes Ashbery's extreme self-consciousness—"he cannot be aware of anything without also being aware of [himself] perceiving it"—and boldly offers a psychological explanation for the poet's "disjunctive techniques," arguing for the "psychological logic of [Ashbery's] interruptions": "a break almost always occurs just as a crisis of revelation approaches" in a sort of "psychic censorship" (118, 120). As Williamson and Vernon Shetley have articulated most convincingly, Ashbery fragments and filters the autobiographical in his poetry for a complex of aesthetic, philosophical and temperamental reasons. Shetley, drawing together Perloff's and Vendler's insights, argues that "the poet of linguistic freeplay exists in Ashbery, but exists in combination with, and in some sense permits the existence of, the Keatsian lyricist" (Shetley 131).

In the one major study of Ashbery that relies in part on biography, John Shoptaw's *On the Outside Looking Out*, a primary interest is the poet's sexuality. Shoptaw brilliantly decodes Ashbery's cryptographic methods of revising clichés and familiar phrasing as "misrepresentative," and frequently uncovers covert expressions of homosexuality—at the risk, at times, of reducing Ashbery's poetics to a principle of repression (2–4). Although some of the early poetry does seem to suggest and disguise homosexuality at once, Ashbery overtly expresses it when he writes in *Flow Chart* (1991): "there are so many other, nicer things to be doing! . . . . / . . . sucking each other's dicks is only one" (*FC* 184). In typically avoiding explicitly sexual or other confessional themes, the poet has motives other than avoiding social stigmas.

Asked in an interview in 1985 whether he dislikes a particular kind of poetry, Ashbery answered "poetry that is called Confessional." And as Shetley has noted, Ashbery defined himself in the 1950s against the dominant poetic mode of Robert Lowell (109). Yet, comfortable as usual with apparent contradictions, Ashbery then remarked irritably in the same interview:

> I've probably written some confessional poetry myself only nobody recognizes it as such. You can't be a part-time confessional poet or a part-time anything else once you're labeled. But in general, the way that kind of poetry turns out doesn't please me; it's not that . . . I'm against trying to deal with one's life in poetry. (Murphy 23)

Prodded further by interviewers, Ashbery has explained that he is not anti-biographical but is attempting, perhaps surprisingly, to provide a widely accessible experience in his poetry:

> [O]f course I find my experiences interesting: they are the only ones that I've had. My life is very important to me. . . . I don't want to go into statistics too much other than alluding to common experiences which everybody has, so that someone who doesn't know me will know what I'm talking about. (Murphy 21)

> What I am trying to get at is a general, all-purpose experience—like those stretch socks that fit all sizes. Something which a reader could . . . maybe get something out of without knowing . . . my history, or sex life, or whatever. (Poulin 251)

We are familiar with the stylistic methods Ashbery uses to create powerful alternatives to confessionalism, from his shifting pronouns—which variously address readers (as "you"), ask readers to identify with figures in the poem and with the speaker ("I, we, he, she, they"), and conflate the speaker's experience with the reader's ("you," used in the conversational sense, which implies the interlocutor is like "me")—to his dramatic, Bakhtinian variety of discourses and voices. Yet a persistent personal thread runs through the beautiful tangle of Ashbery's poetry, drawing out experiences that, the poet hopes, are universal. Herd puts this point succinctly: "Ashbery is antipathetic to confessional poetry because it fetishises the individual, and...so...denies poetry its broader social function" (Herd, *John Ashbery* 20). Douglas Crase, a personal friend of Ashbery, also articulates the poet's ambition to communicate, the opposite of the apparent narcissistic tendency of his poetry to look inward: "We are used to hearing of poets so private they speak for us all. We are not used to hearing, however, that John Ashbery is among them.... The difficulty...is that his poetry is *so* public, so accurately a picture of the world we live in, that it scarcely resembles anything we have every known" (Crase 30–31). In *Flow Chart*, the speaker proposes "distill[ing] whatever happened to me," hoping that, "maybe if I reduced it / all sufficiently, somebody would find it worth his while, i.e., exemplary" (*FC* 135).

One "distilled" experience repeatedly presented in Ashbery's poetry is a rural childhood, among farms and old family homes. Some of his most intense and lyrical poetry arises from this experience. Like Ashbery, many Americans have left a rural family home, in the process of growing up and moving to cities—as individuals and as a nation. In his poetry, rural scenes are the location of personal and cultural youth, and a complicated nostalgia for them is expressed from a mature, rueful, urban perspective. In a poem whose inclusive title proposes a universal scope, "Whatever It Is, Wherever You Are"—in which Ashbery uses the pronouns "we" and "you" but never an "I"—he characteristically locates the reader's childhood and family history in the sort of place he grew up in, in "faraway summer evenings," "out in back" of a house full of benevolent "ancestors" (*AW* 63). In writing the poem, Ashbery said, "I was thinking about [relatives] I hadn't known, like my paternal grandfather, who died when I was a baby.... Living in these old houses that have been family homes, I have a sense of past lives..." (MacArthur 197). Here he may refer to four houses: his present home in Hudson, his maternal grandparents' houses in Rochester and Pultneyville, and his parents' farm outside Sodus (where his paternal grandparents had also lived). Though Ashbery is not the speculator in old houses that Bishop and Frost were, in 1979, he found a sort of replacement for his childhood homes when he bought, and then restored, the run-down house in Hudson, which reminded him of his maternal grandparents' homes.

In a letter to artist R.B. Kitaj, who did a painting for the cover of *Houseboat Days*, Ashbery quotes John Donne, "'we are born but to the liberty of the house' (sermon of March 28, 1619), which is a certain amount of liberty after all," and remarks, "houses seem to be a recurring theme in my poetry" (December 7, 1976, AM 6.24,

Houghton Library). When I asked him about this, Ashbery reflected: "Donne's saying we're all under house arrest, basically, since, I mean, we can go outside, but we can't really get away from our situation, our mortal situation, that we're going to die" (MacArthur 200). Williamson notes: "The past in Ashbery is often—as in Stevens' 'The Auroras of Autumn'—a house. It encloses and protects unchallengeably. . . . But if we lived in it entirely, we would be dead. We need to separate ourselves from it in order to live" (139).

As a young man, Ashbery was certainly eager to leave his father's farm, and the small town of Sodus. He explained his desire to go to New York after college:

> we [he and the other New York poets] wanted to live in the metropolis. I had had the experience of being in a little society of kids when I was very young [in Rochester] and then when I moved permanently to Sodus, there really wasn't anybody to play with and I felt isolated and lonely and wanted to be surrounded by the social possibilities of the city. (MacArthur 197)

When I visited Sodus in 2003, the local residents I met at the public library were obviously proud that Ashbery had grown up there. But they also admitted to finding his poetry rather mystifying, and displayed some small-town prejudice; one man hinted that Ashbery had "strange sexual preferences."

Perhaps the most direct reference to the liberation Ashbery may have felt leaving home appears in "A Wave": " 'I have been free ever since / To browse at will through my appetites' " (*AW* 85). Yet these lines appear within a powerfully nostalgic passage enacting a dream of return, through orchards to a farmhouse like his father's. More than Frost or Bishop, Ashbery articulates not only nostalgia for rural life and the attempted, ambivalent return, but also the liberating escape to the city that necessarily intervenes. The impulse to leave operates in both directions, as in "Pyrography"; the city and the country define each other, neither one fully satisfying. Somewhat like Bishop, Ashbery lacked in his adult life the kind of close extended family he grew up with, which may strengthen his attachment to his childhood landscape and homes. As he told me in recounting his family history, he is "the end of the [Ashbery] line" (MacArthur 178).

As an art critic, Ashbery has often chosen to write about landscape painting; his taste for the genre may also originate in his rural childhood. He writes in "Litany," "We feel we have more in common with a / Landscape, however shifty and ill-conceived, / Than with a still-life" (*As We Know* 96). Ashbery reflected to me, "I guess the landscape of that region [of his childhood] was imprinted on me, maybe without my realizing it, and I've remained attached to it" (MacArthur 188). As an epigraph to an essay about Neil Welliver, a contemporary American landscape painter whose work was included in the U.S. bicentennial exhibition for which Ashbery wrote "Pyrography," he offers the following from William James:

> 'Scenery seems to wear in one's consciousness better than any other element in life. . . . I have often been surprised to find what a predominant part in my own spiritual existence it has played, and how it stands out as almost the only thing the memory of which I should like to carry over with me beyond the veil, unamended and unaltered.'

Certainly this suggests Ashbery's own preoccupation with landscape. The poet admires Welliver for combining a traditional interest in landscape with the technical innovations of Abstract Expressionism:

> he paints large-scaled landscapes of an unspoiled American wilderness . . . but . . . the tone of the work seems . . . to refer . . . to mid-twentieth century abstraction, particularly the "all-over" canvases of Jackson Pollock. How can this be, we wonder? For "we" are accustomed to dealing with one idea at a time, at least when those ideas are proposed by our artists, and the spectacle of one of them keeping two or half-a-dozen ideas aloft simultaneously, of according equal importance to all of them, makes us uncomfortable. For situations that are a common feature of daily life seem strange and even threatening when beamed back at us by the mirror of art.
>
> Having accepted in the relatively recent past that painting can be . . . something we call abstract . . . and . . . that descriptive, figural painting . . . did not on that account dry up and blow away, we are hard put to see how Welliver can deliver both propositions without asking us to choose. ("Neil Welliver," AM 6.2, Houghton Library)

This passage should alert us to the impatience Ashbery feels at being pigeon-holed himself as wholly experimental and postmodern. In reading a poet whose "mind / is so hospitable, taking in everything / Like boarders," almost any critical emphasis can feel like a limitation (*Houseboat Days* 38).[30] Stylistically, Ashbery is the most experimental major American poet since T.S. Eliot, but simultaneously, in some of his most experimental poems, he meditates lyrically on the American rural landscape, "according equal importance" to his rural childhood and to his innovative poetics. The rural landscape of his childhood, and his affinities with Romantic landscape meditation and rural poetry, are highly significant and moving themes in the wide and dazzling range of reference of his poetry.

CHAPTER 1

Robert Frost: "The Ruined Cottage" in America

I dwell with a strangely aching heart
In that vanished abode there far apart
On that disused and forgotten road.

—"Ghost House" (1901)

There is a house that is no more a house
Upon a farm that is no more a farm
. . . .
Here are your waters and your watering place.
Drink and be whole again beyond confusion.

—"Directive" (1946)

My father could hardly pass an abandoned farm without wanting to own it.

—Lesley Frost[1]

A Rootless Youth: San Francisco to New England

The pathos of Frost's poems about the abandoned farmhouse originates in the poet's autobiography. Throughout his life, beginning with his urban youth in San Francisco and New England, Frost and his family struggled to find and keep a home, and moved a bewildering number of times. The poet came to see rural New England as a refuge from that experience, first as a tourist and outsider, and as a man of greater leisure than his neighbors in Derry and later in the White Mountains of New Hampshire. The imaginative scene of the abandoned or ruined farmhouse in his poetry evokes at once Frost's own family history and his dark romanticization of America's rural past, as he transposed Wordsworth's "The Ruined Cottage" onto the cellar holes and abandoned farms of the American landscape. The scene symbolically encompasses Frost's greatest personal and poetic ambitions, failures, and losses. His unsettled life also gave the poet peculiar insight into the restless and problematic relationship of the American people to the national landscape, given ambivalent expression in "The Gift Outright."

To counteract Frost's popular reputation, it is necessary to review the poet's experiences of moving, of keeping house and home, and of trying out farm-life before his move, at the age of twenty-six, to the Derry farm. His story begins in San Francisco, where Frost was born in 1874. In 1880, San Francisco was the ninth largest city in the United States (pop. 233,959). It had grown rapidly since the Gold Rush; in 1850, the population was 21,000 (U.S. Census Bureau). Frost was born to William Prescott Frost, Jr., and Isabelle ("Belle") Moodie Frost, a teacher and a native of Leith, Scotland, who came to America at the age of twelve. His mother had had some reservations about marrying William Frost (see Frost's poem "The Lovely Shall Be Choosers"), with good reason. A devout Presbyterian, Belle Frost became a Swedenborgian in San Francisco under the influence of her reading of Emerson. She would raise her son on Emerson, Wordsworth, and Poe, among other favored poets.[2] Her husband, an outstanding scholar at Harvard, had also become "a successful poker player, a heavy drinker, and a frequenter of brothels" during his college years, and during the Civil War, he had tried to join the Confederate Army to rebel against his parents (he would later name his son Robert Lee). As soon as he could, he fled his native Massachusetts, "bitterly scornful of…strait-laced and puritanical mores." Not long after his son was born, he took up his vices again in San Francisco. He was an aggressive journalist, an athlete, and an aspiring politician (Thompson, *Early Years* 1–5).

With these ill-matched parents, Frost would have an unsettled childhood. While Belle was pregnant with Frost, the couple moved four times in five months—partly, according to Thompson, because Belle was not a good housekeeper. After Frost was born, Belle told her son later, her husband's violence sometimes made her fear for her life and her infant son. Pregnant with a second child, Belle left her husband in the spring of 1876, taking two-year-old Robert back east with her. She returned to San Francisco later that year, with a high school friend, Miss Blanche Rankin, who came west as a companion, and perhaps protector, to Belle and her two children (Frost's sister Jeannie was born in 1876). Reunited, the Frost family continued to live in fear of the black moods and heavy drinking of Will Frost, who also had difficulty supporting the family; he hoped to profit from investments in silver mines, and was increasingly ill with tuberculosis (Thompson, *Early Years* 8–15, 18, 19).

Family tensions were aggravated by the provisional nature of the Frost household. The Frosts moved six times in the next nine years, sometimes living in fancy hotels, but more often in cheap and cheerless apartments. For the Frost children, each move may have inspired insecurity about their parents' capacity to provide for them, and some hope that the family's situation might improve. During these years, Frost also had his first experience of rural escape, from the tense household dominated by his father. In the summers of 1882 and 1884, Belle and her children vacationed on a ranch in Napa Valley, leaving Will Frost behind in the city. On the ranch the boy happily dabbled in poultry-farming, a hobby he kept up for a time in a tiny backyard in San Francisco (Thompson, *Early Years* 486–487, 33, 47). Frost's idyllic visits to the Napa ranch seemed to make a deep impression, and may lie behind a recurrent dream of escape he had, which featured a landscape like Napa Valley or the Sierras, and led to the only story the young Frost wrote while he lived in San Francisco (see Thompson, *Early Years* 37–38, and Munson 28–29).

The Western chapter of Frost's life ended in May 1885 when Will Frost died, at the age of thirty-four, of tuberculosis exacerbated by drinking. Belle Frost found herself with "only eight dollars in cash" (Thompson, *Early Years* 45). Robert, his mother, and his sister Jeannie took the train back east to Lawrence, Massachusetts, where Will Frost had been raised and where Frost's grandparents (who paid for the train fare) still lived. Belle Frost was apparently quite anxious about the reception she would receive, and about supporting her children. As Guy Rotella puts it, "The Frost family's version of the classic American journey West for freedom, fame and profit had failed, and [Frost developed an] association of death and displacement with the collapse of his father's hopes" (246).

When the Frosts retreated east, they were not headed for a New England rural idyll, but to the industrial city of Lawrence, Massachusetts, about twenty-five miles north of Boston, which was by 1890 the sixth largest city in the United States (pop. 448,477). Frost would visit Boston throughout his youth—to look for work, take exams, or just tour the city—and while he attended Harvard from 1897 to 1899, he lived in Cambridge. In 1880 and 1890, Lawrence itself made the list of the 100 largest urban areas in the United States (it was sixty-fourth), with a population of 44,654 in 1890 (U.S. Census Bureau). Also by 1890, Massachusetts was the second-most urbanized state in the union (Brown 139). Jeffrey Meyers gives an apt description of Lawrence circa 1885, when the Frosts arrived there from San Francisco:

> Its leading citizens, people of British origin, felt superior to the recent immigrants, who worked in the shoe and paper factories and in the mills that had made the place a world center for the manufacture of textiles.... There was nothing poetic about the blue-collar mill town, with its poor, run-down tenements in the working-class areas and the scattered churches and small shops of the obstinately provincial middle class. [Frost at first] disliked the Yankees, who seemed closed and narrow compared to the generous, big-hearted Californians, and could not get used to their stiff ways, nor to the dark skies and severe winters of the Northeast. (16)

Though Frost later wrote a poem about his own escape from the mills, "The Lone Striker," Lawrence seemed to inspire few of his poems. He remembered it as an "industrial city," where labor disputes were common (*CPPP* 759–760). For the most part, he would call Lawrence home from 1890 to 1899, from the ages of sixteen to twenty-five.

In Lawrence, and briefly in Salem, New Hampshire, Belle Frost struggled to support the family as a schoolteacher. Meyers suggests that, "Frost felt angry about the degrading poverty of his family" (33). The Frosts continued to move often, sometimes under threat of eviction. When Frost was twelve, he began to contribute to the family income, taking up various jobs from 1892 to 1899, working in the mills, as a handyman in tourist resorts in Maine and New Hampshire, and later as a teacher (Thompson, *Early Years* 61; Rotella 246–247). The family's financial instability and cramped urban apartments led to a desire for rural leisure. According to Thompson, Frost began to imagine and idealize a farming life that would require little work and allow him to cultivate his talent for poetry—a life of rural retreat, which had so appealed to him as a boy in California and New England, would let him play at rural life, rather playing servant to other tourists (see Thompson, *Early Years* 96).

While Frost lived in Lawrence, he enjoyed a few limited experiences of farming and of rural New England. In the summer and early fall of 1885, Frost visited his Uncle Ben and Aunt Sarah Messer's farm in Amherst, New Hampshire, and it apparently made a deep impression on him:

> For the poor relations from California this move to Amherst, New Hampshire, provided the first glimpse of the rural North of Boston region...so strikingly different from the only other farm they had known, the Bragg ranch in Napa Valley[.] [Frost] and his sister found life on this New Hampshire hillside very pleasant after...being cooped up with their grandparents [in Lawrence]....[Ben Messer] seemed to enjoy educating these city children in country lore. (Thompson, *Early Years*, 52–53)

The Messer farm differed wonderfully from the "two shabbily furnished rooms" of the Lawrence apartment where the family moved that fall from San Francisco. We begin to see how Frost may have idealized the New England farmhouse as a symbol of family stability and financial security, in contrast to the transient, urban homes of his childhood, associated with relative poverty and frequent, involuntary movement, and finally with his father's death (Thompson, *Early Years* 54, 85–88).

In the summer of 1891, Frost worked on a farm that took in summer tourist-boarders in Windham, New Hampshire. Apparently put off by the crudeness of his fellow hired hands, he left after three weeks because he had trouble, as he did his whole life, getting up early, particularly to do farm work. In 1892, Frost briefly attended Dartmouth College without finishing the fall semester; he spent much of his time going for walks in the woods (Thompson, *Early Years* 137–146). In the summer of 1893, Frost enjoyed, for the first time in eight years, an extended stay on a farm, this time in Salem, New Hampshire. He had "volunteered to live [there] as caretaker and protector" to the mother and sisters of his future wife, Elinor White, who were summering there; Elinor later joined them. Frost planted a vegetable garden and spent a great deal of time reading (Thompson, *Early Years* 103, 105–106).

The summer of 1893 began a pattern of rural vacations for Frost. To be near Elinor in a White Mountains tourist resort in 1895, he spent part of the summer living alone in an isolated cottage—"an abandoned farmhouse...owned by the 'natives[,]'" as Frost later described it, near Lake Winnepesaukee, New Hampshire (Thompson, *Early Years* 203; *The Letters of Robert Frost to Louis Untermeyer* 355).[3] Staying alone in the house, Frost was apparently terrified at night, having spent most of his life in cities or towns (Thompson, *Early Years* 205–207).

More or less as a tourist, Frost experienced these rural retreats in the 1890s as welcome interruptions to a cramped and uncongenial urban life. When he married Elinor in December 1895, the ceremony took place in a Lawrence office building. The newlyweds lived there for seven months with Frost's mother, where the three also set up a school, which soon failed. It wasn't until the summer of 1896 that the young couple had a honeymoon, at a small rented cottage in Allenstown, New Hampshire, which Carl Burell had found for them. Burell, Frost's friend from high school, worked in a box factory in Pembroke. He was also an amateur botanist and spent much of his spare time teaching the Frosts about the region's native wildflowers. Frost became enthusiastic about botanizing, a rural diversion associated with Romantic poetry in a book Burell lent him, Mrs. William Starr Dana's *How to Know the Wild Flowers.* He found quoted in it many botanizing poets he admired, as well as an author then new to him, Thoreau, who had escaped into what he called wilderness, much as Frost dreamed of doing (Thompson, *Early Years* 217–218, 272).

Newly married, however, Frost had considerable worries about how he was going to support his wife and, eventually, children, and he had a competing desire to devote time to poetry. The idyllic summer of 1896, and his readings in botany, may have confirmed an impression that, not only was rural life *the* subject of poetry, but only a rural life would make writing possible. If so, he needed to find a way to spend more time in the country. At the summer's end, the young couple moved into their own apartment in Lawrence, where their first child, Elliott, was born. But the appeal of rural life had struck them both, and in the summers of 1897 and 1898, they rented a house at Salisbury Point in Amesbury, Massachusetts.

Frost's health problems made the countryside especially appealing. In the summer of 1898 and again in March of 1899, Frost fell ill with what he feared might tuberculosis. His doctor told him that "The best remedy would be an entire change in Frost's living habits...some activity such as farming, which would keep him out-of-doors and give him plenty of exercise" (Thompson, *Early Years* 250). He had been living in Lawrence and in Cambridge part of the year, attending classes at Harvard. On his doctor's advice, in the spring of 1899, Frost moved with his wife, their son Elliott, and daughter Lesley, to a farmhouse in Methuen, just a few miles outside of Lawrence, to try poultry-farming.

The Methuen farm enterprise lasted only a year and a half. Frost's mother fell sick with cancer in the spring of 1899, and Frost himself became very sick with hay fever. And tragically, Frost's son Elliott died of cholera at the age of four, in the summer of 1900. Frost felt he could have prevented the boy's death by seeking a doctor sooner, and Elinor was apparently inconsolable (as is the wife in Frost's poem "Home Burial"). The Frosts were evicted from the Methuen farm for failing to pay rent and letting "nearly three hundred White Wyandottes [chickens]" wander the place. Elinor's mother and Frost's grandfather came to the rescue, when Mrs. White found the Derry farm and William Frost Sr. agreed to buy it for his grandson and his growing family. Frost and his wife both loved the Derry farm at first sight (Thompson, *Early Years* 258–263).

Here we might recapitulate the hopes and experiences Frost brought to Derry in the fall of 1900, with the intention of farming and devoting himself to poetry. During childhood vacations to Napa Valley in 1882 and 1884, and in explorations of rural New England in the 1890s, mostly on summer vacations, Frost had developed a taste for rural retreat, first as escape from the city and his parents' marital and financial troubles and, later, from his own responsibilities. He had, in addition to some dabbling in poultry-farming in Napa Valley and San Francisco as a boy, one and a half years' experience as a poultry farmer in Methuen, which had ended in eviction (Thompson, *Early Years* 260). He had a recently acquired taste for the literary leisure activity of botanizing. His mother had raised him on Emerson, who pronounced in "Nature" that rural New England was the rightful realm of the poet, not of the farmers who legally owned the land, and on Wordsworth, the Romantic exemplar of "a poet living in [rural] retirement" (Preface to "The Excursion," Wordsworth 604). Frost had also published five poems in leading literary magazines: "My Butterfly," "The Birds Do Thus," "Caesar's Lost Transport Ships," "Warning," and "Greece" (Cramer 26, 198, 203–205). Of these, two had a rural bent.

On the other hand, circumstances did not bode well for the venture in Derry. Frost's Derry neighbors viewed him skeptically as an outsider—a green, comparatively affluent, young man who did not understand the challenges of farming in New England—and his grandfather insisted that his more practical friend Burell live with the Frosts to help out. Elinor was not much better than Frost in this regard, apparently; of little practical help, like Frost's mother, she was not an enthusiastic housekeeper (Thompson, *Early Years* 282, 263, 265). Rotella suggests that "Perhaps this [move to Derry] felt like a reversion to the position [of farmer] from which his grandfather had risen, as [Frost's] failure to graduate from Harvard might have seemed a falling off from his father's attainment" (248). Frost seemed to feel that failure loomed for a number of reasons. Although he excelled in high school (he was co-valedictorian with Elinor), he took degrees neither at Dartmouth nor Harvard, and he would not gain significant recognition as a poet until the age of thirty-nine. His grandfather's and his in-laws' reservations about Frost's reliability as a breadwinner, which Parini details, were warranted (72). Given Frost's tendency to put poetry before farming, it is no surprise that after five years of increasingly desultory effort, he gave up farming in Derry and began to teach at a private school down the road, Pinkerton Academy.

In 1900, Frost had suffered the death of his first child, quickly followed by his mother's death soon after he moved to Derry. Frost himself continued to feel weak and ill. Still fearing that he might have tuberculosis, he may have been haunted by parallels to the fate of his father—seriously ill, somewhat at odds with his wife, unable to support his family adequately. Coincidentally, when Frost suffered a "bout with pneumonia during March and April of 1907 [that] was very nearly fatal," he was thirty-three years old; his father had died of tuberculosis at thirty-four. Thompson suggests that, when Frost's grandfather bought the Derry the farm for him, Frost felt he was telling him to " 'Go out and die. Good riddance to you.' " The pressure of these circumstances and worries combined, according to Thompson, to make Frost find suicide, in the "fall and early winter [of 1900 and 1901] more and more attractive." During this depression, Frost wrote the sonnet, "Despair," which he did not publish in his lifetime, and perhaps also began "Stopping by Woods on a Snowy Evening," which can be read as an evasion of a suicidal impulse (Thompson, *Early Years* 229, 335, 120 269–272).

When Frost moved to Derry, his memories of homes would have been of frequent moves from one small, cheap apartment to another, punctuated by infrequent rural retreats. In his twenty-six years, he had moved more than twenty-six times.[4] Before and after the Derry years, the Frosts—both the poets' parents and the poet's own family—illustrate Auden's claim that, for Americans, "to move on and make a fresh start somewhere else is still the normal reaction to dissatisfaction or failure" (360). Although such moves may certainly begin with "dissatisfaction or failure" (recalling that Auden saw the ubiquitous abandoned house as a sign of this tendency in America), it can also become a chronic form of restlessness, an inability to settle, to dwell. And it can feel necessary to a successful career as a public poet or academic, as it apparently was for Frost, who moved often when his poetic career took off, traveling much of the year to give readings and lectures.

Out of literary ambition, Frost had wanted to move away from the Derry farm well before he did in 1909; he hoped to sell the place to finance a move. By the spring of 1906, as he related to Thompson, he thought it might be

> time he stopped pretending he was a farm-poultryman. Everyone in the region knew he did very little farming.... After the annuities [from his grandfather's will] had begun to come in, he had gradually permitted his brood of Wyandottes [hens] to decrease...given the choice, he would prefer to live in New York City as a salaried contributor of prose and verse to a publication like *The Independent*...in 1903,...he had taken his family to New York City and spent a pleasant but futile month there. If other choices existed, he did not know what they might be. Looking around somewhat desperately, he...appl[ied] for a position as a teacher[.] (Thompson 315–316)

Also, first in 1906, Frost began to escape the summer hay fever season in the White Mountains of New Hampshire, a resort locale that would provide him with enough poetic inspiration (particularly for his dramatic monologues) to rival the Derry landscape.[5]

However, the conditional terms of the will of Frost's grandfather, who died in the summer of 1901, specifically constrained his grandson to live in the rural isolation of Derry for ten years before the farm would become legally his:

> "I give [my grandson]...the free use and occupancy of said farm for and during the first ten years beginning at the time of my decease.... At the end of said ten year term, I devise to him the fee in said farm...[and] an annuity of $500 annually for and during said ten year term, and from and after the expiration of said ten year term an annuity of $800 annually for and during the term of his natural life." (qtd. in Thompson, *Early Years* 275–276)

With these conditions, his grandfather had effectively given Frost a ten-year sentence to live on the farm, with a generous allowance, after which Frost would acquire ownership of the farm and a greater annual allowance.

In the introduction to journals that she kept in Derry as a child, Frost's daughter Lesley writes: "The farm I am writing about might well be called 'The Gift Outright' to my father and mother. 'The land was ours before we were the land's'" (Francis n. p.). The Derry farm was a gift, more or less, from Frost's grandfather. The terms of his will, at once generous and demanding, are strikingly similar to the terms of the Homestead Act, which required five years' residence and improvement of land before an individual could claim legal ownership ("The Homestead Act"). "The Gift Outright," as I argue below, is concerned with such land grants. William Frost Sr., formerly a farmer himself, was behaving toward his grandson somewhat like the U.S. government had toward settlers, in encouraging the population of Western territories by European-Americans and the displacement of Native Americans. Frost, like some other Americans who gained title to land under the Homestead Act, sold the farm as soon as he legally could, to finance another new venture: the launch of his poetic career.

But first, from 1901 to 1906, Frost gave himself to the land with some ambivalence, at his grandfather's invitation and rather at his insistence. And gradually, the Derry farm, and the fading rural life it seemed to exemplify, made Frost into its poet. His grandfather's will effected a reversal of fortune for Frost. Following a childhood and youth marked by financial insecurity, Frost would have, for the rest of his life, a small guaranteed income. And in ten years he would own the Derry farm itself. Although Thompson lingers on Frost's irritation at the terms of his grandfather's will, and at the large amount his grandfather left to charities, Frost must have felt some gratitude to him as well, not least for the poetry inspired by his enforced residence in Derry.

By the summer of 1909, soon after the Frosts had moved into an apartment in Derry Village, Frost was already entertaining the idea of buying new property, at Lake Willoughby, New Hampshire, although he had no capital and the Derry farm was not yet his legal property to borrow against. Almost as soon as the terms of his grandfather's will allowed him, he sold the farm. As mentioned in the introduction, Frost took the title for his second book *North of Boston* from "a Boston newspaper advertisement" for properties in the region (Cramer 28–29). Imaginative and actual property speculation became "a new hobby...which [the poet] continued to indulge throughout the rest of his life" (Parini 104).

The poem "On the Sale of My Farm," which Frost wrote in November 1911, was not published until after his death in 1963 (first in Thompson's biography), perhaps because the poem bids farewell to the landscape Frost credits elsewhere as the source of so much of his poetry—or perhaps simply because the title belies Frost's popular reputation as a farmer-poet. Its rueful tone and Yeatsian meter differ from the mitigated nostalgia of Frost's other early poems about abandoned farms:

> Well-away and be it so,
> To the stranger I let them go.
> Even cheerfully I yield
> Pasture, orchard, mowing-field,
> Yea, and wish him all the gain
> I required of them in vain.
> Yea and I can yield him house,
> Barn, and shed, with rat and mouse
> To dispute possession of.
> These I can unlearn to love.
> Since I cannot help it? Good!
> Only be it understood,
> It shall be no trespassing
> If I come again some spring
> In the grey disguise of years,
> Seeking ache of memory here.
> (*CPPP* 519)

The speaker cedes his farm "to the stranger" and nature "even cheerfully," as Frost himself may have when he sold the Derry farm to finance his dream of launching his poetic career in a major city. "Well-away" seems at first a polite way of saying "good riddance." For Frost, the material rewards of keeping the farm were paltry. Ticking off the items that the speaker says he will not really miss, what is left of the farm? The "ache of memory"—which expresses the deep attachment Frost already had to his memories of Derry. He would imaginatively return to the farm countless times, without revisiting the actual landscape until 1938. Perhaps in 1911 Frost anticipated, in Walsh's words, how much "calculated use [he would make] of his farm past," in later "disguise of years."

Abandoned Houses and Cellar Holes

Keeping in mind the ubiquity of the abandoned farmhouse in the New England landscape (as detailed in the introduction), and Frost's experiences of rural life before and during the Derry years, we may approach Frost's poetry about the abandoned New England farmhouse with new insight. In it we will see that, with complex and shifting tones, he transposes "The Ruined Cottage" onto the American landscape to reflect the fact that hope and inspiration are inextricably tied up with loss and failure in the scene of the American abandoned house. The poems "Ghost House," "The Black Cottage," "The Generations of Men," "A Fountain, a Bottle, a Donkey's Ears and Some Books," "The Census-Taker," "The Need of Being Versed in Country Things," and "Directive" draw on Frost's childhood and adult experiences of hopeful new starts in new homes (especially in Derry and also earlier in San Francisco and elsewhere in New England); of voluntary abandonment and eviction; of failure and loss; of the early breakup of Frost's family with the death of his father; of his parents' incompetence in providing secure homes; of his own fears about supporting his family; of cultural nostalgia for an abandoned rural life; of the larger problem of homeless during the Depression; of the destruction of dwellings in WWII; and of the later deaths of two of Frost's children and of Elinor Frost. In these poems, Frost recreates and memorializes the scene of the abandoned farmhouse in its essential loneliness, as a source of peculiar personal and cultural consolation and inspiration.

Frost began writing "Ghost House" in 1901 (*CPPP* 15–16). It is set "under the small, dim, summer star[,]" possibly that first summer in Derry that followed a winter of loss and grief for his son and mother (li. 21). The second poem in *A Boy's Will*, it introduces the book's half-abandoned rural landscape, following "Into My Own," whose speaker fantasizes about "steal[ing] away" into the country. But the woods do not "[stretch] away unto the edge of doom" as he wishes (*CPPP* 15). What the speaker of "Ghost House" finds, when he does steal away, is "a lonely house," actually a cellar hole inhabited by ghosts (li. 1).

As mentioned in the Introduction, the cellar hole that inspired this poem, left after a fire in 1867, was just across the road from the Derry farm. To Frost it may have seemed a literal symbol of a family's failed or abandoned effort to keep a farm. The poet at twenty-seven, a young husband and father, new to farming, finds the scene of an abandoned farmhouse strangely compelling; his youthful speaker (implied by the title *A Boy's Will*) is already nostalgic about failure and loss. The "lonely" "vanished" house may represent a failure to farm in New England's poor soil, and to survive in rural isolation—a venture that many, including Frost's grandparents, had long ago abandoned. Thus Frost's family history in rural New England, as well as the contemporary presence of abandoned farms, may come to dwell in "Ghost House."

In contrast to the end of "The Black Cottage," the speaker gladly remains at the scene of "Ghost House," even after an ominous nightfall, when "the black bats tumble and dart." The recursive rhyme scheme, A-A-B-B-A, also emphasizes return. He is not merely a visitor to the abandoned house, as he always is in later poems, but an inhabitant:

> I dwell in a lonely house I know
> That vanished many a summer ago,
>   And left no trace but the cellar walls,
>   And a cellar in which the daylight falls
> And the purple-stemmed wild raspberries grow.
>
> O'er ruined fences the grapevines shield
> The woods come back to the mowing field;
>   The orchard tree has grown one copse
>   Of new wood and old where the woodpecker chops;
> The footpath down to the well is healed.
>
> (ll. 1–10)

The speaker seems almost grateful that little trace is left of the house. The abandonment or failure of the farm is a sad fact that nature nearly erases, through decay and natural resurgence. The "woods come back" to reclaim the cultivated fields, and "the orchard tree" survives, tended by a woodpecker. In the cellar hole, sweet raspberries grow, and natural overgrowth of the path generously hides or "heal[s]" the shame of the farm's ruin. Perhaps Frost felt shame when he and his parents failed to keep a particular home, or abandoned it. And he may have identified with the imagined grief of the former inhabitants of the house.

This scene must have seemed especially poetic to the young Frost, given his knowledge of Thoreau and Wordsworth.[6] Thoreau had written, in the chapter "Former Inhabitants; and Winter Visitors" in *Walden*, "Now only a dent in the earth marks the sites of these dwellings, with buried cellar stones, and strawberries, raspberries... growing in the sunny sward there" (310). As well, the opening stanzas of "Ghost House" obviously echo lines 28–31 of "The Ruined Cottage": "amid the gloom / Spread by a brotherhood of lofty elms, / Appear a roofless Hut; four naked walls / That stared upon each other!"; lines 453–462, which describe vegetation that "had tempted to o'erleap / The broken wall"; and lines 882–883: "You see that path / Now faint,—the grass has crept o'er its grey line[.]" Buell rightly cites "Ghost House" as evidence of "poetic self-consciousness" and "earnest romantic aestheticism" in Frost's early work—rare in his later poems of the abandoned farmhouse, with their ironic, comic touches, less archaic diction, and darker lyricism (Buell 109).

Yet Frost was already departing from Wordsworth in writing a short lyrical elegy rather than a long dramatic poem about the ruin. The "Ghost House," a stone-walled cellar hole of a vernacular American wooden farmhouse, is overgrown, like Thoreau's cellar hole and like Wordsworth's "lonely Cottage," with berries and vines that begin to hide the walls, fences, well, and paths. In "Ghost House," the lonely scene captivates the speaker, who finds particular consolation in the imagined resilience of American wilderness, which effaces human loss or failure. Frost's attitude here differs from the piteous tone of Wordsworth's "Wanderer," who laments the ruin of Margaret's cottage and the ways that nature reclaims it. However, in "dwell[ing]" in the "Ghost House," Frost's speaker and his ghost companions show the same impractical, sentimental persistence that Margaret does in Wordsworth's poem. Long after her husband has presumably been killed at war, and her oldest son has left to find work far away, " 'She loved this wretched spot, nor would for worlds / Have parted hence.... / In sickness she remained; and here she died; / Last human tenant of these ruined walls!' " (ll. 911–912, 915–916). In the third stanza of "Ghost House," the speaker recognizes something peculiar about his lingering, "with a strangely aching heart." Heartache for something "vanished" implies death, and "dwell[ing]" in a "vanished abode" suggests the paradox of grief for the dead: a preoccupation with what, or who, no longer exists. The ruined landscape's value, then, seems entirely imaginative.

In 1901, the New England farming industry was not flourishing, and Frost had doubts about his own aptitude for farming. However the road to the "Ghost House" may be "disused" and "forgotten," as is the road to the former farm in "Directive," the speaker still follows it. He goes to grieve and be consoled by the "lonely house," the scene of an attempt to make a home, whose shame of failure or abandonment is gradually effaced by the welcome resurgence of nature. In the final stanza, actual ghosts, "[a]s sweet companions as might be had[,]" draw the speaker to the scene (li. 30). The speaker "know[s] not who these mute folk are / Who share the unlit place with" him (ll. 22–23). The cellar hole becomes a sort of grave or memorial for their hopes, and their actual gravestones are nearby, though "mosses mar" the inscribed names. Unnamed, the ghosts of the house became representative figures of failure and loss. If the speaker himself is not a ghost, nor is he with the living; he dwells in a scene that provides no physical shelter and implies failure, abandonment, and death. Like Margaret's attachment to the ruined cottage, the speaker's insistence on dwelling in the ghost house is a sort of heroic, impractical show of loyalty to the dead, to dreams that failed.

As is often the case with Frost, this ruined landscape holds the speaker's, and the reader's, attention because it is a human scene. People have left a meaningful trace on the landscape: the cellar hole. The "mute folk" in "Ghost House" turn out to be "tireless folk, but slow and sad" (li. 26). This may suggest a farming family who worked hard to keep their house and farm, who were slowed and saddened by unknown adversity, perhaps the difficulty of farming in New England. Frost and his wife were certainly "slow and sad" in their first fall and winter in Derry; the most compelling of the ghosts, for the speaker, are "two, close-keeping…lass and lad[.]" There is "none among them [who] ever sings"—if we identify the "lad" with Frost, perhaps he was too sad to "sing" at the time (li. 28). Frost's mother and his son Elliott, recently lost, might also be counterparts for "as sweet companions as might be had." The overt display of failure and loss in nearby abandoned farmhouses and cellar holes, such as the one across the road from Frost's own farm that inspired this poem, haunts the living rural folk in other Frost poems. Similarly, the memory of his parents' and his own failures to keep a house may have haunted Frost. It is the spirit of the former inhabitants of the "Ghost House," embodied in the cellar hole itself, who lived the sort of life Frost was attempting, which captures the earnest speaker's "strangely aching heart."

Frost's second book, *North of Boston* (1914), closely followed the publication of *A Boy's Will* (1913), but moves away from Wordsworthian sentimentalism. It introduces a more ambivalent evocation of the landscape and inhabitants of rural New England. Two poems in *North of Boston* from the Derry years about an abandoned house and cellar hole, "The Black Cottage" and "The Generations of Men," are distinguished by great tonal differences from "Ghost House" and from one another.

Frost began "The Black Cottage" (*CPPP* 59–62) around 1905 or 1906 in Derry, and it was one of three poems written there that led to *North of Boston* (Cramer 36, 29).[7] It is the first evocation of an actual abandoned house in Frost's poetry, rather than a cellar hole, and, like "Ghost House," it obviously echoes Wordsworth's "The Ruined Cottage," though not in descriptions of the ruined house. Instead "The Black Cottage" is modeled on a dramatic dialogue in Wordsworth's poem. Written in more idiomatic blank verse, it grows directly out of Frost's acquaintance with long-time residents of rural New England, and thus registers more local, ambivalent attitudes about the abandoned landscape.

A minister-guide figure speaks most of the lines, telling the speaker, an apparent outsider or newcomer, about the cottage and its former inhabitant, a Civil War widow. The outsider, minister, and widow parallel the tourist-narrator, the Wanderer, and Margaret in "The Ruined Cottage." (In an early, shorter version of "The Black Cottage," with a more nostalgic tone, an old woman still lives in the house [see Thompson, *Early Years* 592].) The outsider figure, who likely stands in for Frost and frames the poem with its opening and closing lines, is carefully distinguished from the native minister-guide—in contrast to "Directive," in which a single authoritative speaker, more closely identified with Frost, is the reader's dubious guide. In "The Black Cottage," the outsider only describes the physical appearance of the mysterious cottage, while the minister details and meditates on the cottage's history, including the way of life the widow represented, now "forsaken" like her home (li. 34). Like Wordsworth's poem, and like "A Fountain…," "The Black Cottage" focuses on the house's former inhabitant as much as on the abandoned house itself. But unlike the speaker in "Ghost House," who "dwells" there with his "sweet companions," the minister and his companion come as intruders to the cottage.

As in "Directive," the syntax of the opening lines of "The Black Cottage" backs up to the abandoned cottage, as we move backward, in memory and time, to find it:

> We chanced in passing by that afternoon
> To catch it in a sort of special picture…
> …
> Set well back from the road in rank lodged grass,
> The little cottage we were speaking of,
> A front with just a door between two windows,
> Fresh painted by the shower a velvet black.
> (ll. 1–2, 4–7)

Even before the widow is mentioned, Frost anthropomorphizes the cottage, describing it somewhat like a face: the windows eyes, the door a mouth. But the cottage offers no welcome to the curious pair, only a "vague parting in the grass / That led us to a weathered window sill" (ll. 12–13). The two men rudely peer inside because, as the minister says, "'No one will care[,]'" but respectfully they do not go in, as the widow's absent sons "'won't have the place disturbed'" (ll. 11, 21). The widow of "The Black Cottage," based on Mrs. Sarah J. Upton, a Civil War widow of Derry, strikingly resembles Wordsworth's Margaret. The widow lost her husband to the Civil War, and her sons left to work far away, while Margaret lost her husband Robert to war (a sort of poetic fusion of the American and French revolutions), and her eldest son to "a distant farm" where he found work (ll. 676–677, 846, 760). There may also be parallels to Frost's family here; again, Frost's father tried to join the Confederate side in the Civil War, and then moved "west," where one of the widow's sons has ended up in the poem.

In the poem, the widow's sons abandon the cottage; like Margaret, the widow never left it. Although the minister respects the widow, she is not venerated like Margaret, but depicted as too naïve for contemporary times. This neglect of the cottage is directly connected with the neglect of the widow:

> 'But what I'm getting to is how forsaken
> A little cottage this has always seemed;
> Since she went more than ever, but before—
> I don't mean altogether by the lives
> That had gone out of it, the father first,
> Then the two sons, till she was left alone.
> (Nothing could draw her after those two sons.
> She valued the considerate neglect
> She had at some cost taught them after years.)
> I mean by the world's having passed it by—
> As we almost got by this afternoon.'
>
> (ll. 34–44)

These lines again remind us of Wordworth's Margaret, who lived on at her cottage as it fell to ruin, pathetically hoping to see, at any moment in the distance, her husband or son returning to her. For the minister and his companion, the cottage is almost irresistible, as "Ghost House" is for the speaker of that poem. The rest of the world passes it by, but some are attracted by its persistence in neglect. The minister links the widow's intractable beliefs to the state of her cottage: "'The warping boards pull out their own old nails / With none to tread and put them in their place. / She had her own ideas of things, the old lady'" (ll. 49–51).

In a startling shift, the minister moves from the subject of the widow to an extended fantasy of ruling "a desert land" that might remind us of Shelley's "Ozymandias" (ll. 111–124). He imagines this geographically isolated kingdom, cut off by snowy mountain ranges, as he sits on the doorstep of an abandoned cottage in a relatively deserted area of New Hampshire, where farming was no longer viable, and which few "'would covet or think it worth / The pains of conquering to force change on / [with its] Scattered oases where men dwelt[,]'" or used to dwell (ll. 117–119). In this "desert land," "The Black Cottage" is a sort of oasis where the widow hung on, queenly in her small dominion—but "forsaken."

As snow-covered mountains wall off the desert, bees in the cottage wall protect it from those who would change it, or even from those who, nostalgic for the way of life it represents, would invade it. The sudden appearance of the bees cuts off the minister in mid-sentence ("'the sand storm / Retard mid-waste my cowering caravans— / There are bees in this wall'" [ll. 123–125].). Like the glory of Ozymandias, the minister's fantasy is doomed to failure and oblivion. The bees' threatening presence may also signal that the minister cannot realize his fantasy in abandoned rural New Hampshire. He and his companion cannot stay at the abandoned cottage, whose windows glare like eyes gleaming with anger: "We rose to go. Sunset blazed on the windows" (li. 127). It is hard to imagine Wordsworth interrupting and ending such a reverie so abruptly. Frost's ending makes "The Black Cottage" eerie, like "Ghost House" and the ghostly former farm in "Directive," and less inviting. At the end of this poem, the minister and his companion retreat abruptly, almost in flight. And clearly, the traditional rural life the cottage represents, and the widow's naïve beliefs, have been abandoned. The cottage now is almost haunted, reverting to nature like "Ghost House," and it fiercely deflects the invasive, nostalgic curiosity of outsiders.

In the more comic blank verse poem "The Generations of Men" (*CPPP* 74–81), ironic and reverential attitudes are expressed toward an abandoned house, combined with self-conscious, mocking references to rural tourism in New England.[8] Auden considers it to be "one of [Frost's] best long poems" (348). Parts of the poem anticipate "Directive," and may also reflect Frost's own experience of falling in love with his future wife, going on long walks in rural areas outside Lawrence, and fantasizing about the possibility of moving to the New England countryside of his ancestors. In the poem, a young man and a young woman, two distant cousins who share the name of Stark, meet alone at a cellar hole.

The original title, as noted in the introduction, was "The Cellar Hole." The opening lines directly refer to the New Hampshire governor's invention of "Old Home Week" and its ancestral preoccupations, which will be lightly mocked throughout:

> A governor it was proclaimed this time,
> When all who would come seeking in New Hampshire

Ancestral memories might come together.
And those of the name Stark gathered in Bow,
A rock-strewn town where farming has fallen off,
And sprout-lands flourish where the ax has gone.
Someone had literally run to earth
In an old cellar hole in a by-road
The origin of all the family there.
Thence they were sprung, so numerous a tribe
. . . .
Nothing would do but they must fix a day
To stand together at the crater's verge
That turned them on the world, and try to fathom
The past and get some strangeness out of it.
(ll. 1–10, 14–18)

These lines poke fun at the earnestness of a large, scattered family of native New Englanders who, at the behest of the governor, takes over an entire village for a week, hunting up their roots in the ruins of an ancestral home among abandoned farms. The Stark descendants had planned, rather ridiculously, to gather at the edge of the seemingly unremarkable cellar hole. There are many comic touches in the poem, mocking nativist pride—the male cousin draws "his passport" to prove he is a Stark, and later the female cousin tells him that he " 'riddle[s] with [his] genealogy / Like a Viola' " (ll. 49, 56–57). Frost may mock himself and other Wordsworthian poets here—as a poet, he profited from visiting cellar holes, trying to "fathom / The past and get some strangeness out of it." And again he echoes Thoreau, who observed, in *Walden*, the surviving descendant of a family lying on his belly, looking into the cellar of his family home, recently burnt down, "as if there were some treasure . . . between the stones, when there was absolutely nothing but a heap of bricks and ashes. The house being gone, he looked at what there was left" (308).

The hole in Frost's poem is also, as the young man says, " 'the pit from which we Starks were digged' " (li. 94). Mocking claims of lofty ancestry, this line also suggests a grave. He imagines that he can see the ghosts of their ancestors there, and describes them to his cousin: " 'a little, little boy, / As pale and dim as a match flame in the sun[,]' " and " 'Granny' " Stark, whom he at first mistakes for " 'Grandsir Stark' " (ll. 99–100, 106). Recalling how tenderly the speaker of "Ghost House" evokes the ghosts of that cellar hole, we might take the ghosts of "The Generations of Men" somewhat seriously. The small boy may remind us of Frost's first son Elliott, who had died at the age of four. And the grandparents Stark, whom the young man caricatures as pipe-smoking cider-drinkers (Granny later speaks a sort of rural dialect), may remind us of Frost's grandparents, the most recent New Hampshire farmers in his family.

The poem takes a more serious turn when the young man says "'we can't stay here for ever[,]'" but seems to long to do so (li. 120). The young woman wants to leave, but the young man keeps her there when he claims to hear the voices of his ancestors, and becomes a sort of medium for their speech. The voice of Granny Stark speaks through the boy in the commanding language of a guide, anticipating "Directive," and tells him to build upon the cellar hole:

> 'take a timber
> That you shall find lies in the cellar charred
> Among the raspberries, and hew and shape it
> For a door-sill or other corner piece
> In a new cottage on the ancient spot.
> The life is not yet all gone out of it.
> And come and make your summer dwelling here,
> And perhaps she will come, still unafraid,
> And sit before you in the open door
> With flowers in her lap until they fade,
> But not come in across the sacred sill—'
> (ll. 160–170)

Perhaps rural New England life might be renewed, if only by summer tourists, some of them natives now living elsewhere. Though Frost himself never built a summer home, after he left Derry he bought several New England farms that he would use as summer homes, just as the Vermont Board of Agriculture hoped summer tourists would. The comic tone of the poem recedes further here, and a question the boy poses to the girl near the end—"'Will you leave the way to me?'" (li. 205)—also anticipates the dubious guide-figure of "Directive." This particular cellar hole scene may recall the Derry farm, as "Directive" does—it was "a new cottage" of sorts on an old spot, built in 1884, just across the road from the cellar hole of the Merriam house, which burned down in 1867; some of its charred timbers may have remained in Frost's time.

Frost would continue to move away from Wordsworthian sentimentalism as he rewrote "The Ruined Cottage" in an early-twentieth-century American context, developing a blend of self-conscious humor about rural tourism and pathos for such scenes, in later work. By the time he published his fourth book *New Hampshire* (1924), he had achieved considerable success, which also required the Frosts to live a more unsettled life. Upon their return from England in 1915, the Frosts bought a farm in the White Mountains, in Franconia, New Hampshire, and lived there for a year and a half. This was the last extended, uninterrupted period Frost would ever spend on an isolated farm in New England. He would own others, but the pattern of residence in 1920 at his farm in South Shaftesbury, Vermont, became typical: "the Stone Cottage on the farm in South Shaftesbury became for Frost more like a hostelry, intermittently visited, than a permanent home. He rested briefly there between trips to far-scattered colleges" (Thompson, *Years of Triumph* 158). Frost taught at Amherst College from 1917 to 1920, and from 1921 to 1923 he was a poet in residence at the University of Michigan, returning to New England in the summers; in Amherst alone, the Frosts lived at four different addresses in these years (Thompson, *Years of Triumph* xii–xiii, 706).

In a long blank-verse dialogue poem from *New Hampshire*, "A Fountain, a Bottle, A Donkey's Ears, and Some Books" (*CPPP* 196–200), Frost's peculiar blend of mockery toward rural tourism in New England, and reverence for the abandoned house as a source of poetry, clearly anticipate "Directive." "A Fountain..." has received little critical attention, though Randall Jarrell admired "the 'Books' part of it" (Jarrell 39). As in "The Black Cottage," the first speaker in "A Fountain..." is a curious outsider led by a guide to an abandoned house or cellar hole. Raymond Holden, a close neighbor in Franconia in the White Mountains and Frost's frequent hiking companion, provides some relevant context:

> "He [was] fascinated by the half-known, half-forgotten relics of New Englanders of an earlier day...[and] often told me of the legend he had heard when he lived in Derry...that the Mormons had once built a stone temple in the forest somewhere in New Hampshire, the ruined altar or font of which was sometimes stumbled upon by hunters...[Frost] and I never took a walk without the sometimes spoken and sometimes tacit understanding that we were looking for that altar. We never found it....The only reference to this romantically elusive spot in [his] work is, so far as I know, in the poem "A Fountain, a Bottle, A Donkey's Ears, and Some Books." (qtd. in Thompson, *Years of Triumph* 563–564)

Holden's reminiscence encourages a biographical reading of poems like "The Generations of Men" and "A Fountain...," whose speakers hunt for ruins and relics on their rural walks. Frost would also make symbolic use of the lost stone font in "Directive."

In "A Fountain...," the outsider-speaker never finds the fountain he is looking for, and, as in "The Black Cottage," he learns the history of the area from his guide. When the speaker mentions wanting to see "'a stone baptismal font'" left by the "'early Mormons,'" Old Davis, his misleading guide, refers to it scornfully as "'that old bathtub[;]'" he says it might be lost in the woods, perhaps had "'sprung / a leak and emptied...forty years / Can do a good deal to bad masonry'" (ll. 10, 9, 15, 21, 24–26). Instead, Old Davis shows him silly tourist attractions: the shapes of a bottle and a donkey's ears (referring to the story of Midas), both traced on the landscape. The speaker mocks these as "likeness[es] to surprise the thrilly tourist," and Old Davis, in leading him to them, apparently tests the speaker's sophistication and knowledge of the area (li. 40).[9] The bottle traced on the landscape, which Old Davis shows to the speaker, is, of course, as empty as the elusive fountain. (Both fountain and bottle may remind us of the "brook that was the water of the house" and the "broken drinking goblet like the Grail" in "Directive" [ll. 50, 57].)

After these detours, Old Davis finally leads the speaker to an abandoned house that once belonged to a female poet, which turns out to be a veritable fountain of poetry. Like the guide in "Directive," Old Davis leads the way down a road the speaker "didn't recognize, /.... to where it ended at a house / I didn't know was there" (ll. 65, 68–69). This road should remind us of the "disused and forgotten road" to "Ghost House" and of the road to the "farm that is no more a farm" in "Directive" (li. 6). The speaker admires the house, saying, "I never saw so good a house deserted" (li. 71), which may recall Frost's attachment to his Derry farm after he sold it. Like "The Black Cottage," this abandoned house resists intruders:

> 'Excuse me if I ask you in a window
> That happens to be broken,' Davis said.
> ....
> 'I want to introduce you to the people
> Who used to live here....
> You must have heard of Clara Robinson,
> The poetess who wrote the book of verses
> And had it published. It was all about
> The posies on her inner window sill,
> And the birds on her outer window sill,
> And how she tended both, or had them tended:
> She never tended anything herself.
> She was "shut in" for life. She lived her whole

> Life long in bed, and wrote her things in bed.
> . . . .
> 'Our business first's up attic with her books.'
>
> We trod uncomfortably on crunching glass
> Through a house stripped of everything
> Except, it seemed, the poetess's poems.
> (ll. 72–73, 75–85, 88–91)

The name of Clara Robinson refers to an actual poet from Lawrence, Massachusetts, "who never had a book of poems published in her lifetime"; later she taught at St. Lawrence University, which Elinor Frost attended, in Canton, New York. Robinson's daughter, Ethel Robinson Murphy, became a published poet (Cramer 73). And, of course, the last name, isolation, and domestic subjects of the "poetess" remind us of a more famous New England female poet, Emily Dickinson, whom Frost greatly admired; he also followed biographical readings of her work (*LRFLU* 203). Finally, the "poetess" may be a figure for Frost himself, and her house may correspond to the Derry farm. While Frost lived in Derry, he was nearly as obscure as Clara Robinson.[10] Frost, like the "poetess," did not "tend [much of] anything" on his farm after 1905.

Just before he guides the speaker to the Robinson house, Old Davis mocks him, " 'Give you your books!' " (li. 59). Perhaps he does lead us to Frost's books, in a sense. Parallels to Frost's own poetic career, and perhaps to Dickinson's, emerge in the rest of the poem. Retreating, like Midas, from the city of material wealth to the poetic wealth of the country, the speaker finds that the attic of this secluded, abandoned house is almost spilling with poetry—in the "books" section Jarrell admired. The books might remind us of Dickinson's fascicles, though there are many more copies of these:

> A whole edition [of books] in a packing-case,
> That, overflowing like a horn of plenty,
> . . .
> Had spilled them near the window toward the light
> Where driven rain had wet and swollen them.
> . . . .
> They had been brought home from some publisher
> And taken thus into the family.
> Boys and bad hunters had known what to do
> With stone and lead to unprotected glass:
> Shatter it inward on the unswept floors.
> How had the tender verse escaped their outrage?

By being invisible for what it was,
Or else by some remoteness that defied them
To find out what to do to hurt a poem.
Yet oh! The tempting flatness of a book,
To send it sailing out the attic window
Till it caught wind, and, opening out its covers,
Tried to improve on sailing like a tile
By flying like a bird (silent in flight,
But all the burden of its body song),
Only to tumble like a stricken bird,
And lie in stones and bushes unretrieved.
Books were not thrown irreverently about.
They simply lay where someone now and then,
Having tried one, had dropped it at his feet
And left it lying where it fell rejected.
. . . .
"Take one," Old Davis bade me graciously.

"Why not take two or three?"
. . . .
All the way home I kept remembering
The small book in my pocket. It was there.
The poetess had sighed, I knew, in heaven
At having eased her heart of one more copy—
Legitimately. My demand upon her,
Though slight, was a demand. She felt the tug.
In time she would be rid of all her books.
(ll. 93–95, 97–98,101–121,
124–125, 133–139)

The initial figure of harming the verse—the temptation to throw one book of poetry out the window—changes into a figure for sending poetry out into the world. The book becomes like a bird, a figure for the poet. Flung out the window, the books might have lain "in stones and bushes unretrieved," but instead, they are still sitting in the attic, some of them tried and rejected. Yet the poems make a claim "legitimately" on the speaker, who is glad for the dead poetess that she won another reader in him.

Frost would have felt similarly when his own books (Frost had to subsidize the publication of *A Boy's Will*) first found enthusiastic acceptance with readers. Frost wrote this poem "in the early 1920s" (Cramer 72), only ten years or so after his first book had finally brought him, at the age of thirty-nine, the poetic success he had long sought and almost despaired of. As late as 1957, he remarked that, when he had published *A Boy's Will* in England, he had "already [been] almost too old to bet on" (Thompson, *Years of Triumph* xii). In the early 1920s, perhaps Frost still felt elated at having emerged from the obscurity of his life in Derry, flung his books of poetry on the world, and seen them take off.

"A Fountain..." may pay homage to Derry and the poetic inspiration that memories of his life there continued to yield. In the abandoned Robinson house, the books of poetry are the only things of value left. Likewise, poetic inspiration was what Frost took with him when he left the rural isolation of Derry. Poetry survived his own neglect of the Derry farm, which was in disrepair when he sold it. The attacks on the Robinson house by "boys and bad hunters" did not harm "the tender verse," whose "remoteness...defied them[.]"

If the poem echoes the fate of Dickinson's poetry and its complicated publication history, Frost may have wanted to perpetuate a legend of New England poets who write for themselves, in isolation, and eventually are celebrated by the larger world. In the early twenties, Frost felt increasingly confident that "In time [he] would be rid of all [his] books" in the best possible sense; he was selling them, as he had aspired to do in 1913, "to the general reader who buys books in...thousands" (*SL* 98). Having set out looking for a baptismal fountain, with its implications of salvation and perpetual refreshment, the speaker finds, instead, an abandoned house full of poems. For Frost, the farm he sold in Derry was a great source of poetry.

A further departure from the Romantic nostalgia of "The Ruined Cottage" is Frost's far less celebratory poem of an abandoned house, "The Census-Taker" (*CPPP* 164–165). This blank-verse poem, which can also be traced to Frost's time in the White Mountains, describes an area where forests had been clear-cut, a destructive process used by the timber industry in New Hampshire in the late nineteenth century (Brown 43). In the first edition of *New Hampshire*, Frost made a note to line 209 of the title poem, "Whole townships named but without population[,]" as referring to "The Census-Taker" (Cramer 63). As cited in the introduction, a symbolic demographic shift was recorded in 1920, when the majority of Americans, for the first time, were living in urban areas (U.S. Census Bureau). Frost had begun "The Census-Taker" by 1920, when he sold his Franconia farm (Cramer 66).

The poem offers Frost's starkest portrait of rural New England as an abandoned wasteland, not a landscape that might attract tourists longing to return to rural life. In its title and lack of place-names,

"The Census-Taker" suggests a broad claim about the cultural significance of the abandonment of rural New England. Census-taking is notoriously difficult, perhaps especially in the United States, where populations shift quickly and frequently. The census-taker goes over unlikely territory to see whether a population has appeared, persisted, grown, or disappeared. Frost's poem underscores how quickly a particular house in a clear-cut forest had been abandoned: "This house in one year [had] fallen to decay" (li. 50). The speaker, who is the census-taker, may have seen the house the year before. He "declare[s]" of the whole region near the poem's end: "'The place is desert'" (li. 57), recalling the minister's imagined kingdom of a "'desert land'" in "The Black Cottage."

The census-taker seems strangely obsessed with the hopeless search for men to count in "the waste." We know, from line eleven, that the house and landscape are empty of people, yet the poem persists for fifty-three more lines, as the spooked speaker assures himself again and again that no one is here:

> I came as census-taker to the waste
> To count the people and found none,
> None in the hundred miles, none in the house,
> Where I came last with some hope, but not much
> After hours' overlooking from the cliffs
> An emptiness flayed to the very stone.
> I found no people that dared show themselves,
> None not in hiding from the outward eye.
> (ll. 9–16)

Any people he may encounter are ghostly, as in "Ghost House" and "The Generations of Men." If they would not "dare" show themselves, perhaps they are, or ought to be, ashamed for laying waste to the forested landscape and then abandoning the house.

In this lonely, eerie scene, we encounter a ramshackle house of the sort we might find in Elizabeth Bishop's work:

> a slab-built, black-paper-covered house
> Of one room and one window and one door,
> The only dwelling in a waste cut over
> A hundred square miles in the mountains[.]
> (ll. 2–5)

If this house, like "The Black Cottage," resembles a face, it is one-eyed, with its single window. The crudely constructed dwelling, surrounded by axed tree trunks, may have housed a crew of lumberjacks. Although the speaker laments the felled trees, he seems equally concerned about the absent people, and describes the mute, dead forest like a field of wounded, dismembered, and dead men.

> every tree
> That could have dropped a leaf was down itself
> And nothing but the stump of it was left
> Now bringing out its rings in sugar of pitch;
> And every tree up stood a rotting trunk
> Without a single leaf to spend on autumn,
> Or branch to whistle after what was spent.
> (ll. 18–24)

Although the poem describes a New Hampshire landscape, the recent memory of the battlefields of WWI—where Frost's dear friend, the English poet Edward Thomas, was killed—lingers in the background. Like men killed in battle, these trees were felled violently and now they bleed "sugar of pitch." They have lost their ways of telling the season, which is deathly autumn. "The Census-Taker" was first published for an audience with the war on its mind, in the *New Republic* on April 6, 1921; the issue included editorial debates about the Treaty of Versailles.

The wind points up the self-serving, violent behavior of the men who used to live there, as it swings the door of the house:

> a door
> Forever off the latch, as if rude men
> Passed in and slammed it shut each one behind him
> For the next one to open for himself.
> I counted nine I had no right to count
> (But this was dreamy unofficial counting)
> Before I made the tenth across the threshold.
> (ll. 27–33)

In the evocation of unfriendly ghosts and loneliness, and the negative diction emphasizing the scene's abandonment (the word "none" appears nine times, "not" ten times, "no" seven times, and "nothing" three times), "The Census-Taker" uses language similar to "Directive." But this abandoned house offers no hope or remedy for confusion. There is only shame, decay, and an eerie sadness. The artifacts of the former life of the house are not spiritually significant, as they are in "Directive," but violent. "[T]he pitch-blackened stub of an ax-handle / I picked up off the straw-dust covered floor" is only good for "arm[ing] myself against such bones as might be" there (ll. 44–45, 43).

> I thought what to do that could be done—
> About the house—about the people not there.
> This house in one year fallen to decay
> Filled me with no less sorrow than the houses
> Fallen to ruin in ten thousand years
> Where Asia wedges Africa from Europe.
> . . . .
> The melancholy of having to count souls
> Where they grow fewer and fewer every year
> Is extreme where they shrink to none at all.
> (ll. 48–5, 361–63)

For the census-taker, this recently abandoned lumberjacks' shack in New Hampshire is no less tragic than the ruins of Mesopotamian civilization, perhaps recalling the minister-guide's fantasy of a vaguely Biblical kingdom in New England. These lines elevate the cultural value of the American landscape, of this ruin of a brief, environmentally rapacious settlement. Unlike a farm, of course, this house did not fall to ruin after generations, but was abandoned when the short-term profit of clear-cutting had been realized. Not only do Americans abandon a landscape after "dissatisfaction or failure," as Auden pointed out, but after a profit from exploiting natural resources has been made, which may finance new ventures.

Although the census-taker criticizes the lumberjacks as "rude men," he is lonely even for such rough characters, and may identify with them. Any place where people have lived, the speaker suggests, however carelessly and temporarily, in American fashion, always feels deserted in their absence. The speaker also honors the "rude men" of rural New Hampshire by comparing their demise to that of great dynasties, and their abandoned house with the ruins of ancient civilizations. Given the choice, the census-taker would prefer that such settlements, and perhaps the forest itself, persist. In the rather flat last line—"It must be I want life to go on living" (li. 64)—the speaker seems almost desperate for survival of any sort. The strangely repetitive observations about the absence of people, and the last line, may have seemed especially poignant in the aftermath of WWI, when memories of pointless carnage in the trenches were vivid. The speaker also simply wants life in rural New England to endure, specifically in the White Mountains. But there is no real hope of that here; this abandoned house offers no imaginative solace, and nature has not been able to heal the shame of abandonment, as it did in "Ghost House," and as it will in "The Need of Being Versed in Country Things."

The final poem in *New Hampshire* (*CPPP* 223), "Country Things" may recapitulate some central themes of the volume, particularly the state's depopulation and abandoned landscapes, as in the title poem. "Country Things" was first published in *Harper's Magazine* in December 1920. A long opening article in the issue, "Hail, Columbia!" by W.I. George, a British writer exploring the United States, noted: "The city-bred American . . . feels a romantic attraction for the wooden cottages that lie between New York and Maine" (6). He also announced, "New England is dead. It is being slain by Newer England; by an industrial New England" (9).[11] On its surface, "Country Things" would have appealed to such a contemporary audience nostalgic for old New England, although the poem actually rejects simple nostalgia.

The poem seems to return to the Derry landscape, perhaps to the same scene that inspired "Ghost House." The prominent barn "across the way" (li. 5) in this poem, left after the house burnt down, may correspond to the barn connected to the Derry farmhouse, which is larger than the house, and stands across the road from the cellar hole. In the spring of 1905, the house in Derry was threatened when the annual spring bonfire of dead leaves, near the cellar hole of Merriam's original house, got out of control (Thompson, *Years of Triumph* 301).

Whereas the sentimental speaker in "Ghost House" is nostalgic about the vanished farmhouse, and the minister-guide and speaker in "The Black Cottage" are compelled by and slightly fearful of the cottage, the speaker in "Country Things" seems to believe, with the phoebes pictured in the poem, that "there was nothing really sad" about the abandoned and decaying farmhouse. Sadness is ascribed to the scene only by human beings, especially those not "versed in country things." "Being Versed in Country Things" means accepting that ruin, failure and loss are both natural and accidental—part of the regenerative order of things—and, incidentally, sources of artistic inspiration. There is, the poem suggests, some comfort in the persistence and recovery of nonhuman life. And Romantic aesthetic value and consolation can be found in the scene of a ruin.

The phoebes have made themselves happily at home in the barn and among the ruins of the farm, and the lyrical rhyme scheme suggests song:

> Yet for them the lilac renewed its leaf,
> And the aged elm, though touched with fire;

> And the dry pump flung up an awkward arm;
> And the fence post carried a strand of wire.
>
> (ll. 17–20)

The lilac, elm, pump, and fence wire offer the birds perches, just as the barn is a place to nest. The birds do very well with what for human beings is ruin. The sexual pun on "country" in the title also emphasizes that the business of nature is regeneration.

A bird is often a figure for the poet, particularly in the work of Frost. In the complicated syntax of the final three lines, the speaker expresses both the phoebes' cheerful attitude and human sadness, but seems to endorse the former:

> For them there was really nothing sad.
> But though they rejoiced in the nest they kept,
> One had to be versed in country things
> Not to believe the phoebes wept.
>
> (ll. 21–24)

As a poet in Derry, Frost had perhaps at first "too much dwell[ed] on what has been" and later "rejoiced in the [house he] kept" with his growing family, as he recovered from the losses of his son and mother, and encountered reminders of his own and his parents' failures in keeping homes, in the grave-like cellar holes that also recalled the abandonment of farm life by many in New England (li. 16, 22). At the same time, he was versed enough in Romanticism and New England history to find a great deal of poetry in the scene of the abandoned farmhouse. As he wrote to Louis Untermeyer, in reference to the poem, "My house may only be a one-room shack but it is not the Poor House: it is the Palace of Art" (*LRFLU* 304–305). Nonfunctional as a farm or a home, the burned-down farmhouse in "Country Things" has much consolation to offer the poet and the phoebes, his representatives.

"The Gift Outright": Key West in 1935

Turning from *New Hampshire* (1924) to "The Gift Outright" (*CPPP* 316)—a poem concerned not with abandoned houses in particular, but with larger American attitudes toward the entire national landscape that such ruins imply—we seem to leap forward some forty years. That is, many readers' primary association with the poem is the fact that Frost recited it at President John F. Kennedy's inauguration in 1961. In that context, it is often interpreted as triumphant nationalism, even a celebration of colonialism (especially in light of Frost's later, casual suggestions that it concerned the Revolutionary War, which oversimplify the poem). Other readers are preoccupied with the fact that "The Gift Outright" was first published in the spring of 1942—not long after the United States had joined WWII, in an issue of the politically minded *Virginia Quarterly Review* that was focused on the struggle of the war.[12] The poem's ambiguous closing lines suggest measured uncertainty about the outcome of the war and America's future.

Without dismissing the interest of such readings, it is worth going back further, first to the probable context of the poem's composition during the Great Depression in Key West, when the impoverished island was in the throes of a New Deal experiment. Thompson cites the poem as written in 1935, and according to Robert Faggen,[13] Frost likely began "The Gift Outright" one night in 1935, after listening with fascination to Jessie Porter, a fifth-generation native of Key West, recount the island's history for hours. Frost was especially interested in the Native American history of the island, and in the fact that "The pirates who founded the city were apparently from Boston" (*LRFLU* 251). Porter would have detailed the island's settlement, perhaps first by the Aztecs, followed by the Spanish, Cubans, Bahamians, and eventually, the U.S. Navy (Boulard 117).[14] With certain variations, this parallels the history of the conquest of the much of the present United States.

I hope to demonstrate that, although "The Gift Outright" is certainly aligned with a colonial perspective, the poem does not simply overlook the tragic fate of Native Americans, nor does it simply endorse Manifest Destiny. A common assumption that Frost was a racist nationalist[15] overdetermines readings of the poem, which takes on the whole narrative of colonialism—especially in the cryptic line thirteen, "(The deed of gift was many deeds of war)[.]" The poem also implicitly draws on Frost's own restless, rootless life, explored in earlier poems about abandoned houses, as emblematic of a disturbing national attitude.

In Key West, Native American history would likely have engaged Frost's interest deeply, as it had in his youth in the California. Brutal government policy toward Native Americans was not ancient history for Frost. Born just ten years after the Sand Creek Massacre of 1864, he was two years old in 1876, the year of the Battle of Little Bighorn, otherwise known as Custer's Last Stand; he was sixteen in 1890, the year of the Wounded Knee Massacre. As Dee Brown details in *Bury My Heart at Wounded Knee*, 1860–1890 was

> an incredible era of violence, greed, audacity, [and] sentimentality....During that time the culture and civilization of the American Indian was destroyed, and out of that time came virtually all the great myths of the American West...the white man's curiosity about Indian survivors reached a high point, [and] enterprising newspaper reporters frequently interviewed warriors and chiefs and gave them an opportunity to express their opinions on what was happening in the West[.] (Brown xi)

Growing up in California, where much of the Native American population had been decimated early, Frost developed a sympathetic fascination, however romanticized, with the natives of North and Central America, and likely followed reports about Native Americans in the newspapers for which his father wrote. The cherished childhood dream mentioned earlier, which he developed into his first story, featured "a tribe of Indians who were the only inhabitants of a secret valley [where they] had escaped from their enemies....Occasionally their braves made sorties.... [and] always returned victoriously" (Thompson, *Early Years* 38). In a high school debate in 1890, Frost made a strong defense of progressive land policy for Native Americans based on Helen Hunt Jackson's *A Century of Dishonor: A Sketch of the United States Government's Dealings with Some of the Indian Tribes*, and his earliest poem, written around the same time, was a romantic portrayal of the Aztecs' heroic, if temporary, defeat of the Spanish, "La Noche Triste."[16]

In thinking about the European colonization of North America as he composed "The Gift Outright," Frost, who thought so much about real estate in his own life, would have thought about land grants, hinted at in the phrase "deed of gift." Above I compared the terms of Frost's grandfather's will to the Homestead Act. Ten percent of the area of the United States, or 270 million acres, was settled under the Homestead Act—partly, of course, with the intention of permanently displacing the Native American population ("The Homestead Act"). Royal land grants were also instrumental in establishing the first British colonies in North America, where the poem begins, "in Massachusetts, in Virginia" (li. 4, *CPPP* 316).

In a notebook that almost certainly dates from this time in Key West, we find Frost reflecting on aspects of American colonial history amid the frightful atmosphere of the mid-1930s, arising from the worldwide Depression and the belligerent dictatorships of Hitler,

Mussolini, and Stalin. The notebook includes drafts of his "Letter to the Amherst Student," in which he defines his poetics and politics in this context: "The background is hugeness and confusion shading away from where we stand into black and utter chaos; and against the background any small man-made figure of order and concentration" (*CPPP* 740).[17] Language that appears in "The Gift Outright" is embedded in critical reflections on the unsettled national character, and on the role of U.S. government policy in the settlement of the continent:

> We moved over in 1630 but we havent [*sic*] brought all our things over yet. We havent [*sic*] finished moving. {A lot of ideas are still to coming to us...}
>
> ....
>
> Land has been taken up by trial and error. When the error has been excessive and especially when the government has been a party to the error by advertising {promoting agriculture in} the desert and letting {permitting} the railroads ~~adver~~ promote agriculture in the desert no question but that the government should do something to correct the error. The government ~~is to blame for~~ would have been to praise for having established watches to keep ~~people from~~ going into some land just as it is for having set up light houses to keep people from ships from going ashore. The state is in a position to see more widely than the people can for themselves: and to see further forward. A man should [~~illegible~~] take the thought for his children. The state may well take the thought for his grand children's grand children—that is if it expects its flag to wave a thousand years.
>
> It may prove beyond the power of stateliness to make forests grow where there is ~~no~~ {small} water. At least this can restore the buffalo grass to attach the soil in place from wind water. (*NBRF* 388, 393)[18]

While implicitly endorsing the European-American settlement of the continent, these notebook entries straightforwardly criticize historical U.S. land policies. Such policies encouraged settlement of areas unsuited for intensive agriculture, destroyed natural ecosystems like the prairies that sustained the buffalo and forests like the one described in "The Census-Taker," and created wastelands, contemporaneously, in the catastrophe of the Dust Bowl that began in 1931, displacing hundreds of thousands, and eventually inspiring government-mandated programs to prevent soil erosion.

Frost argues here that the state has an obligation to address the problems of the Depression, some of which resulted from misguided land policy, to better provide for its citizens. In doing so, he seems to echo the native American proverb: "Treat the earth well: it was not given to you by your parents, it was loaned to you by your children. We do not inherit the Earth from our Ancestors, we borrow it from our Children." Perhaps in accordance with his sense of the failures of historical U.S. land policy, however, Frost was also skeptical about the wisdom of the New Deal.

At the time, Key West was undergoing one of the most publicized and controversial experiments of the New Deal, in response to severe bankruptcy and poverty that were remarkable even in the Depression. The city had "declared Key West in 'a state of emergency'" in the summer of 1934, when "at least eighty percent of [Key West's] inhabitants [were] on the welfare rolls." First the state of Florida, and then the Federal Emergency Relief Administration (FERA), had taken control of the island's affairs (116). The situation was national news, and a chief strategy for recovery, conceived largely by FERA administrator Julius Stone, was to attract as many tourists as possible to the island. A clean-up, construction and advertising campaign (including ads in the *New York Times*, which Frost and Bishop may have seen) was phenomenally successful, almost doubling the number of visitors in the winter of 1934–1935, compared with the previous winter (Boulard 122). Frost and his family were among them, having come, on doctors' advice, to escape the Vermont winter.

The Frosts had become ever more unsettled in the decade since the publication of *New Hampshire*, due to Frost's many teaching and lecturing commitments. Newly arrived in half-abandoned Key West, Frost was fascinated not only by Jessie Porter's stories about the island's history, but with its present, "the politics and economies of Key West" (*LRFLU* 251). He was displeased with FERA's extensive authority and with the public art projects in Key West—Ernest Hemingway, Wallace Stevens, and John Dos Passos were critical as well (Ogle 174). They were not alone in seeing Stone as dictatorial. In the 1930s, many concerned for the needy were also uncomfortable with Roosevelt's liberal use of executive power. Historians of the New Deal note the similarity of the Civil Conservation Corps camps—which operated in Key West, and which were strictly governed and created in part to decrease crimes committed by the poor and desperate—to prisons (see John A. Pandiani, and my discussion of Bishop's "In Prison" in Chapter Two). Such camps today might be interpreted by leftist intellectuals in light of Agamben's theory of biopolitics and the concentration camp—"the politicization of bare life as such."[19] As Frost wrote to Untermeyer, "They [FERA's employees] are mildly and beneficently dictatorial.... Their great object they say is to restore the people to their civic virtue. When in history has any power ever achieved that? You see how much I am interested" (*LRFLU* 251). Referring to statistical estimates that ten to fifteen million Americans were entirely dependent on the government for basic sustenance, Frost suggests ironically in a notebook that the New Deal camps were no better than slavery (*NBRF* 291).

"Civic virtue" is one theme considered in "The Gift Outright," which evokes the early careless attitude of the American people toward the American landscape. Frost brings the full force of his personal unsettled history, his wry yet sentimental interest in real estate, his opinions about the rather desperate state of the nation in 1935, the history of Key West, and the larger colonial history of North America, into the composition of the poem. The colonial era of royal land grants is when the blank verse poem begins, before the Revolutionary War:

> The land was ours before we were the land's.
> She was our land more than a hundred years
> Before we were her people. . . .
> . . . .
> But we were England's, still colonials,
> Possessing what we still were unpossessed by,
> Possessed by what we now no more possessed.
> Something we were withholding made us weak
> Until we found out that it was ourselves
> We were withholding from our land of living,
> And forthwith found salvation in surrender.
> (ll. 1–3, 5–11)

Undue attachment to England, and weak allegiance to North America, in other words, "made us [colonials] weak / Until we . . . . surrender[ed]" ourselves to the land—not, of course, to the British. Deed to the land, through land grants, precedes love of the conventionally feminized land. Annette Kolodny invokes the poem in her study of persistent metaphors of sexual subjugation in the literature of exploration and colonization, *The Lay of the Land* (Kolodny 10). Yet the usual trope of man subduing the feminized landscape is subverted here, as "we" must learn to surrender to the land. These lines can be read as more dynamic romantic metaphor; a legal union such as marriage precedes full physical and emotional surrender, and acceptance of the saving fact of mutual commitment. Frost had had an analogous experience in Derry, where he gradually gave himself over to the farm and the surrounding landscape, according to the Homestead Act–like limits of his grandfather's will, and the farm yielded his most fruitful poetic years—not to mention the early and happiest years of his marriage.

Such historical and biographical context bears on our reading of the last five lines of the poem, in their extraordinary tonal ambiguity:

> Such as we were we gave ourselves outright
> (The deed of gift was many deeds of war)
> To the land vaguely realizing westward,
> But still unstoried, artless, unenhanced,
> Such as she was, such as she would become.
> (ll. 12–16)

The speaker is aligned with the perspective of the Anglo-American colonist, for whom the wars against Native Americans (more than the boasted defeats of the British, the French, and the Spanish) were a national sin only to be mentioned in parentheses. The phrase "vaguely realizing westward" describes the haphazard, provisional manner, typified perhaps by the Louisiana Purchase, in which the United States acquired the Western territories. But these closing lines, considered with the poem's title, suggest first that the land was a gift given without condition, and thus the colonists may not have merited it, and second, that "we" were no great gift to the land.

Here Frost employs "such" in the critical or apologetic sense noted in the Oxford English Dictionary: "*such as one* or *it is*: having the character that he (it) has, no more and no less; used chiefly with a depreciatory or contemptuous reference, or apologetically." The speaker implies that early Americans were not a great people—nor would their descendants necessarily become so. When Frost wrote the poem in 1935, amid the Depression and the environmental disaster of the Dust Bowl, he did not seem to think that America had achieved greatness—there is equivocation, even contempt, in the line, "such as she would become."

Kennedy sensed that the poem did not quite strike the triumphant note he wanted for his inauguration. After suggesting that Frost read the poem, he asked him to change the last line to the "more positive-sounding…'such as she *will* become'"—which Frost did, rather awkwardly, when he read it (Thompson, *Later Years* 278). The slight shift from past conditional to simple future tense at Kennedy's inauguration tips us toward the conventional reading of the poem as an unfinished narrative of nationalist glory. Such a reading was less tenable in 1935 than in 1961, when, after the victory of WWII, amid unprecedented prosperity, "our mood [was] high"—as Frost wrote in the lesser, triumphant poem he composed for the occasion, "For John F. Kennedy His Inauguration" (*CPPP* 436–437). He only read the first few lines of the dedicatory poem "before abandoning it (apparently because of bright sun) to recite 'The Gift Outright'" (Thompson, *Later Years* 280). The former poem, conventionally enough, argues that the American Revolution marked "the beginning of the end" of colonialism, and the poet heralds, for President Kennedy, "a next Augustan age / . . . . A golden age of poetry and power[.]"

That is not, however, the apparent theme of "The Gift Outright." The speaker's measured contempt for "we" ("colonials") in line twelve might well arise from the "deeds of war" in line thirteen, which "we" performed to earn the dubious right to claim the land as "our" legal property. "[D]eed" in the first sense, the title to a piece of property, was explicitly gained by deeds in the second sense, acts of war—"we" sacrificed ourselves for the land in attacking others who claimed a prior right to it. Finally, we need not read line fifteen as simply expressing the Emersonian view that America had no native culture, and needed to create one, to proclaim final independence from Europe. At the beginning of his career with "Into My Own," Frost declared a wish that the woods still "stretched away unto the edge of doom," and a longing to escape the "highway where the slow wheel pours the sand" (*CPPP* 15). Faggen also suggests that Frost was charmed by the idea of Key West before colonization. The poet might rather have preferred the land "still unstoried, artless, unenhanced," in the affirmative sense of artless as "unartificial, natural," and against the pejorative sense of "enhance" as "make to appear greater; to heighten, exaggerate" (*Oxford English Dictionary*). In another notebook entry written around the time he composed "The Gift Outright," Frost sounds closer to Mary Louise Pratt's concept of the contact zone, pre-contact, than we might ever expect him to get, when he takes it for granted that

> The History of the United States of American begins has begun with the sentence: There were two great cities flourishing in ~~the New World~~ and three great peoples approaching civilization in the New World when Columbus found it in 1492. The cities would compare in importance with any but even the best of the line in Europe such as London Paris and Madrid. ~~No word of them came to Columbus—nor word of Columbus to them~~. They were as blissfully unconscious of Columbus him [sic] as he was unblissfully? unconscious of them. (*NBRF* 324)

This entry appears in Notebook 22, in which Frost was also meditating on the New Deal; again we see the continuity of his thinking about American history.

Like many of Frost's most famous poems, including "The Road Not Taken," "The Gift Outright" means different things to different people, bearing out at least one popular reading—as a narrative of triumphant colonialism—that is contradicted by a deeper analysis, partly because of its subtle use of deceptively simple diction. Further, it resonates very differently according to the context in which it is read. Too often, our readings of Frost are overdetermined by our preconceptions about who the poet was. Aware that Frost's sense of American history was less than glorious, and that the poet's own relationship to the American landscape was unsettled, we should register that "The Gift Outright," among other themes, offers some critique of colonialism and of the environmentally destructive tendencies of U.S. land policy.

"Directive": The Legacy of Derry in 1946

The remarkable blank verse poem "Directive," often considered to be Frost's last great poem, is obviously the culmination of Frost's meditations on the vernacular ruin of the American landscape, the abandoned house (*CPPP* 341–342). It was first published just after the end of WWII, on the first page of the winter 1946 issue of the *Virginia Quarterly Review*. Many articles in the issue dealt with the global legacy of WWII, and in a long essay, Max Lerner took up the question, "Are We a People Without a History?"[20] In the *Review*, Frost's poem might have been read as a "Directive" for the country, and even as a response to Lerner's implied question: what is America's history?

Like "The Gift Outright," "Directive" exemplifies Frost's knack for conflating his own and larger cultural experiences of the American landscape. The cryptic opening phrase, which can be read as an imperative, or as a descriptive phrase—"Back out of all this now too much for us"—may attest to the overwhelming tragedy of the 1930s and 1940s, the unspeakable nature of the Depression and the war's unprecedented destruction (both associated with the abandonment and destruction of dwellings), and the impulse to retreat from it all. Widespread homelessness and unemployment, as well as the war, were very recent memories for the contemporary audience of "Directive." A poem that immediately precedes "Directive" in *Steeple Bush* (1947), "One Step Backward Taken," expresses a sense of "universal crisis" and a feeling of having narrowly escaped complete catastrophe (*CPPP* 340).

During the period of the Depression and the war, Frost had suffered a series of crises and devastating personal losses, which contrasted dramatically with his great public success as a poet. These losses, which more or less destroyed his family, bear directly on the poem, which he wrote thirty-five years after he sold the Derry farm, in 1946. In 1933, Frost became very ill, at the age of fifty-nine; he still feared he might have tuberculosis. One result was that the Frosts began wintering in Florida, from 1934 on (Thompson, *Years of Triumph* 391, 405). In 1934, Frost's fifth child, Marjorie Frost Fraser, died at the age of twenty-nine, a few months after giving birth to her first child, from complications that could have easily been prevented. Frost and his wife were heartbroken. Less than three years later, in 1938, Elinor Frost died after suffering seven heart attacks in three days, without saying a final goodbye to her husband of forty-three years. Frost had been sick before Elinor died, and became seriously ill after her death. In the 1930s, Frost had become increasingly well known, and his life became increasingly peripatetic. Elinor had been the most consistent presence in his life; Frost had rarely spent a night apart from her. According to Thompson, Frost blamed himself for Elinor's death because she had her first heart attack climbing the stairs to their Gainesville apartment, after a tiring day of viewing prospective houses to buy. At the time, Frost was also on bad terms with his other daughter, Irma, and with his son Carol, both of whom suffered from mental illness (Thompson, *Years of Triumph* 407–408, 494, 485–486, 495–496).

As time went on, Frost came to see Derry as the most stable and happiest home his family had ever had. In 1938, soon after Elinor's death, he made a trip to Derry, his first visit there in many years. He meant to keep a promise to Elinor, who had asked that her ashes be scattered "among the alders alongside the bank of Hyla Brook" on the Derry farm. As Thompson relates, "Over and over again [Frost] had said to Elinor and others that the days they had spent on that farm were in retrospect the most sacred of his entire life. He had kept the images of house and barn and orchard and pasture and mowing-field so vivid in his consciousness" (Thompson, *Years of Triumph* 507). His sad and solitary pilgrimage to Derry, which failed in its mission because the farm's new owners were unfriendly to Frost, is indisputably behind "Directive." An unusually sympathetic, eloquent passage in Thompson, detailing the trip, reads as if taken by dictation from Frost (see Thompson, *Years of Triumph* 507–510). After the painful visit to Derry, Frost returned to his Gully farmhouse in South

Shaftesbury, Vermont, but could not bear to stay where he had lived with Elinor. Instead he slept at his former farm nearby, then the home of Carol's family. Not knowing what else to do with it, for a time he kept the urn of Elinor's ashes in the cupboard in his bedroom (Thompson, *Years of Triumph* 511).

Another horrific blow came in October 1940, when Carol committed suicide (Thompson, *Later Years* 70). As with the deaths of Elinor and his son Elliott, Frost felt somehow responsible, as he confided to Untermeyer: "I took the wrong way with him. I tried many ways and every single one of them was wrong" (*LRFLU* 322). On a September day in 1941, he went with Carol's widow, Lillian, and his grandson Prescott, and buried the ashes of Carol and Elinor, without religious ceremony, in the cemetery of the First Congregational Church in Bennington, Vermont. When Frost published "Directive," only two other family members survived from the Derry years: his daughters Lesley and Irma. In 1947, Frost made the sad decision to have Irma institutionalized, as he had done with his sister, Jeannie, in 1920 (Thompson, *Later Years* 163). These losses add poignancy to Frost's dedication of *Steeple Bush* to his grandchildren.

A number of critics, when they consider "Directive," remark in passing that it echoes earlier Frost poems about abandoned or ruined houses.[21] Some also notice that it seems to recall Derry, but prefer not to explore the connection (Parini 363). As I have suggested above, nearly all of Frost's poems about abandoned farms can be traced to the Derry landscape itself, or to the White Mountains he discovered during the Derry years. Of course other New England landscapes, as well as memories of Frost's childhood homes, may inform the poem. While the poem's realm of reference is not limited to the landscape of Derry, however, it is deeply illuminating to recognize that "Directive" leads us to an abandoned farm strikingly like Derry. Robert Lowell calls it "an aging Frost's 'Tintern Abbey'—written as he journeyed home to the destroyed homestead of his early marriage, his lost wife and children" (208). In "Directive," Frost apparently conflates his own farm with the ruined cellar hole of the Merriam farmhouse, as he may have done in "The Need of Being Versed in Country Things." Frost began his life in Derry in despair and left it in hope, and the landscape became "sacred" to him over the years.[22]

The personal significance of Derry for Frost, including the deaths he had suffered in the unsettled years since he sold the farm, would resonate with American readers with comparable experiences of loss and displacement, including Elizabeth Bishop. Such readers of

"Directive" would, like Frost and Bishop, idealize rural houses as emblematic of traditional dwelling. The landscape of "Directive" is based on a particular farm where one young family spent its best years—a family whose members, when the poem was written, were scattered, estranged, or dead. Not a few abandoned houses in America share a similar history. For Frost, Derry had become an imaginative home, somewhat like the fragile "crypto-dream-house" that Bishop would memorialize in the late poem "The End of March." "Directive" evokes a sort of dream landscape that paradoxically represents hope, poetic inspiration, failure, and loss.

In "Directive," which, as Blanford Parker notes, is "a New England term for a guidebook.... The poet gives the impression that he is re-enacting a journey that he has already taken, going down a road which is no longer mysterious to him... he has become a kind of master arranger of all the circumstances of the trip" (184). The speaker of "Directive" is an authoritative guide to the abandoned house. In effect, Frost's speaker has become his own guide: "if you'll let a guide direct you / Who only has at heart your getting lost" (ll. 8–9). This contrasts with "The Black Cottage" and "A Fountain...," in which an outsider figure is led by a native guide to an abandoned house. By this point, Frost had transformed himself from an outsider to a seemingly native representative of rural New England. The guide is not quite trustworthy, however. Frost's speaker lures his readers, with the hope of finding simple nostalgic comfort and real shelter, to the eerie scene of the abandoned farmhouse:

> Back out of all this now too much for us,
> Back in a time made simple by the loss
> Of detail, burned, dissolved, and broken off
> Like graveyard marble sculpture in the weather,
> There is a house that is no more a house
> Upon a farm that is no more a farm
> And in a town that is no more a town.
>
> (ll. 1–7)

Somewhat like "The Black Cottage," the poem backs up to reach this imaginative scene, not arriving at the house itself until the fifth line. The phrases "Back out" and "back in" direct the reader out of present, overwhelming circumstances, into a time simplified by time's passage, symbolized in the easing of grief like the wearing-away of "graveyard... sculpture." In 1946, many readers may have wanted to escape into nostalgic visions of the past, but where Frost leads us is not so comforting. Instead, it might remind us of the utter destruction of houses and whole towns, in the relentless bombings of Europe.

Recalling Frost's nine years on the Derry farm, the abandoned rural scene we are asked to go "back" to is also metonymic for what was becoming the national past, as the population shift from rural to urban areas continued. Houses were no longer houses, farms no longer farms, towns no longer towns. "All this" loss and change we might want to simply "back out of" or turn away from, finding an imaginative escape in a Romantic ruined landscape with darker contemporary relevance. The past Frost directs us back to is "made simple by the loss / of detail[.]" Frost had lived in Derry in a time of comparative peace and security, before the horrors of both world wars, before the Depression, in a progressive era when Americans may have felt some legitimate hope about the future. But even then, rural life was being abandoned; simple nostalgia is only possible if we forget such inconvenient details.

The paradoxical description of the abandoned house in "Directive" is reminiscent of "Ghost House," whose speaker dwells in a house that vanished long ago, and also of "The Census-Taker," whose speaker speculates at length about the people who abandoned the house. As Frank Lentricchia puts it, "It is difficult to feel nostalgic about the trip...through decay and destruction" (113). But the speaker may be nostalgic about the decaying landscape because, for Frost, the abandoned house and the Derry landscape had become such rich sources of poetry, and Derry was so deeply associated with his family.

"The road there," to the former farm, which shows "the wear of iron wagon wheels[,]"[23] ought to remind us of the dusty road to the dead female poet's house in "A Fountain..." This road "May seem as if it should have been a quarry[,]" which again suggests that the poem burrows deep into memory and back in time (li. 10). A quarry can be worked profitably for a long time, as the Derry landscape had yielded many of Frost's poems. Who travels this road of memory is watched, perhaps by ghosts, "from forty cellar holes / As if by eye pairs out of forty firkins" (ll. 21–22). The ghosts of this abandoned landscape, as in "The Black Cottage," are alert to intruders. The speaker emphasizes that his interest is in the landscape's past, not its present, when he dismisses the woods thus: "Where were they all [the rustling trees] not twenty years ago? / They think too much of having shaded out / A few old pecker-fretted apple trees" (ll. 26–28). This detail recalls Frost's sad pilgrimage to Derry in 1938 with Elinor's ashes, when the poet found the alders overgrown and the apple trees in the orchard neglected (Thompson, *Years of Triumph* 508).

Recalling the deserted scenes of "Ghost House," "The Black Cottage," and "The Census-Taker," the speaker persistently directs the reader toward the haunted rural past:

> Make yourself up a cheering song of how
> Someone's road home from work this once was
> Who may be just ahead of you on foot
> Or creaking with a buggy load of grain.
> (ll. 29–31)

For Frost, such a road as this, the Londonderry Turnpike, was once his "road home from work," when he was teaching, still living in the Derry farmhouse; in the Derry years, he also drove a horse and wagon (Thompson, *Early Years* 267). But in the atmosphere established by the ghost-eyes from "forty cellar holes," forty shells of former homes that may also remind us of the bombings in Europe, it is sad and eerie, rather than cheerful, to imagine someone walking or driving just ahead, because it now leads to the imagined scene of a ruined former home.

Reflecting on the symbolic richness of the abandoned house by this point in Frost's poetic career, it seems perfectly reasonable that being lost in such a landscape means being "lost enough to find yourself" (li. 36). This is what happened to Frost in Derry, where, in loneliness and fruitful isolation with his young family, he gradually discovered his poetic voice and subject matter—and feared he would never succeed as a poet. This line also echoes Thoreau, who made sacred the idea of retreat into rural New England in *Walden*. In "The Village," Thoreau writes, "Not till we are lost, in other words, not till we have lost the world, do we begin to find ourselves, and realize where we are in the infinite extent of our relations" (213). Frost enacted a Thoreauvian fantasy early in "Into My Own," in the speaker's fantasy of "steal[ing] away" into the woods—losing himself—to become "more sure of all I thought was true" (*CPPP* 15). We also think of St. Paul, whose salvation was more dramatic and meaningful because he had not followed the righteous path all his life. The hopeful attempt, the experience of loss and failure, and belated success, had been great sources of inspiration in Frost's poetry, embodied for the poet in the Derry landscape.

If we are now lost enough to find ourselves, the speaker directs us to "put a sign up closed to all but me" (li. 38). When Frost visited Derry in 1938, according to Thompson, he felt that "the [farm's new] owner was the trespasser," not Frost himself (Thompson, *Years of*

Triumph 507). Claiming imaginative ownership of the Derry landscape, Frost apparently left that day knowing "he still owned everything he wanted of this farm. What was left was merely a profanation, a desecration, of what was his" (Thompson, *Years of Triumph* 510). This far into the poem, the speaker directs the reader to settle in: "Then make yourself at home" (li. 39). But there is no house or home, only memories and broken artifacts:

> First there's the children's house of make believe,
> Some shattered dishes underneath a pine,
> The playthings in the playhouse of the children.
> Weep for what little things could make them glad.
> (41–44)

These lines seem to describe an area where Frost's children played, beneath a pine in Derry: "The carpet of brown needles had served as a picnic ground for the Frosts even when the youngest child had to be carried to it on the father's shoulder" (Thompson, *Years of Triumph* 508). The pathos of the command to weep for the children's simple pleasures is underscored by the fact that two of the four Frost children had died, at the ages of twenty-nine and thirty-four. Remembering the sufferings of Marjorie and Carol Frost, and Irma's mental illness, Frost himself might be inclined to "weep for what little things could make [the children] glad" in their childhood.

Again noting the paradox of taking comfort in such a scene, Lentricchia writes that we are "firmly situated in country hospitable only to the imagination" (39). And before consolation is offered, the reader of "Directive" is commanded to share in the speaker's grief, first for the children's lost happiness, and then for the cellar hole:

> Then [weep] for the house that is no more a house,
> But only a belilaced cellar hole,
> Now slowly closing like a dent in dough.
> This was no playhouse but a house in earnest.
> (ll. 45–49)

Why should the cellar hole bring tears? In the earlier poems, it is never quite so sad as here. It would likely have reminded contemporary readers of houses abandoned during the Depression and, especially, of the bombed-out buildings of Europe; all too often, only cellars remained. Frost's speaker asserts that the ruin (unlike the children's playhouse) was a real home, not a Romantic ruin to be appreciated only aesthetically, as a sort of playhouse for tourists. If this "house that is no more a house" is also modeled on the Derry farmhouse and the cellar hole across the road, it would recall for Frost the loss of his wife and children and of the house itself. Perhaps Frost also felt guilty, knowing that his family had never found a home so beloved as Derry, which the poet's ambitions had led them to leave. The process of a cellar hole becoming overgrown, like recovery from loss and guilt, is indeed slow, "closing like a dent in dough," gradually effacing the impression made on the landscape by the abandoned house. Again Frost echoes Thoreau, who writes in *Walden*, "Now only a dent in the earth marks the sites of these dwellings" (310).

Finally, the speaker guides us to the heart of the poem, which, in Lowell's words, "sadly, rurally, and covertly repeats the Legend of the Grail, here only a hidden household drinking cup" (Lowell 208):

> Your destination and your destiny's
> A brook that was the water of the house,
> Cold as a spring as yet so near its source,
> Too lofty and original to rage.
> . . . .
> I have kept hidden in the instep arch
> Of an old cedar at the waterside
> A broken drinking goblet like the Grail
> Under a spell so the wrong ones can't find it,
> So can't get saved, as Saint Mark says they mustn't.
> (I stole the goblet from the children's playhouse.)
> Here are your waters and your watering place.
> Drink and be whole again beyond confusion.
> (ll. 49–52, 55–62)

The brook the reader is led to—"your destination"—recalls not only "West-Running Brook" and "Hyla Brook," but the "stone baptismal font" that the speaker seeks and does not find in "A Fountain . . ." The "broken drinking goblet like the Grail" should also remind us of the empty bottle figured in the landscape in that poem, and of Wordsworth's broken drinking cup in "The Ruined Cottage." In "Directive," as in these other poems, the "brook" and "spring" are symbolic "source[s]" of Frost's poetry, and here we are "so near its source, / . . . lofty and original": the abandoned house, the cellar hole, the Derry landscape. Frost has taken the lost Mormon font he never found in the White Mountains and placed it in the central imaginative scene of his poetry. As Mark Richardson remarks, "*poetry* has been the 'water' of this 'house that is no more a house' [his italics]" (Richardson 242).

With rich tonal complexity, Frost also takes up in "Directive" the themes of *The Waste Land*, making his claim, amid rural desolation, to offer mitigated hope. As Lentricchia writes, in this poem "linguistic playfulness and the grimmest of issues are the most compatible friends" (113). Here in the peculiarly American scene of an abandoned farm, there is water; here is what Eliot seeks but cannot promise. "A broken drinking goblet like the Grail" will provide renewal and reintegration, reviving the saddened visitors to this landscape of failure and death. Readers may find this source of salvation, however, only if they are willing to get lost, following a dubious guide into an unpromising landscape, far out in the abandoned New England countryside. The spell the goblet is under refers to Mark 4:11–12, and perhaps to the reputed obscurity of Eliot's poem. Frost may lightly mock the legend of the Grail, as the speaker offers salvation in a child's toy cup, not an ancient relic. Extending the idea expressed in Mark to the poem, the speaker suggests that only some readers will grasp the salvation offered by "Directive."

Frost seems to offer the poem as a kind of spiritual salvation and consolation to those left of his family, and to his canniest and most sympathetic readers. Frost's attachment to Derry partly resolves the apparent paradox of finding consolation in a house that no longer exists—the poet found great inspiration in the scene of the abandoned house, in the deep pathos of the lonely Derry scene. What Frost preserved in his memories of Derry offers him comfort, even poetic salvation. As well as the reader's, this is the poet's "water and [his] watering place[,]" where he imaginatively returns to "Drink and be whole again beyond confusion."

In "Directive," written roughly eight years after Frost's visit to Derry with Elinor's ashes, the lost, consoling landscape becomes an entirely imaginative one, only to be found, and re-created, in poetry. Most of Frost's poems of abandoned houses were, of course, completed after the poet left Derry, and so evoke a distant landscape.[24] "Directive" sounds a new note of deep loss, personally associated, perhaps, with the deaths Frost suffered in the 1930s. "Directive" is finally Frost's most self-conscious and intense invocation of the scene of the abandoned farmhouse, and of the Derry landscape. As such, it is equally a scene of loss and displacement, which would have resonated especially with the poem's contemporary audience, after the end of the Depression and WWII.

Frost comes full circle from "Ghost House" to "Directive." At the end of both poems, the speaker longs to remain, and entices the reader to remain as well. But in "Directive," the speaker guides the reader through an elaborate rhetorical journey to arrive at the abandoned house, whereas the speaker of "Ghost House" dwells there from the first line—as Frost lived in Derry when he began the earlier poem. In "Directive," the same and more recent ghosts and memories of Derry are again "the sweetest companions" the speaker has, but the Romantic, sentimental tone has been transformed into an ironic, dark, even bitter acknowledgment of loss and decay, as memory becomes the only consolation. The scene of the abandoned farmhouse—with its personal associations with the home Frost sold in Derry, and its cultural associations with the abandonment of rural areas in New England and elsewhere in the United States, and with homelessness during the Depression and the destruction of WWII—proved to be one of the richest sources of his poetry, partly because of its associations with what we might call a failure to dwell.

CHAPTER 2

Elizabeth Bishop: Incarnations of the "Crypto-Dream-House"

As a house, it was more like an idea of a house than a real one.... It could have been a child's perfect playhouse, or an adult's ideal house—since everything that makes most houses nuisances had been done away with.

—"The Sea & Its Shore" (1936)

My house, my fairy
palace, is
of perishable
clapboards....

—"Jerónimo's House" (1946)

On the hills a million people,
A million sparrows, nest,
Like a confused migration
That's had to light and rest,

Building its nests, or houses,
Out of nothing at all, or air.

—"The Burglar of Babylon" (1965)

the farmhouse, dumb numb and dumb
and let's hope, blind and deaf

—"Just North of Boston" (1970s)

And look! my last, or
next-to-last, of three loved houses went.

—"One Art" (1976)

I wanted to get as far as my proto-dream-house,
my crypto-dream-house, that crooked box
set up on pilings

—"The End of March" (1976)[1]

A Lost Home and a Fairytale Orphan

Over the course of her writing career, Bishop was even more preoccupied with the image of the rural house than Frost. Some of the same historical episodes—the Great Depression and the New Deal, whose effects she also observed in Key West, and WWII—influence her depiction of the image of the fragile or neglected house. And, as with Frost, Bishop's personally unsettled circumstances led her to find the scene compelling. In considering why rural houses, from Nova Scotia to Brazil, appealed so much to Bishop, and in exploring their consoling and disturbing qualities in her poetry and prose, it is impossible to follow the chronology of her life and the sequence of her published work at once. An important aspect of her creative process is the way that times and places—as inspiration for her writing about dwelling—overlap in a Bachelardian manner, without regard to chronological sequence. As Bishop wrote in an undergraduate essay, with remarkable prescience about the development of her writing, the meaning of experience shifts and changes according to psychological, not chronological, schedules ("Dimensions for a Novel," Bishop 70.9). She may have written this essay as she attempted to write a novel about her childhood in Great Village, Nova Scotia, "Reminiscences of Great Village." In Bishop's work, personal anxieties about dwelling blend with cultural ones, in North and South America and in Europe.

To most readers of Bishop, the sad facts of her early life are familiar. Born in 1911 in Worcester, Massachusetts, she lost her father when she was eight months old.[2] Gertrude May Boomer Bishop, Bishop's mother, was unhinged by the death of her husband, and soon returned to her parents' home in Great Village with her young daughter. Eventually she left Elizabeth there, with her parents, for several years.[3] In 1916, when Bishop was five years old, her mother was declared insane and permanently institutionalized in Dartmouth, Nova Scotia. Bishop continued to live with her maternal grandparents in Great Village until the fall of 1917, when her paternal grandparents took her away to live with them in Worcester, Massachusetts (Millier 2–3, 19, 28).

In the posthumously published story "The Country Mouse," which Bishop began in the 1950s in Brazil, she compared the experience of moving to Worcester to "being kidnapped." She was miserable there, and often ill (Millier 253, *CPr* 14). After nine months, she was allowed to go live with her Aunt Maud Boomer Sheperdson, her mother's elder sister, and her husband George, in Revere, Massachusetts. As a result of recurrent illness—eczema, asthma, and bronchitis—Bishop was often confined to bed, and did not attend formal schooling until the age of fourteen (Millier 28–30). Bishop would live with her aunt and uncle from the age of eight to sixteen, in Revere and then in the more middle-class Cliftondale. Bishop "[l]ater said emphatically that Maud, along with Grace in Great Village, had saved her life" (Millier 28). She returned to "spen[d] two months of each summer [in Great Village] from 1918 until 1923" (Millier 19). In 1923 she began to attend a summer camp in Cape Cod, where she returned for five years (Stevenson 26–27).

As a young writer who felt homeless, Bishop recounted her childhood homes in remarkable detail, especially Great Village.[4] She evokes her grandparents and their small colonial house, and the very small village itself, in several prose pieces, including "In the Village" and the short memoir "Primer Class," both written in her first years in Brazil, and "Memories of Uncle Neddy," completed in Brazil in 1962 (Millier 253, *OA* 406). She also lovingly describes her maternal grandparents' house in the unpublished "Reminiscences of Great Village," which she began in the spring of 1934, during her final year at Vassar (Millier 60). The early draft begins with an epigraph by Gerard Manley Hopkins: "Enough: corruption was the world's first woe," from "On the Portrait of Two Beautiful Young People (A Brother and Sister)." As Hopkins elegizes the "young delightful hour" pictured in the portrait, later corrupted by time and the adult world, so Bishop evokes the brief and, comparatively, happiest time in her childhood.[5]

In "Reminiscences," Bishop portrays a quiet existence in Great Village, primitive and utterly charming. Just two houses had electricity; her grandparents' house was not one of them. There were only two "electric lamp posts" in the whole village. Its two general stores, in which assorted goods were organized haphazardly, amused and pleased her (as similar stores would later in the Florida Keys, described in the unpublished "5/10,000 Islands" [Bishop 53.3], and in Brazil, in "A Trip to Vigia" and "To the Botequim & Back").

The rustic buildings of Great Village claim much of Bishop's attention in "Reminiscences." Her descriptions of the village electrical plant and the parlor of her grandparents' house give two prototypes for the small rural shacks and houses that appear throughout her poetry and stories:

> The electric light plant was a small barn-like building, shingled and already turning grey…we could see it through the trees at the end of the garden. Outdoors, at its back, was a large, black round boiler, covered with mysterious holes….
>
> Over the door of the electric light plant hung, under another tin frill, the biggest light-bulb in the village—a monster, exceedingly brilliant, with nothing to light up but the doorway and the under branches of a couple of elm trees. (Bishop 54.13)

In Great Village, even the electricity was primitive, almost unnecessary,[6] housed in a small wooden shack. Its generation, for the child narrator, was a notable daily event.

A dwelling in Bishop's later work that may be traced to these Great Village scenes appears in "The Sea & Its Shore" (1936). The mysterious activities of a man named Charlie Devereux, who looks after the boiler, anticipates the figure of Edwin Boomer, who lives in a similar shack in the story. The electric light plant and boiler also anticipate the strange wooden structure described in the poem "The Monument" (1938).

In depicting the Boomer house itself in Great Village, Bishop evokes an intimate, almost spooky atmosphere:

> We seldom talked much in the evenings. Now and then my grandfather would read out loud, either from [Robert] Burns or the Bible….
>
> At night the windows became more impenetrable and confining…the walls were there but dimmed and softened, *thinned* by the Lamp Light, while the windows were a curious confinement Black and gleaming, and giving back to us darkened and jagged reflections of ourselves….
>
> I used to look at my sorry reflection—there I was, and what had I done all day? There was my grandmother in the next window—what had she done? Here we all were, all darkly together. (Bishop 54.13)

This description of the house and its black, reflective windows is reminiscent of Frost's 1916 poem, "An Old Man's Winter Night"

(*CPPP* 105–106). In both Frost's poem and Bishop's prose, there is a vague sense of threat from the night outdoors.

Perhaps initiating Bishop's fondness for one-room shacks, a small room in the Boomer house becomes a sort of separate dwelling for the narrator, which she appreciates for its size, simplicity, and seclusion.

> For some reason or other I always felt that the parlor belonged to me . . . it seemed much more secluded than any other place in the house. It seemed removed from the whole house and village, and in our parlor was the one place where I could think about the village people and my own family as from a distance. Sometimes, especially that winter [of 1916–1917?], I used to go in there and sit in a rocking chair just behind the window curtains and look out at the lace-covered view they gave me, like any curious old lady. (Bishop 54.13)

Like the shacks in "The Sea & Its Shore" and the late poem "The End of March," and like the one-room cell in the story "In Prison," the parlor seems to belong to the narrator alone, as a place of solitary retreat from other people. Yet its small size, with its close walls and ceiling, offers a compensating intimacy:

> The parlor was almost square, with four large square windows, two on either side of the corner of the house. The ceiling was low, covered with white paper decorated with silver stars. I could touch it easily with my hand. In the living room the ceiling, covered with the same paper, was even lower[.] (Bishop 54.13)

These rooms, with their intimate scale, were the scenes in which Bishop first contemplated the loss of her mother and her own status as an orphan in the care of her grandparents. Bishop's attention to the physical space suggests the way a lonely child takes an interest in her surroundings, to make up for a lack of company.[7]

The décor of the Boomer parlor also reflects Bishop's taste for simple, primitive interiors. Like the Key West houses that Bishop describes with delight in her prose piece "Gregorio Valdes" and the poem "Jerónimo's House," the Boomer parlor was decorated sparely:

> The only concessions we made to village fancies were the series of coral fans and woven grass fans, two enormous shells and a screen from India. These things had been brought home to us by Great-Uncle Will (Grandmother's younger brother who was a missionary) on one of his furloughs, and because of their foreignness and rare colorings they

> acquired in the parlor an air of value, almost as if we possessed works of art.
>
> The pictures in the parlor were limited to portraits. (Bishop 54.13)

One of these portraits was of her own mother as a child of eight, done by a traveling artist in a primitive style that Bishop later admired in artists such as Valdes.

Memories of Great Village, which Bishop would idealize and evoke in real and imagined houses, are also associated with the comforts of a close family and community. In "Manners," a poem that includes the epigraph, "For a Child of 1918," published in 1965 (*CP* 121–122), Bishop comically, tenderly evokes the communal, neighborly life of Great Village, which was changing even when she was a child. A dust-raising automobile makes it hard for the grandfather and granddaughter in the poem to greet passersby—exemplifying the tendency of modern technology to transform traditional social conduct, and, sometimes, to alienate people from one another. Similarly, the late poem "The Moose," which conflates two bus rides Bishop took from Nova Scotia to Boston in 1946 and 1970, closes by evoking the sharp scent of gas, thus linking departure from home with automobiles: "an acrid / smell of gasoline" (Millier 182–183, *CP* 173).

Although some critics tend to see Great Village as a site Bishop primarily identifies with the traumatic loss of her mother, her deep affection for Great Village as an idealized home is evident in her published prose as well. Her attachment to her maternal grandparents, especially after the loss of her mother in 1916, is poignantly clear in "Primer Class": "Until I was teased out of it, I used to ask Grandmother, when I said goodbye [on the way to school], to promise me not to die before I came home" (*CPr* 7). Several unfinished and uncollected poems, including "Syllables," "The Grandmothers," and "For Grandfather," and especially "A Short, Slow Life," also express great affection for this set of grandparents. In the latter poem, cruel Time removes the inhabitants of a cozy house—which perhaps expresses the way that Bishop as a child understood, or rather did not understand, why she had to leave Great Village (*EAP* 107).

The move to Worcester seems to have been at least as traumatic as the loss of Bishop's mother. As she described Worcester in "The Country Mouse," the somber atmosphere of the large colonial house there contrasted terribly with the familiar warmth of Great Village:

> The front of the house looked fairly familiar, very much the same kind of white clapboard and green shutters that I was accustomed to, only

> this was on a much larger scale, twice as large, with two windows for each of the Nova Scotia ones and a higher roof.
>
> ....
>
> I had been brought back unconsulted and against my wishes to the house my father had been born in, to be saved from a life of poverty and provincialism[.]...With this surprising extra set of grandparents, until a few weeks ago no more than names, a new life was about to begin. It was a day [the day of her arrival] that seemed to include months in it, or even years, a whole unknown past I was made to feel I should have known about, and a strange, unpredictable future.
>
> The house was gloomy, there was no denying it, and everyone seemed nervous and unsettled. There was something ominous, threatening, lowering in the air. My father had been the oldest of eight children. All of them were dead, except for three[.] (*CPr* 17–18)

The similarity of the façades of the two houses is a wistfully noted detail, since Bishop's paternal grandparents were initially strangers to her, and they disregarded her attachment to her maternal grandparents and Great Village—seeing her, indeed, as a "Country Mouse" who needed to be raised and educated according to their more modern, upper-class standards.

By 1917, Worcester was already becoming suburban:

> The old white house had long ago been a farmhouse out in the country. The city had crept out and past it; now there were houses all around and a trolley line went past the front lawn with its white picket fence. There was no doubt but what the neighborhood, compared to the old days, was deteriorating. The Catholics had been trying to buy the house for years; they wanted to build a church there. All the time I was there the subject was under debate—to sell or not to sell. However, there were still fifteen acres of land, an old apple orchard behind the house, and tall chestnut trees up on the hill. The life my grandparents still led was partly country, partly city. There were hens and two cows, and a large barn also up on the hill. (*CPr* 18)

The sense of instability Bishop felt in Worcester may have been exaggerated by the frequent discussion about selling the house, which was losing its idyllic rural character. Her happiest moment in Worcester was when her grandfather gave her a gift, of "two hens and a rooster," associated with the "country" side of their life, and perhaps, for Bishop, with the close rural family of Great Village (*CPr* 30).

As in Great Village, Bishop took refuge in the Worcester house in the little-used "front room" or parlor, perhaps because it was more old-fashioned than the rest of the house and may have reminded her of the Boomers' parlor:

> it was my favorite [room]. This was before the days when people were conscious of preserving the character of old houses. Perhaps because this room was so little used, it had been preserved by accident. The antique furniture was upholstered in gray blue, the walls were papered, and it all went together. There were even some paintings I now realize were primitives, in gold frames on the walls, done by an ancestress. It was a quiet room, and I could sit on the carpet there undisturbed and think. *(CPr 25)*

Like the Boomers', this secluded parlor is associated with undisturbed thinking, just as small, secluded houses and shacks became places where, as an adult, Bishop imagined she could most freely read, think, and write. Lacking intimacy, she could also find solace in the old-fashioned, cozy room.

If, however, the Boomers' primitive house in Great Village was the model for a small, charming rural house with a close family and neighbors, the Bishops' prosperous Worcester house may have become a model for a more ominous, confining dwelling that helped inspire Bishop's desire for travel as escape, depicted earliest in "Once on a Hill," discussed below. In Worcester, Bishop became very sick, and spent much of her time confined to bed in her room, or to the house itself.

After nine months, it was a great relief for the young Bishop to move in with her Aunt Maud and Uncle George Sheperdson, in Revere, Massachusetts. The Sheperdsons, who provided Bishop with relative stability, were poor, though her paternal grandparents helped them support Bishop, and they lived among poor Italian and Irish immigrants. In her unfinished memoir about this time, "Mrs. Sullivan Downstairs," which she wrote in Brazil in the early 1960s, Bishop seems captivated with the distinctive neighborhood. She describes her aunt and uncle's rundown clapboard house, and then the neighborhood:

> They lived in the upstairs apartment of a two-family house on the outskirts of an old but hideously ugly city north of Boston. The house had been built, I suppose, around 1905 or 10; it was clapboard, painted a dirty yellow, with white trim.... I could draw the floor plan now....
>
> It was a medium-poor section of a very poor town.... The streets were steep, unpaved and there were no sidewalks.... Here and there [was] a really old house, perhaps what once had been an old farmhouse,

> but they were very run down. A few of the young and more energetic men, like my uncle, did have vegetable gardens,—but no attempts were made to brighten up the front of these houses and tenements. They all gave immediately on the [street] anyway—& perhaps it was too hopeless. (*EAP* 197–198)

This description reveals some distaste for squalor, yet in the memoir of Revere, Bishop reinforces an association that she often makes between relative poverty, familial intimacy, and neighborliness, especially compared with the austerity and loneliness of the large home of the wealthy Bishops in Worcester.

While she lived with her aunt, Bishop began to take an interest in poetry. Maud Sheperdson gave her niece Victorian poetry to read, and Bishop memorized a great number of poems, going through "a Shelley phase, a Browning phase, and a brief Swinburne phase," and she began to write poetry herself, at the age of eight. At summer camp in Cape Cod, she read Harriet Monroe's *The New Poetry: An Anthology*, published by Macmillan in 1917, which may have introduced her to Frost's poetry (Brown 291–292).

She had also begun to read Hans Christian Andersen and the Brothers Grimm early in childhood, and identified with the orphan characters in fairytales, who often, secretly, have noble blood or otherwise romantic histories, and who have often lost their homes. In Revere, becoming friendly with a girl poorer than herself and with a poor immigrant woman, Bishop was reminded of fairytales:

> Many poor Italians lived around us, and some not so poor.
>
> ....
>
> Mrs. Constantina looked like a witch, very bent, straggled hair....I was as afraid as all the other children of "Old lady Constantina" but [one day] suddenly I realized she was *smiling* at me. It was like a fairy tale. Mrs. C turned into the *good* fairy under my eyes and very formally presented me with [a] tomato plant and several pats on the cheek with her muddy hand. My aunt could scarcely believe this; but there was the tomato plant to prove it....
>
> Across the street lived Barb'runt, whose name of course was really Barbara Hunt and who was probably, I realized much later, a bastard. She lived in one of the old houses, high, three-storied, narrow, set on one side of the hill[.]
>
> ....
>
> [She] was a sort of standby for me when I got too lonely...and we lent her books—she was bright and a great reader but had almost nothing of her own, poor child....[She had] A horribly strange grim unlovely cold family—Barb'runt was obviously the brightest member

> of it but I didn't even feel the mystery or romance of her sad situation then—we were both orphans, that is, almost fairy princesses and living here just temporarily—that was our great bond although we took it so much for granted we never once referred to it as far as I remember. (*EAP* 200–202)

One fairytale that Bishop read deeply did not feature a princess, however. The Grimm tale her work alludes to most often is "Hansel and Gretel," in which the siblings are driven away from their father's cottage by an evil stepmother because the family is too poor to feed them. They get lost in the forest, are nearly eaten by a witch who confines them to her house and stable, and then return home to reunite with their father after the death of their stepmother. The story is alluded to in one poem from Bishop's first book, *North & South* (1946), "Sleeping Standing Up," and in the early story "The Farmer's Children" (1939), and perhaps obliquely in the later poem "The Prodigal" (1949).[8]

The early poem "Once on a Hill" (*EAP* 5–7), written in tetrameter quatrains rhyming A-B-C-B, also alludes to "Hansel and Gretel," evoking a prison-like house, reminiscent of the witch's house and stable in the fairytale, and perhaps of the Bishops' Worcester house. Bishop probably wrote "Once on a Hill" in the 1920s. In the poem, the speaker is kidnapped by a sort of wizard who resembles "The Pied Piper," and also her paternal grandfather as described in "The Country Mouse": he had "thick silver hair and a short silver beard [which] glittered . . . a powerful but aging Poseidon" (*CPr* 13–14).

We might read this poem as reimagining Bishop's involuntary move from Great Village to Worcester, which the child-narrator of "The Country Mouse" perceives as a kidnapping. The wizard-figure resembles not only Bishop's grandfather but also the evil stepmother and the witch in "Hansel and Gretel." Bishop makes adjustments to the fairytale's plot in the poem that parallel her own circumstances as a child.

In "Once on a Hill," her imprisoned, lonely speaker, a Hansel figure, longs desperately for the friend (or sister) he imagines may be outside. The voice of the unknown friend is lost in the wind; in the fairytale, Hansel and Gretel tell the witch that their voices are only the wind, when they first arrive and nibble at the gingerbread house. The witch lures them to stay with her by giving them shelter and a delicious meal. Then she locks up Hansel in a stable and tries to fatten him up, intending to eat him, while she feeds Gretel almost nothing and makes her work like a slave. In "Once on a Hill," the wizard-figure lures the speaker to the small house and locks her inside, apparently in the midst of a forest, among "curious and shady trees" (li. 44). It is also fragile, like a gingerbread house, as if only "touch[ing] the walls / Or push[ing] against the window" might yield a way out; the speaker wants to "break down the door" for the friend she thinks she hears in the wind (ll. 53–54, 62). (The house also resembles the fragile one-room shacks that Bishop describes later in "The Sea & Its Shore" and "The End of March," and the house in Great Village as described in "Reminiscences.") The poem ends not with a happy return home to the family cottage, as in the fairytale, but with a hopeless sense of the futility and danger of escape. Similarly, as a six-year-old child, Bishop may have felt it was impossible to escape from her paternal grandparents' home in Worcester, where she was ill and confined in bed, to return to Great Village, which she would have thought of as home.

Countering the sense of the prison-like house in "Once on a Hill," another juvenile poem written in tetrameter couplets, "I introduce Penelope Gwin" (*EAP* 2–4), inaugurates Bishop's love of travel as escape. In a comic mode, the poem celebrates escape from oppressive domesticity and family difficulties, and perhaps from heterosexuality, through travel. It also includes several illustrations apparently cut out from a children's book, including one of a penguin, "Our Heroine." The poem's title may refer to the 1920s French slang of *pingouin* for a lesbian, referring to the black suits and white shirts in style then among French lesbians,[9] which Bishop may have learned at boarding school.

> I introduce Penelope Gwin,
> A friend of mine through thick and thin,
> Who's [*sic*] travelled much in foreign parts
> Pursuing culture and the arts.
> "And also," says Penelope
> "This family life is not for me.
> I find it leads to deep depression
> And *I* was born for self expression."
>
> (ll. 1–8)

By this point, after the early loss of her mother, the traumatic departure from Great Village, and the miserable time in Worcester, Bishop may have found an escape from "family life" appealing. The poem also registers the class privilege of the traveler, who can afford to escape from an unpleasant home or family.

After introducing this heroine, the speaker recounts some of her own travels, including her delighted discovery of a "Russian Aunt-Eater" (li. 50) (perhaps referring to Bishop's aunt Florence, the "timid, foolish" "Aunt Consuelo" of "In the Waiting Room" [*CP* 160, 159]). The speaker also determines never to marry, rejecting a suitor labeled "German tutor," pictured as a dumb-looking duck with an open bill (li. 57). Humorously, the poem suggests Bishop's early admiration for independent women travelers, her lack of desire for men as sexual partners, and some foreboding that her lack of "family life" and home might mean facing the "stark reality of life" on her own (ll. 58–59). (In a later notebook from 1936, Bishop records her thought that "families seemed to me like 'concentration camps'—where people actually let out their sadistic natures" [Bishop 77.2]).

A Homeless Tourist, 1934–1951

In 1927, the semblance of a "family life" and a stable home that Bishop had, with her Aunt Maud and Uncle George, came to an end (Millier 29). At the age of sixteen she enrolled in a boarding school, the Walnut Hill School for Girls, in Natick, Massachusetts. Throughout the rest of her youth, even when she stayed with her Aunt Maud, and especially with her Bishop relatives, Bishop felt that she was " 'always a sort of guest,' " and during holidays at boarding school and college, she often had nowhere to go. During vacations while she was a student at Walnut Hill (1927–1930) and at Vassar College (1930–1934), Bishop began a pattern of living in hotels and staying with friends at their homes or at rented summer cottages. She was, as Millier puts it, "conspicuously homeless" and "[h]olidays became horrible trials for her" (Millier 31–32). By 1931, both her maternal grandparents were dead (Millier 29).

And so, when Bishop graduated from Vassar on June 11, 1934, her future was entirely hers to decide. This is not so usual for a privileged American college graduate, but the daunting sense of autonomy was more pronounced for Bishop who, wealthy, orphaned, and homosexual, did not really need to work for a living (her father had established a trust fund for her), had little or no guidance from family, and did not intend to settle down by marrying. She became an orphan more officially when her mother died on May 28, 1934.

That summer after graduation, Bishop went to New York. First she stayed at the Hotel Brevoort on East Eighth Street at Fifth Avenue, looking for an apartment. Soon she left the city for Cuttyhunk Island, Massachusetts, where she spent several weeks. For much of the 1930s, when she was not traveling in Europe, the only approximations she had to home were the Murray Hill Hotel, at Fortieth Street and Park

Avenue, and the Hotel Chelsea on West Twenty-third Street (Millier 62, 121). This pattern of homelessness and wandering would not really end until she moved in with Soares in Brazil in 1952.

While Bishop seemed to enjoy aspects of her utter freedom, she also seemed intimidated and morally perplexed by it, especially in the context of the Great Depression, as Millier suggests (Millier 62). Where should she live? What should she do? In the 1930s, she frequently sounds self-conscious about her privilege, particularly in letters to Marianne Moore about her lack of plans (*OA* 34, 41, 42–43). As a student at Vassar, she had inevitably become leftist, as she wrote in her early autobiographical story, "The U.S.A. School of Writing":

> When I was graduated from Vassar in 1934, during the Great Depression, jobs were still hard to find and very badly paid. Perhaps for those very reasons it seemed incumbent on me and many of my classmates to find them, whether we had to or not. The spirit of the times and, of course, my college class was radical; we were puritanically pink. Perhaps there seemed to be something virtuous in working for much less a year than our educations had been costing our families. It was a combination of this motive, real need for a little more money than I had, idle curiosity, and, I'm afraid, pure masochism that led me to answer an advertisement in the Sunday *Times* and take a job. It was with a correspondence school, the U.S.A. School of Writing. (*CPr* 35)

This job, which Bishop kept for no more than a few months (and which brought her into contact with isolated, uneducated writers who had hopes of achieving fame), was the only formal paid work she did throughout the 1930s—though she worked at her writing, of course, and published a number of poems and stories. During the Depression, which only ended with the war, widespread social breakdown was impossible to ignore, as sociologist John A. Pandiana describes it:

> untold numbers of Americans abandoned both civility and conventionality in the face of desperate economic conditions. Arraignments for family abandonment in New York City nearly tripled between 1928 and 1931. By 1933, fully one-third of America's work force was unemployed.... [By 1931] The total number of transients in the USA was estimated to approach two million.... Family and work, two of the most basic social institutions, were collapsing[.] (Pandiani 348)

Certainly Bishop's early work does not ignore these widespread calamities. The strange urban creature in the wonderfully surreal poem, "The Man-Moth," is the product of a newspaper misprint for "mammoth";

he is also, among other things, a homeless man who takes refuge in the subways. Following the moth aspect of his nature, he creeps up the sides of tall buildings toward the moon, and "Then he returns / to the pale subways of cement he calls his home" (ll. 25–26, *CP* 14). During the Depression, Bishop's sense of being a homeless orphan, though, significantly, a privileged one, would have found a distorted reflection in the plight of the homeless and unemployed.

I linger on this context because we do not always remember that Bishop came of age as a writer during the Depression and the rise of fascism, and that she composed a number of the poems for her first collection, *North & South* (1946), amidst the economic and social breakdown in New York and Key West, and in a Europe that was consciously preparing for war. In startling ways, her early poems and stories register contemporary anxieties about homelessness and unemployment, the ominous development of fascism and militarism in Germany and Italy, the outbreak of the Spanish Civil War, and Italy's invasion of Ethiopia. One reason we may not always connect her early work to such dramatic historical context is the late date of her first book: her poems had been appearing in major magazines for a decade when *North & South* was published. And her early stories were only collected posthumously in *The Collected Prose*. A few scholars, notably James Longenbach and Betsy Erkkila, have considered Bishop's early poetry within the political context of the 1930s, "locat[ing] Bishop's work within the debates about the relation between literary modernism and the American—and international—Left." The tendency of many critics, however, has been to focus on what seem to be the purely aesthetic, surrealist elements in Bishop's writing from this period,[10] and to characterize her later work in Brazil, from the 1950s and 1960s, as a political awakening (Erkkila 285).[11]

Yet the apparent aesthetic-political dilemmas of late modernism in the 1930s were very real to Bishop. As Longenbach has argued, "The problem for Bishop, early and late, was not her values as such but her discomfort—nurtured in the thirties—with the conventions of political poetry.... [F]rom the beginning of her career, Bishop was 'more interested in social problems' than, in retrospect, she would allow" (Longenbach 468–469). He refers here to statements Bishop herself made, much later in life, about politics and her poetry. For instance, she said in the 1960s: "Politically I considered myself a socialist [in the 1930s], but I disliked 'social conscience' writing" (Brown 293).

As a young writer, Bishop consciously approached the apparent dilemma of any ambitious, socially aware author of the time, who also admired the implicitly elitist aesthetics of high modernism: how to allow politics to affect her writing. For a sophisticated writer, of course, this is not a simple problem, and it seems hasty, on the one hand, to fault her early poems for their "Eurocentric aesthetics," and, on the other, to praise Bishop for eventually "moving…toward a more socially embedded and class-conscious art" (Erkkila 290). Bishop felt drawn not only to the poetics of T.S. Eliot, whom she interviewed as an undergraduate at Vassar, but she also found a hero in W.H. Auden, admiring his politics and poetry, and in college she helped found a leftist magazine, *Con Spirito*, with Mary McCarthy and Muriel Rukeyser (Millier 48). She did not closely imitate Auden's voice or style, in its direct appropriation of jargon and topical themes, but her fondness for writing formal, rhymed poems in the 1930s may owe something to him.[12] And she disliked some of the more overtly political writing of some of her peers, including Rukeyser.[13]

The development of her political thinking, and the formative influence of the 1930s and WWII, emerge in a 1964 letter about her early work, which she wrote in Brazil to the poet Anne Stevenson, her first biographer:

> [W]ell, at the time I was writing the poems I like best, I was very ignorant politically and I sometimes wish I could recover the dreamy state of consciousness I lived in then—it was better for my work, and I do the world no more good now by knowing a great deal more. I was "left" because my friends were, mostly—although of course we all felt the effects of the [D]epression profoundly, and ever since noticing the split in my own family and going through my Shelley period, around 16, I had thought of myself as a "socialist."
>
> ….
>
> I was always anti-communist, I believe—after one or two John Reed Club affairs….
>
> But—before the war—we knew much less. The purges in the 30s were what opened most people's eyes. Here now [in Brazil] it is dreadful for me to see young men I know making the same mistake that U.S. intellectuals were making around 1930. How they can is hard to see.—They seem totally unaware of recent history…one of [Brazil's] greatest drawbacks to any kind of maturity, I'm afraid, is that it has never been through a war.
>
> ("Answers to Your Questions of March 6th," Elizabeth Bishop Papers, Washington University Libraries, Department of Special Collections)

In the 1960s in Brazil, Bishop may have felt nostalgic for a certain creative fertility of the unformed mind; she had written more prolifically in her youth. She implies that, as a young woman, partly because of the economic differences between her maternal and paternal relations and her Vassar experience, she became leftist, and that the experience of the Depression and the buildup to WWII, the Soviet purges of dissidents, and the war itself, were crucial to complicating and moderating her political views. Today we sometimes tend to equate American anti-communism with McCarthyism, but it is important to remember the disillusionment of many American and European communists when Stalin's murderous state polices were revealed in the 1930s. In her notebook from this period, Bishop wrote, "I am sure the time is coming when we shall say: 'Communism: the opiate of the people.' It serves as such a 'clearing-house' already for people, idealistic people, who have nothing really to *do*" (Bishop 72A). Rather than "politically ignorant," then, Bishop seems politically naïve in her youth.

In the 1930s, in some contrast to the more topical poems she wrote in Brazil in the 1950s and 1960s, Bishop resolved these dilemmas in an inimitable manner, through a process she claimed not to understand well herself, as her own personal anxieties and larger cultural crises about fundamental matters of home and homelessness, dwelling and travel, violence and victimization, security and imprisonment, merged in dreamlike, fairytale and surrealist tropes and scenes. She was figuring out, through trial and error, how socially engaged her writing could be without sacrificing aesthetic quality. Throughout, Bishop is responsive to the contemporary pressure on writers to demonstrate social engagement. In January 1937, she sent a poem called "War in Ethiopia" (see *EAP* 24, where it appears without a title), to the American poet and critic Horace Gregory, editor of *Forum and Century*, apparently for a journal issue:

> I don't know who the other poets you are gathering are, or what the material is likely to be like—but in case it's all "social consciousness," etc., and you'd rather keep up a united front, I am sending "War in Ethiopia." Of course it's very out of date, and I am not sure whether my attempts at this kind are much good, but I should like to have you see it, too, and tell me what you think. (*OA* 55–56)

Gregory apparently rejected the poem. Bishop also asked her publisher to include a note, as a sort of an apology for the lack of war poems, on the copyright page of the first edition of *North & South*: "Most of the poems were written, or partly written, before 1942." But as Erkkila astutely points out, "tropes of militarism and violence, sometimes accompanied by dim predictions of apocalypse and doom, pervade the volume" (Erkkila 294). Bishop's claim of political ignorance is also belied by her political-literary activities in college, her avid reading of newspapers, and by some of her letters and journals from the 1930s and 1940s. The journals, in particular, include numerous newspaper clippings about fear of war in Europe, the Spanish Civil War, and the human costs of the Depression in the United States.

Her first published story, "Then Came the Poor," which Bishop wrote at Vassar, evokes the atmosphere of the Depression in the United States more imaginatively than "The U.S.A. School of Writing." Certainly the sense of homelessness and aimlessness Bishop felt as a young woman of leisure in the 1930s coincided and contrasted with the actual homelessness of many poor and struggling Americans during the Depression. From her work with Bishop's notebooks, Alice Quinn concludes that "as a child [she] had to learn to negotiate two worlds—the world of her fairly impoverished aunt and uncle, who brought her up from age seven to sixteen, and the world of her prep school, where the father of a friend was vice president of a company that let her uncle go, and then Vassar" (Quinn 1). "Then Came the Poor" (which appeared first in 1934 in *Con Spirito*),[14] registers some of this anxiety about her privilege.

In the story, a Communist revolution has occurred in the United States, and the "Reds" are killing some of the rich and taking over their property.[15] The narrator, a young man from a wealthy New England family, stays behind when his family flees their mansion, curious to see what happens when "the Poor" arrive. The mansion may be modeled on the Bishop estate in Harwichport, where the poet's paternal grandparents moved after selling the Worcester house. The narrator's sympathies are largely with the poor; Bishop, as we have seen, also favored the close community and family she associated with her more modest childhood homes.

Just as Bishop took refuge in parlors in "Reminiscences of Great Village" and "The Country Mouse," so this narrator hides from his family, as they prepare to leave, in the dark "small Louise [*sic*] Quinze parlor off the hall[.]" In effect, the narrator is orphaned by choice when his family leaves without him. In the meadow outside the house, he waits all night for the arrival of "the Poor." The next day, unrecognized as a son of the house, he joins the "wild, magnificent lawn-party" held by the poor, who dig into the mansion's store of food and liquor. As the story closes, he agrees to share a room with a small, gracious, drunk man named Jacob Kaffir, who takes an implicitly homosexual interest in the narrator: "he gave me a wink I could almost hear. 'Seems like home already, don't it?' " (Bishop 46.2).[16] In its "puritanically pink" message of bravely joining "the Poor"—even abandoning wealth and a stiff, proper family for them—the story also portrays the poor with great warmth and vividness. They humanize the cold, proper, lonely household with their rejoicing and squalor:

> People were coming and going in excited groups, pointing and grabbing and exclaiming, some of them dressed in fantastic costumes put together from the wardrobes of my departed family. It was an [*sic*] hilarious affair. I felt like the host of a house party whose guests had gone mad, which was, nevertheless, a great success. (Bishop 46.2)

The revolutionary reclamation of the mansion in "Then Came the Poor" seems to improve life for the narrator, who in the past was always "scared . . . about a picnic or a party," but so much enjoys this "house party"—just as Bishop's emotional life improved when she moved from her paternal grandparents' house to her Aunt Maud's apartment in Revere.

After she wrote this story and left Vassar, Bishop would have encountered many of the poor and hungry while living in New York, and perhaps she witnessed or read about some of the rent strikes in protest of evictions, which occurred in the early 1930s in the city. She certainly kept up with the news, writing in her journal on May 19, 1935, "You go for days reading the newspaper every morning, feeling a certain responsibility about all over, everyones', [*sic*] predicaments" (Bishop 72A). She also clipped a photograph from a newspaper with the caption, "STILL ON THE ROAD TO SELF-SUPPORT. Dave Sweatman, 72 years old, accompanied by his family and pulling all his worldly goods on a wagon, passes through Memphis, on a journey across the country from Oklahoma, looking for a job as a carpenter or blacksmith. He has refused all offers of Federal relief" (Bishop 72A). Another clipping she saved reads, "as a consequence, the New York taxicab driver cannot be said to exist as a type as he did ten or fifteen years ago, for his ranks are overflowing now with men from other occupations—lawyers, brokers, medical students, engineers, etc." (Bishop 72A). As she said in 1965, "After all, anybody who went to New York [during the Depression] and rode the Elevated could see that things were wrong" (Brown 294). Surely this atmosphere would also have been psychologically depressing for Bishop, who, feeling guilty about her wealth, was trying to decide what to do next.

In 1935, she suspended the question of her future by choosing to travel to Europe—at a time when being a tourist there seemed increasingly ridiculous, even dangerous. With a friend from Vassar,

Hallie Tomkins, she sailed to Europe in July 1935, by chance aboard "the Nazi freighter *Königstein*[,]" where she felt uncomfortable among the mostly German passengers (Millier 86). She stayed abroad nearly one year, visiting Belgium, spending five months in Paris, visiting England and Morocco, and finally spending two months in Spain, before returning to New York in June 1936. She spent the summer of 1936 in a beach cottage in West Falmouth, Massachusetts, and most of the winter of 1936–37 at the Hotel Chelsea in New York. In December 1936, she first visited Key West, where her Aunt Maud and Uncle George had settled. She then returned to Europe in June of 1937, visiting Ireland, England, France, and Italy, and sailed back to New York in early December (Millier 103, 107, 116).

During these years, memories of her childhood were surfacing, perhaps of the traumatic displacement from Great Village to Worcester, and of her mother's descent into mental illness. In 1935 before she left for Europe, Bishop wrote in her journal:

> A set of apparently unchronological incidents out of the past have been reappearing. I suppose there must be some string running them together, some spring watering them all. Some things will never disappear, but rather clear up, send out roots, as time goes on. They are my family monuments, sinking a little more into the earth year by year, boring silently, but becoming only more firm, and inscribed with meanings gradually legible, like letters written in "magic ink." (Bishop 77A)

"The Monument" became the title of a poem in 1937, with its suggestion of writing as memorial, of the persistent significance of the dead, and, in the structure depicted in the poem, of a grave as a final dwelling place. (See also "The past..." from 1935 [*EAP* 23].) The act of dwelling, and images of houses and rooms, gather the weight of memory of personal trauma and war, and of apprehensions about the future, in Bishop's poems written in Europe in this era.

During her first journey to Europe, Bishop was overwhelmed with a sense of what she tentatively identified as homesickness:

> an awful, awful feeling of deathly physical and mental illness.—something that seems "after me.".... When this feeling comes I can't speak, swallow, scarcely breathe. I knew I had had it once before, years ago, & last night, on its 2nd occurrence I placed it as "homesickness." I was homesick for 2 days once when I was nine years old; I wanted one of my aunts. Now I really have no right to homesickness at all. I suppose it is caused actually by the motion of the ship away from N.Y.—it

> may affect one's center of balance in some way; the feeling seems to center in the middle of the chest. (Bishop 72A)

This feeling might also be characterized as a sense of homelessness. Bishop may have felt that she had "no right to homesickness" because she had no home, yet she had been writing, extensively and recently, about the one she once had, in "Reminiscences of Great Village."

In the autumn and winter of 1935 and 1936, during a five month-stay in Paris, Bishop and her former Vassar classmate Louise Crane, an heiress to the paper fortune, shared a luxurious apartment at 58 Rue de Vaugirard. While there, Bishop began at least three poems, "Paris, 7 A.M.," "Sleeping Standing Up," and "Love Lies Sleeping," and the story, "The Sea & Its Shore" (Millier 84). Critics have noted that the "Sleeping" poems (a third is "Sleeping on the Ceiling") and "Paris 7 A.M." "occur within a symbolist and surrealist rhetoric" (Costello, *Questions of Mastery*, 15). Bishop is often "explor[ing], like [Max] Ernst, what can be discerned in between states, half asleep" (McCabe 56).[17] Bishop attended surrealist exhibitions in New York and in Paris she went to André Breton's gallery and met Max Ernst ("Answers to Your Questions of March 6th," Elizabeth Bishop Papers, Washington University Libraries, Department of Special Collections).

In considering the surrealist and dreamlike elements of these poems, I focus here on the way that one of these poems, "Sleeping Standing Up," registers an unconscious or half-conscious unease about the Depression and fears of war in Europe, meditating on a "cottage" that seems under threat of attack in the night, in a nationally unspecified landscape. (Elsewhere I also discuss "Paris, 7 A.M.," "In a Room," and "Love Lies Sleeping."[18]) If some of Bishop's early poems now seem rather cryptic, it is not only because of an evident surrealist influence—though Surrealism was by no means divorced from political realities in the 1930s; Salvador Dali and Max Ernst created paintings anticipating the outbreak of the Spanish Civil War—but because we lack, as early-twenty-first-century readers, collective memory of the global Depression and of the long, apprehensive and violent prelude to WWII in Europe and Asia.

According to historian Eugen Weber, war was regarded as inevitable by many in France in the mid-1930s, in part because Hitler had been able to gain support from Germans who resented the punishing terms of the Treaty of Versailles, which in turn were widely credited with causing a terrible economic depression in Germany. The French press, pacifist groups and the government encouraged fears of new military technology, especially as developed by Germany and Italy.

The Disarmament Conference of 1932–1933 had collapsed when Hitler withdrew from it and then from the League of Nations, in reaction to pressure from France to limit expansion of the German army until 1941 (Brose 190). From then on, "simulated raids and battles in the air designed to test defenses in Britain, France, Italy and Germany received wide press coverage" (Weber 238). In 1934, Winston Churchill was also vocal about his belief that Hitler was building up the German military. Hitler publicly announced Germany's rearmament in March of 1935, and thereafter Germany openly expanded its army and air force, the *Wehrmacht* and *Luftwaffe*, developing and manufacturing large numbers of advanced tanks and fighter planes.

This was the atmosphere in which Bishop recalled her traumatic displacement in childhood, associated with WWI, when she was orphaned and "kidnapped" in 1917. In "Sleeping Standing Up," militaristic diction likely arises from Bishop's awareness of preparations for another war. In "The Country Mouse," she remembers reading as a child in Worcester "the war cartoons, several big books of them: German helmets and cut-off hands haunted us" (*CPr* 28). "Sleeping Standing Up" seems infused with the apprehension, indeed the expectation, of war—a feeling of doom that hung over Europe in the 1930s, characterized by Weber as "a nightmare of fear" (Weber 237).

Bishop began "Sleeping Standing Up" on her first tour of Europe, and continued to work on it during her 1937 trip, when the situation on the Continent had deteriorated further. By this time, Italian and German troops, as well as smaller contingents from all over the world, were fighting in the Spanish Civil War. There was a sense among artists and the general public in Europe that this conflict—especially as Franco was strengthened by the support of Mussolini and Hitler—was the harbinger of wider catastrophic war (Brendon 205–207). In her notebooks, Bishop seems aware of the probability of wider war. Certainly June 1937, shortly after the bombings of Guernica appalled the world and inspired Picasso's painting (which would influence Bishop's later poem from "Roosters"), was an even less auspicious time to embark on a tour of Europe than June 1935 had been. In November 1937, Bishop also visited Rome under Mussolini, where Italy's military readiness was quite visible to a tourist. She frequently made observations in her notebook about uniforms, and while in Italy, she also saw the Italian film, titled *Scipio l'Africano* in its U.S. release in 1937, which Bishop recognized as obvious "Empire Propaganda" glorifying the invasion of Ethiopia (Bishop 77.2). The global rise of bellicose imperialism and fascism was exemplified in the outbreak of war in China, following a conflict between Japanese and Chinese troops in Beijing (then Peking), on July 7, 1937 (Brendon 390–391). The fears of aerial bombardment that Bishop evokes in "Paris, 7 A.M." had been realized—not in France, but in Ethiopia, China, and Spain.

"Sleeping Standing Up" (*CP* 30) shares a bedroom setting with "Paris, 7 A.M." and "In a Room," and in it Bishop returns to the tale of "Hansel and Gretel," as her speaker falls headlong into a childhood dream of seeking a lost home. The title suggests several things: having no place to sleep, sleeping in an awkward position (on a train, for instance), and falling asleep on one's feet. In "Hansel and Gretel," the siblings spend several nights walking in the forest, looking for their father's house. (Bishop wrote in a notebook from 1934 or 1935, "Sometimes a children's book—a fairy tale—might be made to hold things that could only be put into poetry in three life-times" [Bishop 77A.3].) The speaker uses the first person plural, seeming to include all humanity in this experience—everyone lies down to sleep at night, everyone dreams—thus generalizing a sense of anxiety as the earth turns on its axis and "we" fall into disoriented sleep:

> As we lie down to sleep the world turns half away
>   though ninety dark degrees;
>   the bureau lies on the wall
> and thoughts that were recumbent in the day
>   rise as the others fall,
>   stand up and make a forest of thick-set trees.
> (ll. 1–6)

As repressed or latent thoughts rise in the night, up-ending the logic of rational consciousness, in surrealist fashion, that kept them down in waking life, they cluster together, becoming trees in the dense forest of a dream. Some of these "recumbent" thoughts might be, for Bishop, her memory of childhood displacement. Just as the train in "The Country Mouse" moves through "some black hairy forest" on its way south, so in this dream-state in the poem we are carried to the "edge" of a forest that we enter in the next stanzas (*CPr* 14). During the second tour of Europe, Bishop took trains through France and Italy (Millier 127, 129–132), which may have reminded her—especially when traveling through forests—of her "kidnapping" by train in 1917, which she narrated in "The Country Mouse." In the story, Bishop described her child self on the lumbering train on the way to Worcester, helplessly carried away from Great Village: "The train went into a long curve and tried to bend its stiff joints; my sofa tried to throw me off. The walls creaked. *Ee-eee-eee* went our whistle, and I held on for dear life" (*CPr* 14).

But rather than riding a train, we are transported by "[t]he armored cars of dreams," which protect us as we penetrate the forbidding forest of the unconscious. The sturdy six-line stanzas, with line-lengths that advance and retreat (the metrical pattern is roughly iambic hexameter-trimeter-trimeter-pentameter-trimeter-pentameter), counterbalanced by a steady A-B-C-A-C-B rhyme scheme, make steady progress in pursuit of the trail of "crumbs or pebbles" left by "the clever children":

> The armored cars of dreams, contrived to let us do
>   so many a dangerous thing,
>   are chugging at its edge
> all camouflaged, and ready to go through
>   the swiftest streams, or up a ledge
>   of crumbling shale, while plates and trapping ring.
>
> —Through turret-slits we saw the crumbs or pebbles that lay
>   below the riveted flanks
>   on the green forest floor,
> like those the clever children placed by day
>   and followed to their door
>   one night, at least;. . .
>
> (ll. 7–18)

"The armored cars of dreams" in the poem, whose trappings are described with technical terms, suggest that Bishop's awareness of the fearful atmosphere in Europe may have blended with her childhood memories and present feelings of homelessness and insecurity. Photographs of advancing tanks appeared in news coverage of Italy's invasion of Ethiopia and of the Spanish Civil War; Bishop also saved an article in her journal about an eyewitness account of German military exercises, perhaps by a British spy (Bishop 77.2). At the same time, her memories of WWI may come into play, when tanks were introduced into modern warfare and were instrumental in defeating Germany through attacks on trenches (see Foss 95–96, 100). In the poem's setting of the forest, perhaps she was also thinking of the Ardennes in the Rhineland, where Panzer units were established soon after Germany reoccupied it in March 1936.

In alluding to "Hansel and Gretel"—"the clever children"—Bishop includes the reader in the speaker's search; we are passengers or drivers in "ugly tanks" trying to follow the children's trail back to the lost cottage. In the fairytale, the first time the father abandons the children in the forest, they leave a trail of pebbles, which they follow home the next morning. This method of finding the way back home works for "one night, at least[.]" The second time, in the tale, presumably being led in a different direction by their deceitful father and stepmother, they leave a trail of crumbs that the birds eat up, and the pair gets lost in the forest, not finding their way home again until after their stepmother has died. In the poem, "we" glimpse the passing forest, and the way back home, through the slits in a "turret" (the term may refer to the gun sights on a tank and to the raised roof of a passenger carriage in a train), just as Bishop as a child glimpses the dark forest through "the window before the porter had made the beds" on the train in "The Country Mouse" (*CPr* 14).

Dreams, like armored cars, have the power to take us through dangerous territory relatively unscathed (we may be upset when we wake, but we are not physically hurt), and in them we can defy gravity (climbing a ledge of shale, sleeping standing up). The "armored cars," once protective, become "ugly tanks," and seem unnecessarily aggressive and awkward for the task of "track[ing]" mere crumbs or pebbles leading back to a childhood home—unless the goal is to destroy the cottage if it is found:

in the ugly tanks
we tracked them all the night. Sometimes they disappeared,
dissolving in the moss,
sometimes we went too fast
and ground them underneath. How stupidly we steered
until the night was past
and never found out where the cottage was.
(ll. 18–24)

In "Sleeping Standing Up," the way home is pursued in the dream, but it is "never found." The dreamers and the child, in the poem and in "The Country Mouse," cannot steer the "ugly tanks" or the train to find the way back. (Early tanks were notoriously difficult to steer, and even the most advanced tanks of recent years cannot change direction abruptly). The clues marking the way home—the crumbs or pebbles—are lost in the forest floor, or crushed beneath the wheels of the tanks.

In the apprehensive atmosphere in which Bishop wrote the poem, it was anticipated that large populations would soon be displaced and perhaps annihilated. This was already occurring in the civil war in Spain; orphaned children had been brought to London, and Bishop saw some of them at a meeting at the Albert Hall (Millier 123). The rather primitive life of the woodcutter and his children in "Hansel and Gretel," associated with Old Europe, was being threatened by aggressively modern military technology. As in Bishop's juvenile poem "Once on a Hill," the plot of the original "Hansel and Gretel" is halted before the happy homecoming can occur. In the poem, "we" have inexplicably lost the way to the cottage, and the effort to find home again is defeated. Similarly, the average European citizen felt powerless to halt the escalation toward war, which would threaten the lives and dwellings of many. Europe had not yet emerged from the worldwide Depression, as it moved toward war; the woodcutter in "Hansel and Gretel" is persuaded by his second wife to abandon the children because they have too little to eat. The last lines of the poem also suggest that the chance to find the lost home has been "stupidly" wasted. We, the ones driving or riding in the tanks, perhaps the ones directing military and political strategy in Europe, took the wrong direction, and now it is too late; we will never find home and safety again.

"Sleeping Standing Up," then, seems centrally concerned with the Heideggerian problem of dwelling, and resonates deeply on several levels at once: the aesthetic (Bishop's precise, contemporary and lyrical language, and her adoption of the surrealists' freedom of association), the personal (her own unsettled life, leisure and status as an orphan), and the historical (Europe in the 1930s, when dwelling seemed so threatened, which Bishop would express most explicitly in "Roosters," written in Key West during WWII). The poem is the work of a privileged young woman, who was in some ways very isolated and unsettled, yet was also peculiarly sensitive, as a tourist in the 1930s, to the fears and nervous energy of prewar Europe.

"Sleeping Standing Up" was published in *Life and Letters To-day* in November 1938. Though the magazine had been founded, in 1928, on the reputation of established Modernist contributors, particularly the Bloomsbury group, it made "a significant shift in policy" in 1936 when "it announced support for the Republican forces in the Spanish Civil War" (Hoffman 225). A twenty-three-page prospectus about recent contributors to the journal in 1936 gives a sense of the aesthetic and political range and ambitions of the journal. European, British, and American modernist writers of great reputation published in it, as well as surrealists and leftists. In the notes, frequent mention is made of the politics of the contributors and of disturbing developments in Spain and Germany (Herring and Petrie). By November 1938, Germany had declared Austria a province of the Third Reich

(March 1938), Barcelona had been bombed (also in March), Britain had officially recognized Italy's conquest of Ethiopia (April 1938), Nazi troops had invaded the Sudetenland (October 1938), and *Kristallnacht* had occurred in Germany on November 10 (see Brendon 445–491). In this context, readers of Bishop's dreamlike poem of abandonment and involuntary exile would have interpreted the armored cars and tanks not as strange, private tropes, but as images drawn from an increasingly frightening contemporary reality.

By 1938, it would seem absolutely clear that Europe was no place for an escapist tourist. Nor was New York, as the Depression continued, an especially comfortable place to be aimless and affluent. When Bishop returned from Europe, she spent the Christmas holiday with her Aunt Maud and Uncle George, and then checked into the Murray Hill Hotel in New York on December 26. On January 12, she went to Key West, where her aunt and uncle had decided to move (Millier 133–134). The island was as crucial to her experience of the New Deal as it was for Frost, and for the next eight years, she divided her time between Key West and New York.

Bishop had first visited the small town in December of 1936. Counteracting the efforts of FERA, which had been so successful in attracting new tourists (including Frost) to Key West in the winter of 1934–35, a Labor Day hurricane in 1935 had destroyed railroad access to the island; an overland highway was completed in 1938. In May of 1938, Bishop attempted to make a home there of her own, when she bought the house at 624 White Street in Key West with Louise Crane. For a few years, Bishop even had family nearby, as she often saw her Aunt Maud and Uncle George, until Maud died in 1940.

Even once she co-owned a house, however, Bishop remained unsettled in the late 1930s and throughout most of the 1940s. The summer of 1938 was typical: soon after she moved into the house in Key West in 1938, she left it for the summer, and headed north. First she stopped in New York, and then left the city to stay alone in a temporary home she adored, "a tiny shack on the beach at Provincetown, Massachusetts, on property owned by her married friends the painter Loren MacIver and the literary critic and scholar Lloyd Frankenberg" (Millier 140–141). The shack, along with Key West, provides something of the oceanfront setting and perspective for "The Monument," as Millier suggests, which she had begun writing on her second European tour and finished in 1939.

"The Monument" (*CP* 24–25) articulates, among other themes, the intense poetic and artistic appeal that weathered wooden houses and structures continued to have in her work. The poem's initial inspiration came from Max Ernst's *Histoire Naturelle,* in which Ernst uses the technique of frottage: "the artist place[s] paper across wood or other surfaces and objects, and then rub[s] away at the paper with blacklead" (Goldensohn 121). Bishop had been studying Ernst's illustrations in Douarnez, France, and did a frottage sketch for "The Monument" in a Key West notebook. In Provincetown, Bishop found something surrealist about the landscape, which lends the flat, two-dimensional perspective for the poem. She also "loved the provisional, found-object furniture" inside her shack, which echoes the bare, idealized prison cell of "In Prison," and which is almost as open to the outdoors as Edwin Boomer's little house in a description from her notebook (Millier 141–142).

"The Monument," set in a desolate, imaginary landscape, is a dialogue in which one speaker is trying to persuade another to appreciate "The Monument." Its dialogue form, unusual in Bishop's work, recalls Frost's "The Black Cottage." As the minister in Frost's poem calls attention to the cottage, the first speaker in "The Monument" is a guide figure who draws the second speaker's attention to the unspectacular wooden monument:

> Now can you see the monument? It is of wood
> built somewhat like a box. No. Built
> like several boxes in descending sizes
> . . . .
> Then on the topmost cube is set
> a sort of fleur-de-lys of weathered wood,
> long petals of board, pierced with odd holes,
> four-sided, stiff, ecclesiastical.
> . . . .
> The monument is one-third set against
> a sea; two-thirds against a sky.
> (ll. 1–3, 8–11, 18–19)

This description echoes that of the electric light plant in Great Village, in "Reminiscences." Its decorations are also similar to the wooden "scrollwork that looks as if it were cut from paper" in Key West houses, and another Key West house she describes in her prose piece "Mercedes Hospital" (*OA* 68, *CPr* 64). Like those houses, the attraction of this monument is not immediately obvious to an outsider, perhaps because it is wooden and roughly made.

As the outsider in Frost's poem is ignorant about "The Black Cottage," so the second speaker in Bishop's poem asks perplexed questions about "The Monument." It is unclear whether the artifact is a work of art, or whether the viewers are actually inside the scene:

> "Why does that strange sea make no sound?
> Is it because we're far away?
> Where are we? Are we in Asia Minor,
> or in Mongolia?"
>
> (ll. 31–34)

The second speaker speculates that the monument may be in the Middle East, the cradle of European civilization, or in a desolate landscape like Mongolia; and the monument no longer seems like an art object separate from the viewers, but part of a world that the viewers enter into, at least imaginatively. As well as "The Black Cottage," Bishop may echo Frost's "The Census-Taker" here, whose speaker laments the "decay" of the lumbermen's shack in New Hampshire as much as that of ancient civilizations. Bonnie Costello notes that Bishop's poem alludes to a number of other monument poems, "includ[ing] Coleridge's 'Kubla Khan,' Shelley's 'Ozymandias,' Yeats's 'Sailing to Byzantium,' and Stevens' 'Anecdote of the Jar'" (Costello, *Questions of Mastery,* 218). If "The Monument" can be located anywhere, it might plausibly be located in North America, partly because it is made of wood, like the Key West house in "Mercedes Hospital." Remembering that Frost may refer to "Ozymandias" in "The Black Cottage," and recalling Bishop's "Shelley phase," we might speculate that Bishop creates in "The Monument" a warning like "Ozymandias," not about the doomed ambitions of kings, but about the fate and provisional nature of any art work, and of the American dwelling.

The first speaker does not directly answer the second speaker's question, "Where are we?," but designates the site of the monument only geographically: it is on a "promontory," as Provincetown is on Cape Cod. It is also, more fantastically, in "an ancient principality" that recalls "Kubla Khan," but it is much humbler than Coleridge's "pleasure dome." In the next phase of description, the art object is transformed into a Romantic memorial of some sort:

> An ancient promontory,
> an ancient principality whose artist-prince
> might have wanted to build a monument
> to mark a tomb or boundary, or make
> a melancholy or romantic scene of it...
>
> (ll. 34–38, ellipsis in original)

The speaker suggests the monument is an intentionally Romanticized ruin, and it is also associated with a grave. The second speaker comments obtusely that the monument "looks old," and complains it has not been worth his while to come see "A temple of crates," which almost sounds like contradiction in terms. Perhaps only a young or primitive civilization, or one with little chance of enduring, or a surrealist artist, would try to make a temple out of crates.

The first speaker explains the weathering effects on the wooden structure, as does Frost's minister in "The Black Cottage," calling a great deal of attention to the material, and then suggests that this structure only aspires to be a monument. "It is an artifact / of wood" (ll. 51–52):

> The monument's an object, yet those decorations,
> carelessly nailed, looking like nothing at all,
> give it away as having life, and wishing;
> wanting to be a monument, to cherish something.
> The crudest scroll-work says "commemorate,"
> while once each day the light goes around it
> like a prowling animal,
> or the rain falls on it, or the wind blows into it.
> It may be solid, may be hollow.
> The bones of the artist-prince may be inside
> or far away on even drier soil.
> But roughly or adequately it can shelter
> what is within (which after all
> cannot have been intended to be seen).
> It is the beginning of a painting,
> a piece of sculpture, a poem, or monument,
> and all of wood. Watch it closely.
>
> (ll. 57–78)

Costello observes that, "in choosing wood rather than gold as her material, Bishop eschews the idea of mastery or transcendence. Wood as a medium.... has a 'life' of decomposition. Bishop contrasts this natural process to aesthetic duration" (Costello, *Questions of Mastery,* 220, 222). Wood is of course less durable than the stone of the fallen Ozymandias, and wood was, as mentioned in the Introduction, the "universal structural material" of North American buildings in the early history of the U.S. and Canada, including the houses belonging to both sets of Bishop's grandparents, as well as the beach shacks that appealed to her so much. She also associates wooden houses with European villages under attack in "Roosters." In a later poem, apparently for her lover and friend, the Swedish widow of a Brazilian,

Lilli Correia de Araújo, Bishop writes: "Dear, my compass / still points north / to wooden houses / and blue eyes, // fairy-tales" [ll. 1–5, *EAP* 140].

The strange appeal of "The Monument," then, is in its primitive, decaying qualities. Its precisely described boards, which have lost any paint they had through weathering, recall the structures preferred by the narrator of "In Prison" (discussed below), whose narrator hopes the walls of his cell might be unpainted boards—or boards whose paint has worn away, like houses he has seen in "foreign lands"—also like the weathered "warping boards" of Frost's abandoned "Black Cottage." Though the origins of "The Monument" are in Ernst's technique of frottage, this poem is also a monument to the "impermanence and vulnerability" of dwellings and memorials, as Susan McCabe points out, both North American and European (McCabe 60). The assertion that "our lonely monument," in its "melancholy or romantic scene," is "the beginning of a poem" and should be "watch[ed]...closely" suggests the cryptic significance that such weathered, isolated wooden structures or shacks, and their material vulnerability, would continue to have for Bishop. She may have found them especially captivating, as she continued to feel unsettled herself.

If "The Monument" is located everywhere and nowhere, a pair of stories concerned with dwelling, which Bishop wrote partly in Key West before she bought the house there with Louise Crane, seem firmly grounded in the Depression era on the island. "The Sea & Its Shore" and "In Prison" suggest affinities with, and contrasts between, Bishop's own sense of homelessness and aimlessness, and the poverty and homelessness she observed in Key West; these stories, as David Kalstone notes, evoke "extremit[ies] of retreat" (61).

The slow pace of life in Key West, where there were many abandoned buildings in the 1930s, greatly appealed to Bishop. As she wrote her friend Frani Blough shortly after she had moved into 624 White Street:

> One of the reasons I like Key West so much is because everything goes at such a *natural* pace. For example, if you buy something and haven't any money and *promise*, in a most New England way, to bring it around in half an hour, and then forget for two weeks, no one even comments. And as soon as anyone has worked for a week, they "knock off" for two or so, and drunkenness is an excuse as correct as any other. (*OA* 75—76)

The town's intimate scale and neighborliness may have reminded her of Great Village, and the house itself, with its white clapboard façade, recalled her maternal grandparents' house. Notably, Bishop calls this very leisurely pace of life "natural," and must have found, in remote Key West, affirmation of her own leisurely mode of writing (and drinking), in contrast to New York.

Although "The Sea & Its Shore," a parable more than a story about an isolated man with a strange job on the beach, does not announce its historical moment like "The U.S.A. School of Writing," its initial publication in 1937 clarifies the political context:

> "The Sea and Its Shore" was published as the lead story in a volume [*Life and Letters Today*] that *New Masses* literary editor Horace Gregory—in an attempt to articulate a more inclusive Popular Front poetics—presented as a kind of contemporary American writing that is not necessarily "useful" for the purposes of "immediate political action" . . . but is nevertheless dialectically engaged in and with the history of its time. (Erkkila 290)

Bishop had finished the story late in 1936 in New York and Key West. When it was first published, "The Sea & Its Shore" may well have struck readers not only as a parable of literary creation and reception, but as the tale of a poor man with literary inclinations who had been given a job—to keep a public beach free of papers—and a beach shack home through an agency such as the New Deal's Works Progress Administration (WPA). As Bishop said later, "The town [of Key West] was absolutely broke then. Everybody lived on the WPA" (Brown 299).

The unnamed agency that gives a job to the story's protagonist, Edwin Boomer, would be a sort of cross between the Federal Arts Project and the Civilian Conservation Corps (CCC), both of which operated in Key West. The beneficiaries of the "cultural projects" of the WPA were very poor—"90 percent . . . had to come from the welfare rolls" (Mathews 321). A sort of "gallery-workshop" designed to train and employ amateur artists was also opened up in Key West under the auspices of the WPA, probably in an abandoned building (329). Relief organizers were very concerned about the problem of homelessness, and some hoped that the WPA cultural programs would call more attention to it. Harry Hopkins of FERA, who initiated funding for the arts, "talked of using the power of theatre to spotlight tenements so as to encourage the building of decent houses for all people" (Mathews 322). The CCC generally engaged in environmental projects, such as planting trees and building dams (Pandiani 352); a WPA job in Key West may have been to keep a public beach clean. "The accomplishments of the CCC were vast in protecting and restoring forests, beaches, rivers and parks…[it was] the most widely praised of the New Deal Programs" (McElvaine 155).

While Bishop draws on such New Deal programs in imagining Edwin Boomer's circumstances, several critics have also detailed the parallels between his character and Bishop. He has her mother's maiden name and shares Bishop's initials. Paralleling Bishop's motivation of guilt in taking a job in "The U.S.A. School of Writing," Boomer unquestioningly accepts both the solitary job he is given, and a house so basic as to be inadequate. This would seem to be an appealing fantasy for Bishop. He also lives "the most literary life possible," something Bishop was trying to do herself. When she moved to New York after college, she had earnestly drawn up a bibliography of reading material, and took herself regularly to a desk at the New York Public Library, to lend some formal routine to her efforts to develop as a writer. The fragments of text that Boomer finds are usually taken from her own reading at the library (Millier 64–66). (In her notebook from the mid-1930s, Bishop noted "Papers on the beach at Coney Island…. The[y] drift along the beach came from the land. / A thousand morning papers, late editions, sparkling / print upon the seven seas—" (Bishop 77A). One of the bits of texts that Boomer finds, possibly from Ignatius Loyola's *Spiritual Exercises,* he categorizes among the texts "that seemed to be about himself, his occupation in life, and any instructions or warnings that referred to it." It reads: "'The Exercitant will benefit all the more, the more he secludes himself from all friends and acquaintances and from all earthly solicitude, for example by moving from the house in which he dwelt, and taking another house or room, that there he may abide in all possible privacy'" (*CPr* 175–176). The personal message that Boomer takes from this passage implies a desire to devote himself almost religiously to a life of letters, as Bishop was sometimes inclined to do, isolated in his little shack.

But Boomer conspicuously lacks Bishop's independent wealth—a significant deviation from what many take to be closely autobiographical story. This suggests Bishop's identification with the poor she observed and met in Key West, who were living in ramshackle housing, and also perhaps embarrassment about her comparative affluence. Bishop's imaginative "proto-dream-house" in "The Sea & Its Shore" may be based an abandoned shacks in Key West. The house appears on the first page of the story, anticipating the wooden structure in "The Monument" and the beach shack in "The End of March."

It is a home in the barest sense of the term, a small house that has been assigned to Edwin Boomer:

> This house was very interesting. It was of wood, with a pitched roof, about four by four by six feet, set on pegs stuck in the sand. There was no window, no door set in the door frame, and nothing at all inside.
>
> ....
>
> When the wind along the beach became too strong or too cold, or when he was tired, or when he wanted to read, he sat in the house. He either let his legs hang over the doorsill, or doubled them up under him inside.
>
> As a house, it was more like an idea of a house than a real one.... It could have been a child's perfect playhouse, or an adult's ideal house—since everything that makes most houses nuisances had been done away with.
>
> It was a shelter, but not for living in, for thinking in. It was, to the ordinary house, what the ceremonial thinking cap is to the ordinary hat. (*CPr* 171–172)

If this "idea of a house," stripped of all conveniences like furniture, provides no real shelter, it leaves Boomer essentially homeless. For Bishop, this house may also be associated with the summer beach cottages where she stayed during her school years and later. Such cottages were like playhouses, bare of all but the most necessary furniture, eliminating the material encumbrances of wealth and reducing or evading a perplexing array of choices about what to do with her life.[19] Boomer's situation may also anticipate the desire of the narrator of "In Prison" to be incarcerated, which would mean, in a sense, to have one's daily occupations, and one's permanent home, chosen and mandated by a recognized authority.

Two remarkable facts about Edwin Boomer are his apparent lack of volition and his utterly earnest approach to his job. His situation is arranged for him—again, by an unnamed agency, perhaps like the WPA and the CCC—entirely in the passive voice: he "was appointed to keep the sand free from papers. For this purpose he was given a stick, or a staff, with a long, polished nail in the end...he was also given a lantern to carry" (*CPr* 171). (This pointed stick Boomer uses for gathering papers, incidentally, resembles the metal detectors used by beachcombers looking for change.) Boomer also takes pride in doing his job well. During the Depression, many people were humiliated by unemployment and poverty, and WPA administrators such as Harry Hopkins emphasized the importance of providing the poor with jobs, not simple welfare (see McElvaine 265). Similarly, Boomer approaches his job with an exaggerated seriousness: he "might almost have been said to have joined the 'priesthood.' . . . . No poet, novelist, or critic . . . could imagine the intensity of his concentration on the life of letters" (*CPr* 172). Neither the narrator nor Edwin Boomer questions or complains about the isolated situation or frustrations of his job. In the persistent use of the passive voice, the narrator almost relishes Boomer's lack of free will, as the narrator of "In Prison" will eagerly anticipate his incarceration.

His isolation, however, presents certain dangers, as Boomer frequently gets drunk at night in his lonely shack—as Bishop did alone in hotels in New York and elsewhere. She came of age, and began drinking, during Prohibition, and thus may have developed an idea of drinking as a secretive, solitary activity, especially once she began to drink too much. The story is sympathetic, or at least nonjudgmental, in its evocation of Boomer's drinking, which is introduced matter-of-factly:

> Once or twice when drunk (Boomer usually came to work that way several times a week), he had attempted a little rough modeling [making shapes out of wet newspaper]
>
> . . . .
>
> On nights that Boomer was most drunk, the sea was of gasoline, terribly dangerous. He glanced at it fearfully over his shoulder between every sentence he read, and built his fire far back on the beach. It was brilliant, oily, and explosive. He was foolish enough to think that it might ignite and destroy his only means of making a living. (*CPr* 173–174)

This is one of the few explicit references to Boomer's poverty: clearing the beach of papers, and burning them, is "his only means of making a living," which he fears losing.

The story ends with Boomer in his shack, in an image that echoes Frost's "An Old Man's Winter Night" and the portrait of Bishop as a child, with her grandparents, staring at their reflections in the Great Village house in "Reminiscences": "Let us leave him in his house, at four one morning, his reading selected, the conflagration all over, the lantern shining clearly. It is an extremely picturesque scene, in some ways like a Rembrandt, but in many ways not" (*CPr* 180). The dramatic chiaroscuro is like a Rembrandt, if the lantern provides the only light. One of the "many ways" it is not like a Rembrandt is the change in setting: not a Dutch interior, but a fragile wooden shack, open to the elements on what seems to be an American beach. It is the only shelter available to Edwin Boomer, who is probably drunk and lonely; his situation is dire as well as picturesque. Indeed, the narrator's studiously equivocal tone throughout the story wavers between rendering Boomer as comically picturesque and hinting at undisclosed misery.

If the depiction of Edwin Boomer in "The Sea & Its Shore" imaginatively conflates Bishop's own high-minded aestheticism and existential insecurity with the unfortunate circumstances of the poor and unemployed in Key West, "In Prison," which Bishop apparently began in 1937 during her second tour of an increasingly apprehensive Europe, extends the fantasy of having one's home and vocation chosen and provided by an unnamed authority, presumably the state, in this case. The story (which, like "The Sea & Its Shore," is a parable, but with even less plot) begins, "I can scarcely wait for the day of my imprisonment" (*CPr* 181). What the narrator has done or will do to warrant imprisonment is never explained. It is possible that the story also satirizes the CCC camps. "In Prison" was published in the leftist *Partisan Review*, having won the magazine's fiction contest, in 1938.

Bishop finished writing "In Prison" in the U.S. in December of 1937 and January of 1938, when she had returned from Europe and was deciding what to do next. Once she followed her Aunt Maud and Uncle George to Key West, she stayed down the street from her relatives at a boarding house at 529 Whitehead Street, owned by a Mrs. Pindar. Her room there, where she finished the story, was "right across from the courthouse[,]" she reported: "every day I can watch the convicts in their black-and-white stripes, at work. They are allowed to be 'at large' here during the day, and they have to 'report back' to the jail at nine o'clock—otherwise they're *locked out*!" (*OA* 68; her italics). In Bishop's view, the jail in Key West provided a basic home, with a surprising degree of freedom, for its occupants.

In autobiographies, popular literature and film of the era, according to historian Timothy Yates, prison was sometimes depicted as a place where

> the common man, whose circumstances force him into petty crimes and eventually into prison, ends up finding community and fraternity. In men's asylum autobiographies from the 1930s, men often try to avoid release for fear of the economic conditions on the outside or because they have been so thoroughly humiliated by their families, who resent their failures as breadwinners.

A strange depiction of prison from the time, at once critical and affirmative, is the 1932 film *I Am a Fugitive From a Chain Gang*, which Bishop, an enthusiastic moviegoer, may have seen.

As Robert S. McElvaine explains, the film makes a hero of a WWI veteran, James Allen (played by Paul Muni), who wants a better job than the one he had before the war "as a shipping clerk in a shoe factory":

> Jim takes to the road...but is able to find only occasional employment. Finally he becomes desperate and tries to hock his war medal, but finds a case in the pawnshop is already filled with them....
>
> Jim's real troubles begin when Pete [another "bum"] unexpectedly pulls a gun on [a] diner's proprietor and forces Jim to join in a robbery. Showing no concern for the circumstances, a judge sentences Jim to ten years at hard labor...and Jim finds himself on a chain gang. On the surface, *I Am a Fugitive* is an effective attack on the horrors of chain gangs. On a slightly deeper level, it carried a more important meaning to Depression audiences....
>
> While those in power are cruel and unreasoning, the victims show concern for each other and cooperate as much as they can. An older man, Bomber, advises Jim on how to escape and gives him $7, which it took him years to accumulate. Sebastian, a black prisoner, helps Jim bend his shackles. Muni himself presents a more sympathetic character than he had a few months earlier in his more noted role as the Capone-like leading man in *Scarface* (1932). (McElvaine 212–213)

Contemporary audiences may have connected the film's celebration of collectivist opposition to government authority with the 1932 Bonus March of thousands of poor veterans on Washington, DC, where they camped out, creating their own Hooverville, in hopes of relief from Congress; infamously, the protest was violently put down and the veterans' camp destroyed by the army, led by General Douglas MacArthur.

Although the strange, psychologically opaque narrator of "In Prison" actively seeks imprisonment, and is in this way obviously unlike the character of Jim from the film, he longs for the sort fraternal support that Jim finds in prison. He hopes to make "one intimate friend" in prison and says that, "Ridiculous as it sounds, and is, I am looking forward to directing the prison dramatic association, or being on the baseball team!" (*CPr* 190). These desires would seem to reflect a profound isolation in the narrator's life outside of prison, to which the fate of incarceration seems preferable.

While the jail in Key West may have provided a sort of home to poor men, some of the CCC work camps functioned like prisons, according to Pandiani. In 1933, the crime rate fell after years of steady increases, due to the CCC, which took desperate, poor young men—who were statistically most likely to commit crimes—off the streets.

It appears that between 1932 and 1940, one-third to one-quarter of the nation's poor young men were in the CCC:

> CCC enrollees were removed from the general population and isolated in rural work camps. They were subject to military discipline and under the supervision of Army officers. While free time was provided each day and enrollees could leave camp during these hours, for most there was simply no place to go. Weekend passes were available but most boys were far enough from home to discourage regular travel and had little or no money.
>
> These camps, simply by virtue of their geographical displacement, provided the functional equivalent of a prison. . . . The expressed purpose of the program was to provide economic relief for enrollees and their dependents. Unemployed young men from families on relief were paid $30 each month and provided room, board and clothing for the duration of their enlistment, but enrollees were required to allot $25 per month to their families or dependents. (Pandiani 350–351)

The CCC work camps were widely publicized and supported, according to Pandiani. This blend of a social welfare program with virtual incarceration may have contributed to Bishop's strangely idyllic fantasy "In Prison." Surely Agamben, who characterizes biopolitics as "dislocating localization," would recognize the way that Bishop's stories comment obliquely on an economic crisis that revealed the role of a socialist-inflected, capitalist nation-state in controlling the most basic aspects of citizens' lives, while or because it often failed to provide for their basic welfare (Agamben 131).

Bishop's reticent narrator does not reveal his economic status, but admits that:

> The reader, or my friends, particularly those who happen to be familiar with my way of life, may protest that for me any actual imprisonment is unnecessary, since I already live, in relationship to society, very much as if I were in prison. This I cannot deny, but I must simply point the philosophic difference that exists between Choice and Necessity. (*CPr* 181)

Part of the narrator's present "way of life" is living in hotels, as Bishop did in New York and as a tourist in Europe, but there is no element of adventurous travel in the story. His desire to make "one intimate friend" in prison also suggests Bishop's homosexuality, since prisons are usually segregated by sex; the prison imagined by the narrator seems more like a boarding school or a same-sex college such as

Vassar. Poverty and a homosexual "way of life," of course, could also make the narrator feel that larger "society" was like "a prison."

Yet in the story, prisons and schools promise more community than a "hotel existence," living among transient strangers, which the narrator describes as alienating and rather lonely (as Bishop does in "In a Room" and "Love Lies Sleeping"):

> The hotel existence I now lead might be compared in many respects to prison life, I believe: there are the corridors, the cellular rooms, the large, unrelated group of people with the different purposes in being there that animate every one of them; but it still displays great differences. And of course in any hotel, even the barest, it is impossible to overlook the facts of "decoration," the Turkey carpets, brass fire extinguishers, transom hooks, etc.—it is ridiculous to try to imagine oneself in prison in such surroundings!

If Bishop herself is a model for the narrator, her wealth is effaced, as with Edwin Boomer. The burden of choice among different rooms and hotels, and the ever present possibility of traveling somewhere else, obviously set apart hotel life, or the life of an affluent tourist, from prison life. The desire to stop wandering is understandable, but it is free will, and unnamed social constraints, that the strange narrator wants to escape from, into prison.

In the story, Bishop clearly draws on her own observations of prisoners in Key West, some of whom seem to be homeless when they are "locked out" of prison, and most of whom were impoverished, seeking or being ordered to do odd jobs, like the inhabitants of the CCC work camps:

> One must be *in*; that is the primary condition. And yet I have known of isolated villages, or island towns, in our Southern states where the prisoners are not really imprisoned at all!.... [T]hey are deliberately set at large every morning to work at assigned tasks in the town, or to pick up such odd jobs for themselves as they can. I myself have seen them, pumping water, cleaning streets, even helping housewives wash the windows or shake the carpets....
>
> But the prisoners, if such they could be called—there must have hung over their lives the perpetual irksomeness of all half-measures, of "not knowing where one is at." They had one rule: to report back to the jail, as "headquarters," at nine o'clock, in order to be locked up for the night; and I was given to understand that it was a fairly frequent occurrence for one or two, who arrived a few minutes too late, to be locked out for the night!—when they would sometimes return to their homes, if they came from the same district, or would drop down and

> sleep on the very steps of the jail they were supposed to be secured in. (*CPr* 182–183)

With comic earnestness, the narrator clearly sees this kind of imprisonment as inadequately confining. But Bishop also suggests the "irksome," insecure position of men who cannot even rely entirely on imprisonment as a guarantee of shelter—they can leave to work during the day, but if they do not return by curfew, they are homeless for the night, like those who were confined—partly for their own welfare, partly for the security of the state—to the rural CCC camps.

In his fantasy of confinement, the narrator of "In Prison" feels very differently from the speaker of the early poem "Once upon a Hill," who longs to escape from "a tiny house." This contrast in attitude toward confinement and dwelling may relate to the fact that Bishop herself, by the time she wrote the story, had traveled a great deal, as the speaker of "I introduce Penelope Gwin" had longed to do, to escape "family life." The narrator of in "In Prison" desires some authority—conspicuously lacking in Bishop's life—to choose a home for him, once and for all, and to "be *in*" it, for certain and for good. His longing for an end to "half-measures," and to "know where one is at," also suggests Bishop's own desire to settle in a home for a while, to stop living in hotels and traveling—as she attempted to do with Louise Crane at 624 White Street, near her Aunt Maud and Uncle George.

The narrator devotes several pages to imagining what his rustic prison cell will be like, and these descriptions draw on a number of places Bishop had visited in her travels. His fantasies recall Edwin Boomer's wooden shack and also the many hotel rooms and apartments where Bishop had stayed in Europe and New York (perhaps including the scenes of "In a Room" in Seville and of "Love Lies Sleeping"). The narrator continually wavers between speculating about the size, shape, and arrangements of the cell, and insisting that all choices should be made for him. Whatever it looks like, it should be primitive. The cell could have stained or weathered walls, like the shack in "The End of March" and the structure in "The Monument." And, as with Edwin Boomer's shack in "The Sea & Its Shore," the prison cell is associated with literary or artistic creation. Bishop's narrator here, who wants "to be given one very dull book to read, the duller the better…on a subject completely foreign to me[,]" also plans to add his own writings to those he expects to find on the wall of his prison cell (*CPr* 187).

The narrator's ideal room would also have rural surroundings, like most of the houses that Bishop idealized. In writing "In Prison," according to Millier, Bishop "lift[ed] a passage almost verbatim from her travel notebook account of her visit [to Arles in 1937]...to the Asylum of the Mausoleum, to the cell where Van Gogh was confined" (Millier 134–136). Admiring the view of "the kitchen garden of the institution...the open fields [and a] row of cypresses" that he observed from Van Gogh's cell, and drawing on his "foreign" travels, the narrator concludes that "something a little less rustic, a little harsher, might be of more use to me personally. But it is a difficult question, and one that is probably best decided, as of course it must be, by chance alone" (*CPr* 185). This passage continues to suggest that the narrator does not feel quite as flexible as he wants to feel about having his prison cell designed and chosen for him, but he renounces preferences. Still, this prison cell sounds more like a quaint country cottage than an unpleasantly bare room. Again, the narrator is impatient with "not knowing where one is at," and longs for an answer to the fundamental question of the homeless tourist—"Where should we be today?"—which Bishop posed later in "Questions of Travel" (*CP* 93). At the same time, it is tempting to read this passage as a commentary on the CCC camps:

> [I]n the same way that I was led to protest against the ambiguity of the position of those prisoners who were in and out of prison at the same time...I should bitterly object to any change or break in my way of life. If, for example, I should become ill or have to go to the prison infirmary, or if shortly after my arrival I should be moved to a different cell—either of these accidents would seriously upset me[.] (*CPr* 190–191)

At the end of the story, the possibly homosexual narrator seems to refer to the limited options available to the poor, homeless, and unemployed of the era. He admits that he has thought of "joining our army or navy[,]" but fears hard labor, travel, ocean views, and—naturally, given the expectation of wider war in Europe in the late 1930s—"active service" (*CPr* 191). Ocean views would be disturbing to this narrator, as they were to Edwin Boomer, but for different reasons—representing, perhaps, the entire world of choice that he wants to escape. He also anticipates and agrees with the reader's inference that he "would have been happy in the more flourishing days of the religious order," recalling Edwin Boomer's identification with Loyola's advice to sequester himself in a new home, far from friends and acquaintances (*CPr* 191).

The fact that the military and monasteries, like prisons, are segregated by sex may remind us that Bishop was seeking to make a life with a female companion in Key West. Most choices about where to live, and even about what to read, would be decided for the narrator of "In Prison," yet there he could make "one intimate friend." In the voice of its earnest, naïve narrator, the story would seem to blend Bishop's own idiosyncratic, leisure-class problems of being a homeless tourist, orphan and lesbian with the dire circumstances of the poor, whose desperation had landed them in prison or the CCC camps.

As Bishop tried to make a home in Key West, the fragile and dilapidated houses that she discovered there appealed to her extremely. Indeed, the theme of the fragility of dwellings continued to occupy Bishop in the late 1930s and early 1940s, in relation to her own unsettled life, the poverty in Key West and the destruction of WWII. In the winter of 1938–1939, which Bishop spent at her new house in Key West, she began "Jerónimo's House" (*CP* 34), a portrait of a particularly fragile and temporary home (Millier 158).

The poem may be based in part on the house of a local primitive painter, Gregorio Valdes, whom Bishop and Louise Crane had hired "to paint a picture of [their house]" (Millier 139). "Jerónimo's House" echoes Bishop's description of Valdes's house in a short eponymous essay after his death in 1939. Another likely model she observed from her rented room on Whitehead Street in 1938: "Down the street is a very small cottage I can look right into, and the only furniture it contains beside a bed and chair is an enormous French horn, painted silver, leaning against the wall, and hanging over it a pith helmet, also painted silver" (*OA* 68).

The poem's speaker is a poor man named Jerónimo[20] whose house is a "love-nest"; he apparently has a number of children, as his table settings include a tray "for the smallest baby" (ll. 9, 27). In its fragility, this house recalls Edwin Boomer's shack and the humble structure in "The Monument":

> My house, my fairy
>   palace, is
> of perishable
>   clapboards with
> three rooms in all,
>   my gray wasps' nest
> of chewed-up paper
>   glued with spit.
>   (ll. 1–8)

As a "fairy palace" this house also recalls Bishop's childhood fancy in "Mrs. Sullivan Downstairs" that, as an orphan, she was a sort of "fairy princess," like the kidnapped child imprisoned in "Once on a Hill." The frequent use of "my" implies pride in ownership, like Bishop's in her own first house. The odd description of the house in the first stanza resembles the sculptures Edwin Boomer sometimes made out of wet newspaper in his small house. "Jerónimo's House" and Boomer's house and sculptures are made of flimsy materials, carefully formed but easily destroyed:

> At night you'd think
>   my house abandoned.
> Come closer. You
>   can see and hear
> the writing-paper
>   lines of light
> and the voices of
>   my radio
>
> singing flamencos
>   in between
> the lottery numbers.
>   When I move,
> I take these things,
>   not much more, from
> my shelter from
>   the hurricane.
>   (ll. 49–64)

For all his pride in his house, Jerónimo knows it is a temporary shelter that looks "abandoned." And he is, presumably, poor; he listens to the "lottery numbers" on the radio. When he leaves his little house, as he knows he must when a hurricane comes, he will take his few possessions. (Again, the disastrous Labor Day hurricane of 1935 destroyed much of the improvements made by FERA in Key West, and cut off the island for several years.) Like Jerónimo, Bishop had few possessions to tie her to one place. Millier notes that the clavichord she had purchased after college "was for a time the only thing in her life that drew her or tied her to one place or another," and even that she often kept in storage (Millier 82). Oddly, if he has children and a lover or wife, Jerónimo seems not only to doubt the security of his house, but also plans to leave the house alone, which may imply doubt about the relationship that makes this house his "love-nest."

Key West entered a phase of fuller recovery when the United States entered WWII in 1941, as the naval base was revived. As Camille Roman notes, "naval housing in Key West went up in the field across from [Bishop's] 624 White Street house so that the war literally sprang up in her back yard and near her own home. Indeed, she rented her home to [N]avy personnel" (Roman 55). One of the most remarkable poems from this era in Key West is "Roosters," which brilliantly depicts macho, homicidal aggression (probably referring to the Nazis and perhaps to Fascist Italy, which Bishop had observed in her travels) and also subtly critiques compulsory heterosexuality. Roman so insightfully discusses "Roosters" in *Elizabeth Bishop's World War II-Cold War View*, including the ways that dwelling itself is threatened by a warlike atmosphere in the poem, that I will not discuss the poem in detail here (see Roman 50–81).

The revival of the naval base improved the economy in Key West and brought the war home to Bishop; it also helped make Key West a tourist resort for gays. As John D'Emilio and Estelle B. Freedman recount in *Intimate Matters. A History of Sexuality in America*, in the 1940s, military bases provided homosexuals with new places to meet and form communities, as gay districts sprang up in the towns and cities that hosted them. "Truly, World War II was something of a nationwide 'coming out' experience" (289). The incipient gay tourist lifestyle was something that Bishop apparently enjoyed in Key West. A number of drafts and poems from this era, published in *Edgar Allan Poe & the Juke-Box*, are full of sailors, soldiers, drink, sex, and gambling. She conceived the title poem "as a sort of farewell to Key West…intended…to conclude her second volume," *A Cold Spring* (1955); in December of 1953, writing to Robert Lowell, Bishop referred to it as "'that last impossible poem'" (*EAP* 271). It seems to me more frank about sexuality, loneliness, and alcoholism, than anything else Bishop wrote. It seems to reflect on the experience, or observation, of the lonely in the bars of Key West.

Like "Jerónimo's House," Bishop's home with Louise Crane may have felt provisional and insecure. According to Betty Jean Steinshouer, Crane's family kept Louise away from Key West much of the time because they hoped to cure her of homosexuality through psychiatric treatment, and thus kept Bishop in a holding pattern as she tried to arrange their life together (Steinshouer).[21] Bishop's actual residence at 624 White Street was brief, and she sold the house in 1946. Her subsequent moves were often motivated by romantic relationships, as she tried to make or find homes with women with whom she was involved. (She rented out the White Street house in June 1941 to move in with Marjorie Carr Stevens, a woman who was separated from her husband, who was in the U.S. Navy, and living in Key West.)[22] Yet for a time, Key West seemed the best place to make such a home.

The last poem I want to consider from Bishop's Key West era, "Chemin de Fer" (*CP* 8), written in 1945 and 1946, concerns similar personal anxieties about dwelling. In 1940 and 1941, Bishop made two autumn trips to visit friends (Charlotte and Red Russell) in an isolated rural area in Brevard, North Carolina; she was accompanied by Stevens in 1941. Near the small Appalachian town south of Asheville, Bishop encountered "a reputedly crazy hermit woman named Cordie Heiss," whose character and home apparently inspired the poem, and who resembles the isolated figure of Edwin Boomer, and the speaker of "The End of March" (Millier 178). To meet Heiss in her secluded mountain cabin, Bishop and a friend braved a trespassing sign that read: "'PLEASE STAY OUT FROM PROWLING AROUND ON MY LAND. CORDIE.' Elizabeth copied the sign and sketched the cabin with great detail in her notebook" (Millier 161). The poem questions the Thoreauvian isolation represented by the cabin.

In "Chemin de Fer," a solitary speaker follows the "railroad track" and arrives at "the little pond"

> where the dirty hermit lives,
>   l[ying] like an old tear
> holding onto its injuries
>   lucidly year after year.
>   (ll. 1, 8, 9–12)

"[T]he little pond" recalls Walden Pond, and the hermit-like Thoreau is thought to have had homosexual inclinations. As McCabe points out, no sense of communion with nature lessens the hermit's isolation in this poem, as it does for Thoreau (66). In contrast with the isolated artist-figure of Edwin Boomer, who seems relatively content, this hermit both aggressively defends his isolation and seems to regret it:

> The hermit shot off his shot-gun
> ....
> "Love should be put into action!"
>   screamed the old hermit.
> Across the pond an echo
>   tried and tried to confirm it.
>   (ll. 13, 17–20)

Like the pond, the hermit isolates himself because of his distrust of people, his tendency "to hold... onto [his] injuries / lucidly year after year." In these lines, Bishop perhaps voices a self-accusation (whether just or not) for being troubled, year after year, by her childhood traumas, whose effects may have interfered with her attempts to maintain relationships and establish a home; perhaps her sexuality was also a complicating factor.

A hermit rejects relationships, yet this inconsistent hermit does not stop worrying the question of love, even as he tries to scare off the intruding speaker. The gunshot and the shouted imperative contradict each other. If Bishop wanted or felt she had to keep her homosexuality something of a secret, it would sometimes be difficult to put "love...into action." Perhaps it would seem easier at times to retreat into the artist's solitary existence, emblematized by the hermit's rural cabin and Edwin Boomer's beach shack in "The Sea & Its Shore."

Although her poetic career was finally, officially launched with *North & South* in 1946, "Chemin de Fer" dates from Bishop's most unsettled and unhappiest decade, from 1941 to 1951. In these years she continued to move between Key West and New York, and elsewhere along the East Coast, and she also traveled to Mexico. This period included an especially miserable year, from 1949–1950, when she served as poetry consultant to the Library of Congress in Washington, DC. Her last "sustained" relationship with a man ended in 1949, when she broke with Tom Wanning; Millier speculates that "the pain of its ending may also have involved the end of her hopes for a so-called normal heterosexual life" (Millier 219). On the day when Robert Lowell almost proposed to her, as he recalled it, in the summer of 1948 in Stonington, Maine, Bishop had told him "rather humorously yet it was truly meant, 'When you write my epitaph, you must say I was the loneliest person who ever lived' " (*OA* 345).

The beautiful poem, "Over 2,000 Illustrations and a Complete Concordance," which Bishop began in 1945 and finished in 1948 (Millier 179, 198), gives the most poignant expression of the pathos of Bishop's unsettled adult life up to this point. It was included in *A Cold Spring* (1955). The first stanza closely describes the meaningfully arranged scenes in a family Bible; it is likely that Bishop had in mind the Bible her grandfather Boomer sometimes read from in "Reminiscences of Great Village." The second stanza, in marked contrast with the first, presents vignettes from the speaker's travels, which loosely cohere only through the speaker's precise, alienated perspective. (In her journal on November 15, 1937, Bishop noted while sightseeing in Rome: "I recognized many things that had served as illustrations in my Latin Grammars" [Bishop 77.2]). For her travels, there is no official, explanatory "Concordance." The second stanza leads to the brilliant line about the arbitrariness of the speaker's experience, especially the recited itineraries and undigested travels, which opens the third stanza: "Everything only connected by 'and' and 'and'" (li. 65).[23]

In the third stanza, Bishop's nostalgic speaker returns to the Bible, which apparently inspired a desire to travel in the first place, as the gilt edging of the illustrated pages rub off on the reader's hands:

> Open the heavy book. Why couldn't we have seen
> this old Nativity while we were at it?
> —the dark ajar, the rocks breaking with light,
> an undisturbed, unbreathing flame,
> colorless, sparkless, freely fed on straw,
> and, lulled within, a family with pets,
> —and looked and looked our infant sight away.
> (ll. 68–74)

The scene is an illustration from Christ's Nativity, familiarized and domesticated; it also seems a description of a quaint Nativity scene, lit with an electric bulb, that might be placed under a Christmas tree. The plaintive question can be understood in several senses. The tourist-speaker may wish she had also visited Jerusalem, or that she could have thoroughly appreciated the Nativity while it was before her. Another sense may reveal the source of the closing lines' tremendous pathos: the adult speaker, like the lonely Bishop remembering Great Village, deeply longs for the simple childhood scene, where she was part of "a family with pets."

Home at Last: The Brazil Years

When Bishop arrived in Brazil as a tourist on November 26, 1951, she had no intention of staying for fifteen years. She traveled to South America unsure of her future, knowing only that she did "not [want] to settle in New York," which had been her home base from 1945 to 1951 (Millier 235, 245). In the poem "Arrival at Santos" (*CP* 89–90), she chides an exaggerated version of her tourist self, who is disappointed with her first impression of the country:

> Oh, tourist,
> is this how this country is going to answer you
>
> and your immodest demands for a different world,
> and a better life, and complete comprehension

> of both at last, and immediately,
> after eighteen days of suspension?
>
> Finish your breakfast.
>
> (ll. 7–13)

Blissfully, to Bishop's surprise, Brazil did offer her "a different world, / and a better life" almost "immediately," in the person and home of Lota de Macedo Soares, whom she had met in New York in 1942.

With her new and devoted lover, Bishop found her first real home as an adult, in Petrópolis. The romance began with Soares caring for a very ill Bishop at her home, Samambaia; sometime in December, Bishop had an extreme allergic reaction to Brazilian cashew fruit, and stayed there during her recovery. Soares invited Bishop to live with her, and made plans to build a separate writer's studio for Bishop near the house (Millier 243–244, 246). Bishop was ecstatic and deeply grateful.

She was also charmed with the rural setting of the house, which proved, with Soares's company, to be ideal for her writing. The house, designed by the noted architect Sérgio Bernardes, is a very modern structure, perched on the side of a steep mountain, with long low roofs, large glass doors and windows, and a large paved patio. Samambaia was not a neglected house, like so many of Bishop's dream-houses, but it was unfinished. All the time she lived there, it was under continual construction, overseen by Soares. She described the house and its surroundings in "Song for the Rainy Season" (*CP* 101–102), begun in 1954 and published in the *New Yorker* in 1960 (Millier 304); the poem evokes a sense of fertility and intimacy associated with waterfalls and a "magnetic rock," echoing perhaps Frost's "West-Running Brook" and Eliot's *The Waste Land*.

Finding such love and such a home in a small rural community in Brazil furnished an atmosphere in which Bishop began to write about her childhood in Nova Scotia. She had visited Nova Scotia twice not long before she sailed for South America. In the summer of 1951, she went to Sable Island, "where her grandfather Hutchinson had been lost at sea," and to Halifax, where she stayed "across the bay from [the]... hospital in Dartmouth" in which her mother had been institutionalized, a grim reminder of childhood losses (Millier 252). In 1947, on leaving Great Village after her first visit there in fifteen years, she began the elegiac poem, "The Moose." As Bishop settled into her new home in Brazil, her childhood emerged as a constant theme in her thinking and writing. One after another, she began prose pieces about this time: "Gwendolyn," "In the Village," "The Country Mouse," "Primer Class," and "Memories of Uncle Neddy."

And, after years of feeling so unsettled, Bishop was also preoccupied with houses, with dwelling itself and various threats to it. "She said in July of 1955 that she was dreaming of houses almost every night" (Millier 268). Initially, however, she had "difficulty writing poetry about Brazil, [which,] combined with her enthusiasm for recent prose, made her think that her next book would be a volume of short stories" (Millier 253). One of the first poems Bishop wrote in Brazil, "Sestina" (*CP* 123–124), was obviously about her childhood, yet the poem also begins to universalize the theme of displacement in the evocation of a child's attachment to houses. Originally titled "Early Sorrow," the poem was published in 1955. In *Questions of Travel* (1965), Bishop placed it after "In the Village," as Millier points out, and autobiographically, the poem seems to follow the experience described in "In the Village": her mother's last visit to Great Village before she was institutionalized in Dartmouth, Nova Scotia (Millier 267).

Unlike "In the Village," however, "Sestina" is written in the third person, suggesting that Bishop wanted to write a more distanced, more universal parable about children's need for the security of a house. The source of the "Early Sorrow" is unnamed in the poem, as a child's grandmother cries over a teapot and bread, and tries to distract the child, who is drawing "inscrutable house[s]," by reading out of the almanac by the stove (li. 39). The first line—"September rain falls on the house"—may refer to the traumatic September of 1917, when Bishop's paternal grandparents came to Great Village to take her away to Worcester. Perhaps the child's imminent departure, as well as her daughter Gertrude's institutionalization, makes the grandmother cry. "[H]er equinoctial tears" may refer to the autumn equinox, which falls around the twentieth of September (li. 7). From that date, the hours of daylight diminish until the winter solstice, the shortest day of the year. Noted in any almanac, the autumn equinox marks the beginning of the season and of autumn rains, just as some unspoken sorrow marks a turning point for the worse in the poem.

An almanac, whose root meaning is "calendar," forecasts weather, relying on historical trends. In the past, almanacs also provided astrological predictions. And, when people owned few books, an almanac such as Benjamin Franklin's *Poor Richard's Almanac* was sometimes second in importance only to the Bible. In "Sestina," it is an instrument for predicting the sad future that the grandmother somehow anticipated: "*It was to be*, says the Marvel Stove. / *I know what I know*, says the almanac [italics in the original]" (ll. 25–26). This italicized pronoun "*It*" only vaguely hints at the cause of the grandmother's sorrow, of which the child seems ignorant for the moment. The stove and the almanac know, and say so, but they don't say what they know; the reader is in the position of the child, for whom adult sorrows are a secret.

The grandmother repeatedly tries to hide the fact of her sorrow from the child, who draws houses with pathways that lead away from or toward home, like the path from Hansel and Gretel's house, and she includes a man who might be an absent father or the woodcutter-father of the lost siblings in the fairytale:

> But secretly, while the grandmother
> busies herself about the stove,
> the little moons fall down like tears
> from between the pages of the almanac
> into the flower bed the child
> has carefully placed in front of the house.
>
> *Time to plant tears*, says the almanac.
> The grandmother sings to the marvellous stove
> and the child draws another inscrutable house.
> (ll. 32–43)

The child draws house after house, seemingly obsessed with the security and family they symbolize. The sorrowful event acquires the inevitability of the phases of the moon, which fall from the almanac into the child's drawing—hints of the event, planted in the pictures she draws. Surely memories would grow from planted tears, as "Sestina" grows out of Bishop's childhood experience of displacement and loss of home and family.

The theme of displacement, in her own unsettled childhood, also seemed to make Bishop more sensitive to the poverty around her, and to the most vulnerable, poorest children of Brazil. At the same time, she continued to write for an American audience who knew little about the country, and thus acted as a sort of poet-guide to Brazil. (She had a first-right-of-refusal contract with the *New Yorker* until 1962, and continued thereafter to publish many of her poems there [Millier 323].) A theme she continually emphasized in her poetry and prose, as well as comparisons between the country's colonial history and problematic touristic perspectives, was the country's poverty and particularly its tragic consequences for children. She was also involved in caring for "the five children of Lota's adopted son Kylso," who had been crippled by polio, "and Maria Elizabeth, the cook's daughter" (Millier 261, 265–267).

In 1961, Bishop more formally acted as a guide to Brazil for American audiences when she accepted the well-paid job of writing a book for Time-Life, *Brazil*—and came to regret it, because of persistent editorial intervention. In 1961 and 1962, she complained in letters to her Aunt Grace that the editors wanted "ALL of Brazilian history, geography, and politics reduced to pill-form—and all in two or three months." She swore "never again" to do such a project, "not for Time, Life, etc—they are incredible people and what they know about Brazil would fit on the head of a pin—and yet the gall, the arrogance, the general condescension!" ("Letters to Aunt Grace Boomer Bowers," undated 1961, March 25, 1962, Bishop 25.1, 25.9). Something of Bishop's preoccupation with fragile dwellings, however, survives in this caption to a photograph of the hills of Rio from the book:

> the *favelas* of Rio are home to a quarter of its people, who live without running water or sewers literally a stone's throw from luxury apartment houses. Flimsy shanties built of odd scraps, they are inhabited mainly by rural people who come to Rio to find work. Although the *favelas* are no worse than many other city slums, they are more conspicuous—inescapable reminders of the rural squalor behind Brazil's industrial progress. (*Brazil* 138)

Some of the time, Bishop occupied one of these "luxury apartment houses"—Soares's second home was an apartment on the Copacabana in Rio. Needless to say, children growing up in *favelas* were and are subject to extremes of neglect and misfortune to which Bishop was most fortunately a stranger. But she empathized with them, as she had with the poor and unemployed during the Depression in the United States, and the *favelas* in particular engaged her imagination.

"Squatter's Children" (*CP* 95), one of Bishop's earliest poems about Brazil, was "published first in Portuguese in March 1956" (Millier 266) and "directly treats the issue of childhood displacement" (McCabe 183). In *Questions of Travel*, Bishop placed it after the title poem, which closes inconclusively: "*the choice is never wide and never free. / . . . . Should we have stayed at home, / wherever that may be?*" (ll. 65, 66–67, *CP* 94). In relation to that poem, "Squatter's Children" evokes a sad, anti-picturesque reality that an American tourist might contemplate in Brazil.

The children depicted in the poem—which is written in three eight-line stanzas that mostly follow an A-B-C-B-D-D-F-F rhyme scheme—should question the security of their home, but they are naïve and trusting. Their innocence makes them especially vulnerable to the storm that looms and breaks over one stanza into the next, prefigured and emphasized by the recursive, emphatic rhymed couplets that close each stanza:

> On the unbreathing sides of hills
> they play, a specklike girl and boy,
> alone, but near a specklike house.
> . . . .
> A dancing yellow spot, a pup,
> attends them. Clouds are piling up;
>
> a storm piles up behind the house.
> The children play at digging holes.
> The ground is hard; they try to use
> one of their father's tools,
> a mattock with a broken haft
> the two of them can scarcely lift.
> (ll. 1–3, 7–8, 9–14)

The tiny size of the children against the huge hills, from the perspective of the distant observer, underscores their insignificance, as they play in ignorance of looming malevolent forces. "A storm" threatens these innocent, hapless children, like the "September rain" that falls on the house in "Sestina."

The squatter's children's parents can offer them little help or guidance in their play on the hillside, and by implication, in securing their home there—"their father's tools" for digging are broken and too heavy for children. Yet they take their situation lightly. The weather and the children's mother have nothing hopeful or sensible to say in response to their laughter; their "weak flashes of inquiry" are answered by meaningless babble like their own speech ("echolalia"):

> But to their little, soluble,
> unwarrantable ark,
> apparently the rain's reply
> consists of echolalia,
> and Mother's voice, ugly as sin,
> keeps calling to them to come in.
>
> Children, the threshold of the storm
> has slid beneath your muddy shoes;
> wet and beguiled, you stand among
> the mansions you may choose
> out of a bigger house than yours,
> whose lawfulness endures.

Its soggy documents retain
your rights in rooms of falling rain.
(ll. 17, 19–32)

The storm welcomes them, ironically, to their patrimony: no rights to their home, even as the family's flimsy shack almost seems to dissolve in the rain. (The "specklike house" and the "little, soluble, / unwarrantable ark" may remind us of the insubstantial "chewed-up paper / glued with spit" of "Jerónimo's House.") The detached, yet concerned speaker closes the last stanza with sad irony; the children "may choose" a home among the *favelas* that will certainly not be a mansion, and their rights even to that dissolve easily. The worst of it is that their insecure fate is so impersonal and undeserved (as Bishop's had been, in her estimation: " 'my miseries as a child weren't anybody's fault, anyway—most of them were due to chance' " [qtd. in Millier 266]). Any religious consolation to which the squatter's children cling is insubstantial; there may be many mansions in heaven, as in John 14:2, which Bishop alludes to here. But the children's earthly lot is a slum.

"The Burglar of Babylon," written in 1963, also concerns the *favelas* and the tragic fate of one who grew up there. Its form approximates ballad meter, and in the manner of a traditional narrative ballad, it recounts a fatalistic tragedy from the viewpoint of an impersonal third-person speaker. Millier explains the poem's context: "In April 1963, she had watched idly from the balcony in Rio as police pursued a thief over the steep hills behind the building" (Millier 345).[24] The poem falls into a genre of Robin Hood ballads, which renders lower-class criminals heroic.[25] In its form, "The Burglar of Babylon" returns to the Audenesque style of "Chemin de Fer" and "Roosters," and of the juvenile poems "Once on a Hill" and "I introduce Penelope Gwin." As in the earlier poems, there is a childlike, naïve tone, which in this case apparently endorses the sense that the burglar's fate is inscrutable and inevitable.

The burglar, named Micuçú, is a "killer, / An enemy of society," but his criminal behavior is attributed partly to his growing up in the *favelas*:

On the fair green hills of Rio
   There grows a fearful stain:
The poor who come to Rio
   And can't go home again.

On the hills a million people,
   A million sparrows, nest,
Like a confused migration
   That's had to light and rest,

Building its nests, or houses,
    Out of nothing at all, or air.
You'd think a breath would end them,
    They perch so lightly there.
                                        (ll. 21–22, 1–12)

Comparing the poor inhabitants of the *favelas* to "a confused migration" of exhausted sparrows, Bishop gains the reader's sympathy for them. Comparing them to lichen, conversely, she hints at the cold detachment of the rich toward the poor, seeing them as a parasitic growth on the hills of Rio. Conspicuously Bishop chooses the hill of Babylon for her title. It is not inevitable that the poor be thieves in the corrupt city of Babylon, but it is understandable, as the poem outlines the economic inequality embodied in Rio's geography. Members of all classes observe the pursuit of Micuçú, from the inhabitants of the *favelas*, to women at market, to the rich (including Bishop herself).

In turn, Micuçú regards the whole landscape of Rio. Pursued by soldiers, the poor criminal watches the rich at play on the beaches below, and he also hears the barking of mongrel dogs. Failing to find "shelter," he dies with a gun, "just the clothes he had on, / With two contos in the pockets, / On the hill of Babylon" (ll. 143, 150–152). His "auntie" bewails his fate and defends herself, " 'I raised him to be honest / Even here, in Babylon slum' " (ll. 155, 165–166). The poem ends by repeating the first and fifth stanzas, underscoring the predictable form throughout, as if to say: As long as the lives and homes of the poor in Rio are so insecure, such criminals will arise in the slums.

By the time she wrote "The Burglar of Babylon," Bishop had become something of a literary celebrity in Brazil, ever since she won the Pulitzer Prize for *Poems: North & South—A Cold Spring* in 1956 (Millier 255). In 1965, her third book, *Questions of Travel* was published, mostly to great acclaim. But earlier in the year, a debacle about a piece she wrote for the *New York Times Magazine* had turned some Brazilians against her. She was commissioned to write a short article about *Carnivale* on the 400th anniversary of the city of Rio. Her attempts at subtlety and historical scope led the editor to send her a curt telegram: "WE[']RE NOT INTERESTED HISTORY OF RIO" (Bishop 42.14). In the article, she complained of the commercialization of *Carnivale* and at the same time celebrated the events, and Rio's apparently harmonious racial and religious diversity. The reaction in Rio to the article was fierce. Millier suggests that Bishop's "chief literary tools—irony and understatement" had been missed, and progressive Brazilian readers perceived in her celebration of racial harmony in Brazil an acceptance of a racist social structure. For a time, Bishop avoided Rio entirely because of the reaction to the article (Millier 362–366). Her sense that she had a secure home in Brazil seemed threatened.

Throughout all this, Soares was mostly in Rio, thoroughly taken up with the task of developing the Parque do Flamengo. In Bishop's view, Soares was "'killing herself with work,'" and Bishop was at loose ends (qtd. in Millier 367). She spent more and more time on her own at Samambaia and in Ouro Prêto, a mountain resort northeast of Rio. There she also began an affair with Lilli Correia de Araújo. In Ouro Prêto, Bishop fell in love with a fragile house that, for a time, became a second home. In a 1963 letter to her Aunt Grace, Bishop wrote:

> I am going through another wave of nostalgia for the NORTH. Even Lota has asked me to write about the price of a little old house we know of in Connecticut. This is just the wildest day-dreaming—but I'd STILL like to own something in or around G[reat] V[illage], I think... I mean our—your—old house? Would they ever want to sell it? (August 3, 1963, Bishop 25.11)

Instead of buying an old house in the North, Bishop indulged her "dream[s] about real estate" in 1965 when she bought her third "loved house" in Ouro Prêto (Bishop 25.11, *CP* 178). It was something of a "housewreck," a term Bishop coined in a 1964 poem, "Twelfth Morning; or What You Will" (*CP* 110–111), which was originally titled "Real Estate Development, 6 A.M.," hinting at Bishop's fondness, like Frost's, for property speculation in abandoned or neglected houses (Bishop 67.5). The half-ruined seventeenth century colonial house, set on a hill, thoroughly charmed Bishop almost against her will, as she wrote to Ashley Brown:

> I've gone and bought a house. I never intended to. Lota and I have wanted to get an old one on the seashore somewhere, to restore, but had no luck.... It is one of the oldest houses in town, and has all sorts of mysterious stone steps and platforms and cellars—where gold was washed.... Oh dear, I am afraid Ouro Prêto in its tiny way will become the Cornwall or Provincetown of Brazil, and here I am getting into it—but it is a good "investment"; we can always sell it—and one doesn't feel normal in Brazil unless engaged in some sort of real estate deal. (*OA* 435–436)

Like Great Village, Provincetown, Key West, and Petrópolis, Ouro Prêto appealed to Bishop because of its slow pace of life and close-knit community that embodied, or attempted to recreate, a sort of village lifestyle. As in Frost's New England, abandoned towns and short-lived settlements in Brazil offered many opportunities for "real estate deals" for those nostalgic, like Bishop, for rural life. Bishop wrote: "what really won me over, I think, was that it has two large lots beside it that go with it, with very high stone walls around them—perfect for a garden. Also water running through one, a brook on the other side, palm trees, all kinds of fruit trees, etc." (*OA* 435).

Her 1970 prose piece, "To the Botequim & Back," describes the daily walk Bishop took in Ouro Prêto to to fetch milk at a ramshackle general store, which may have reminded her of general stores in Great Village. On her walk, half of the houses she encountered seem to have been abandoned. There were "fields full of ruins. After two hundred years, a few ruins have turned back into houses again" (*CPr* 73). Bishop's own house required very expensive restoration. Once she returned to the United States, the house became inconvenient to maintain and visit, and she finally, reluctantly sold it in 1974 (*OA* 583). It was the suicide of Soares in 1967, of course, that instigated Bishop's permanent move back to the United States, though she would continue to spend some time in Brazil until 1974.

Many readers of Bishop are familiar with the heartbreaking end of Bishop's relationship with Soares. In 1966 Bishop had returned to the United States for her first extended stay in more than a decade, when she filled in for Theodore Roethke to teach creative writing for a semester at the University of Washington. While there, she began a relationship with a younger woman, Suzanne Bowen, which Soares eventually discovered. Bishop returned to Brazil in the summer, only to find the country in increasing political turmoil and Soares in a worsening condition; Bishop's alcoholism was exacerbated by conflict with her. In an attempt to repair the relationship and improve Soares's spirits, they went on a brief trip to Europe; when they returned to Brazil, Soares ended up in the hospital. In 1967 Soares improved for a while, but, joining Bishop in New York in September, she overdosed on Valium and possibly Nembutal, and died after five days in a coma (Millier 374–397).

Return to New England

With the excruciating end of this relationship, Bishop lost the most enduring, loving home she had found as an adult. As she wrote to her friends Ilse and Kit Barker, after her first serious conflict with Soares, she had to leave Samambaia "'in half an hour,' 'after fifteen years with a few dirty clothes in a busted suitcase, no home any more, no claim (legally) to anything here'" (qtd. in Millier 384). She would return, but her lack of legal claim to the house was partly because of the lack of legal recognition of their relationship. In her will, Soares, by prior agreement with Bishop, left Samambaia to Mary Morse and the Rio apartment to Bishop, which she sold. She felt "homeless" again; after her lover's death, she wrote to her Aunt Grace, "I had to move out of Samambaia (forever, I suppose—and I did love that place so)" (January 20, 1967, Bishop 25.15; undated, Bishop 25.16). Bishop also became estranged from Soares's friends and family, who seemed to blame her for the death. "Inventory," the last poem Bishop typed out in her writing studio at Samambaia in 1967, testifies to her sense of homelessness. She lists the few objects and "living cat" she was attached to, and laments, "where—where can I take them next?" (Millier 385; *EAP* 143). (The list recalls the few possessions in "Jerónimo's House.") Where she took some of them next was San Francisco, where she lived with Suzanne Bowen (and her infant son), who crucially helped Bishop through the initial period of grieving; they also spent time in Ouro Prêto. However, they had a bitter falling out in 1970 (Millier 399–431).

And so, in 1970, Bishop moved to Cambridge, Massachusetts, to teach creative writing at Harvard (later she taught at Brandeis University). Initially, she lived on campus at Kirkland House, and then "at 60 Brattle Street near Harvard Square," in an apartment found for her by Alice Methfessel. Methfessel, who was 33 years Bishop's junior, was working as the administrative assistant at Kirkland House when they met. She became Bishop's companion and personal assistant until Bishop's death in 1979, when she became Bishop's literary executor (Millier 432, 435, 442).

Initially Bishop felt extremely unsettled in Boston, and her poetry took a more personal turn in the final decade of her life. She began the last poem in *Geography III* (1976), "Five Flights Up" (*CP* 72), in 1971, when she was staying in an apartment at 16 Chauncey Street belonging to Methfessel (Millier 443). In contrast to the unrealizable fantasy of retreat in "The End of March," "Five Flights Up" is set in an apartment associated with fundamental loneliness and isolation, recalling similar poems from the 1930s: "Paris 7 A.M.," "In a Room," and "Love Lies Sleeping." The time is early morning, the grim moment before dawn. The wakeful speaker, who perhaps has not slept for hours (the first line is "Still dark"), envies a dog and a bird who

> know everything is answered,
> all taken care of,
> no need to ask again.
> —Yesterday brought to today so lightly!
> (A yesterday I find almost impossible to lift.)
>
> (ll. 22–26)

In her grief, Bishop also turned to memories of childhood. In October 1970, she went alone to Great Village, for the eighty-fifth birthday of her Aunt Grace, to whom she had been promising a poem since the late 1940s "'mostly about Nova Scotia and dedicated to you'" (Millier 438, 466). One of the first long poems Bishop completed in the United States, in 1972, was "The Moose" (*CP* 169–173), which she had started in 1946 after a bus trip from Great Village to Boston after her first visit home in fifteen years. The poem begins by beautifully describing the landscape of Nova Scotia, through which a bus is traveling, "past clapboard farmhouses / and neat, clapboard churches" (ll. 21–22). In the "The Moose" Bishop seems to relive the departure from her home in Great Village in 1917, with an elegiac sense of everything and everyone she had left and lost since her maternal grandparents died. Details recall "Once on a Hill," "Sleeping Standing Up," and "The Country Mouse." Houses with comforting dinner rituals, and the remembered murmurings of her grandparents over the sad fates of people they knew, are left behind as the bus, like the train of "The Country Mouse," moves south and west to Boston. Like a jolt back into the present, the speaker's reverie is interrupted abruptly by the appearance of "The Moose" in the road. In some way, the moose seems associated with the beloved past and the lost, primitive home—it is "safe as houses" and emerges from the woods (li. 142). The moose makes the bus stop—stopping the progress toward Boston, away from the past—and then the bus goes on, while the speaker seems to look longingly back at the moose. As in "Manners," the last lines of "The Moose" mark the end of a rural life in Nova Scotia with a sign of the automobile, bearing away those who used to live there, with "an acrid / smell of gasoline" (ll. 167–168).

Throughout the 1970s, while Bishop lived in Cambridge and later in Boston, she took trips north of Boston to rural areas, not as far as Nova Scotia, but to New Hampshire and Vermont, to the island of North Haven, Maine, and frequently to Duxbury, Massachusetts, to the south. At the same time, she was rereading the poetry of Frost, so closely associated with rural New England. As noted in the Introduction, she asked her students in these years to memorize, recite, or anwalyze a number of Frost poems, and she also assigned Randall Jarrell's essays on Frost (Bishop 71.6).

Her interest in Frost seems to date from the 1940s, when she first met and became friends with Jarrell. She had crossed paths with Frost in Key West, and formally entertained him when she was poetry consultant at the Library of Congress in 1949, where he came to be recorded reading his poetry, soon after he had published "Directive." Bishop especially enjoyed the party for Frost afterward, as she wrote to Lowell with evident relish: "I am dying to see you and tell you about the strange tea party for Frost, at which Carl Sandburg suddenly turned up to everyone's horror—everyone who had any sense, that is. It was very funny" (*OA* 196–197). It is tempting to imagine that Frost and Bishop would have talked about New England and Key West, and perhaps shared their fascination with abandoned and neglected houses, with imaginative and actual property speculation. It seems possible that Bishop conceived a deeper respect for Frost's work from this encounter, with encouragement from Jarrell and Lowell. Bishop and Frost met again in Brazil in 1954, when he gave a poetry reading there. She wrote to Marianne Moore, "He is amazing for a man eighty years old, and the audience—mostly Brazilian—liked it very much" (*OA* 297).

During her late years in New England, in the unfinished "Just North of Boston" and "The End of March," Bishop turned again to the themes she shares most with Frost: the idea and problems of dwelling, and specifically the appeal of the abandoned or neglected house. In the course of teaching Frost's "Directive," Bishop asked her students a series of cryptic questions, recorded in her teaching notes: "read it through—what does F. want us to [judge?] by all these? imposters? 1. and what is Frost asking the reader to do? 2. Is it a good idea or not. If it is good, how can it apply to[,] can it be made to apply to the present? past?" ("College Teaching Notes, Exams," undated, Bishop 71.6). Formulating these questions, Bishop seems to register the unreliability of the guide-speaker in the poem. She also seems to imply that the imagined return to the abandoned farm in "Directive" may be "a good idea," but that the contemporary relevance of such a return should be distinguished from its meaning in the past.

When Frost wrote the poem in 1946, the relevant cultural context included the large-scale migration of Americans from rural to urban areas and the consequent abandonment of rural areas (which had begun early in New England), the trauma of the Depression, and the destruction of WWII. In the 1970s, as Thoreauvian retreat became a political and cultural ideal in the United States as part of the "Back to the Land" movement, and as rural tourism became ever more popular, the imaginative return to an abandoned farm in "Directive" did indeed have new implications.

In her most explicit response to Frost, the unfinished "Just North of Boston" (*EAP* 166–167), Bishop seems to register the roadside tourism and commercialization of rural New England alongside the persistence of abandoned farms, thus detailing how the region had and had not changed since Frost lived in Derry. (It is possible that Bishop may have passed, even stopped off to visit, the Derry farm.) Perhaps she wrote the poem around 1973, when she mentioned having recently "seen 'lonely New England farm-houses'" in a letter to Lowell (qtd. in Millier 481). "The miles of roadsigns" in the unfinished poem evidently date from contemporary New England; Bishop may have seen them on Interstate 93 driving south to Boston after a weekend in the country. But other parts of the draft seem to imagine a figure like Frost or even the guide-speaker of "Directive," who leads the reader to "the children's house of make believe":[26]

> at the intersection, just off—
> a barn, a farmhouse—ten yards
>   from the road
> a big old farmhouse all the
>   elms are gone
> but one and it is dead
> Let's hope the farmhouse
> is blind and deaf—it looks it
>
> One can imagine a giant child
> trudging along here, discovering
> all these wonderful toys with
>
> whoops of joy
>
> picking them up ~~and mixing~~
> setting the down, all
> mixed ~~up~~
>
> no one lives there—
> someone sesll [*sic*] home made bread—what home/?
>
> A Cowboy's hat, forty or so ft.
> high
> you can walk inside it
>
> . . . .
>
> a blue-jay shrieks
>
> the farmhouse, dumb numb and dumb,
> and let's hope, blind and deaf
> The barn has just fallen down
>   quite recently
>
> bright as a light, as those
> policecar light
> that policecar light—
>
> The original owners the real world the ??? unobtrusive
> have given up not quite the ghost—the ghost is there—
> ~~(like Vuillard's sister in the wall-paper) NO~~ -
> weak, stunned, dazed, pale, pining
> "gone into a decline" "consumptive"   consumed, all right—

This abandoned farmhouse, with its one dead elm and fallen barn, recalls "The Need of Being Versed in Country Things" as well as "Directive." The surroundings, however—the billboards, the police cars with flashing lights, the contrails from jets in the sky—show complete disregard for the house. Perhaps the speaker hopes the personified farmhouse is "blind and deaf" to its decay and irrelevance.

The "home made bread" is a joke on tourists; there is no authentic home where it is made. As in "Directive," the "original owners" of the abandoned farmhouse are unknown, and they are ghostly. Fragmentary as it is, "Just North of Boston," referring to the title of Frost's second book, suggests how much Frost's poetry haunted the rural New England landscape for Bishop.

A more finished and more personal response to "Directive," however, is "The End of March" (*CP* 70), the penultimate poem of her last book, *Geography III*. She began the poem in the spring of 1974, on a visit to the coastal resort of Duxbury, Massachusetts. John Malcolm Brinnin (whom she had met at Yaddo in 1949) and his partner Bill Read owned a house there, and beginning in 1973, Brinnin, who traveled frequently, made it available to Bishop and Methfessel (Millier 215). The poem is, in many ways, Bishop's finest evocation of the abandoned rural house and its deep appeal.

The poem "started out as 'a sort of joke thank-you note—John B. was so appalled when I said I wanted that ugly little green shack for my summer home! (He doesn't share my taste for the awful, I'm afraid)' " (qtd. in Millier 492). The "summer home" in question was an abandoned beach shack. In its details it recalls a number of houses and dwellings where Bishop had lived, from the Great Village house to the shack in Provincetown, which helped provide the setting for "The Monument," and Bishop's writing studio at Samambaia, which Soares had built for her, near the house they shared for almost twenty years. "The End of March" also resembles the many fragile houses she had evoked in her poetry and prose.

In some ways, the plot of "The End of March" parallels that of "Directive," which is also a journey to a lost home, associated with a family lost to death and mental illness. In an imaginative return, the speaker narrates a walk to an abandoned house on the beach, but the house is never reached. And as in "Directive," the present seems difficult, even overwhelming; the poem offers an illusory escape from it to the remote dream-house. The speaker wants "to get as far as my proto-dream-house, / my crypto-dream-house," and the poem itself evokes the house, but paradoxically it turns out to be "too cold / even to get that far" (ll. 24–25, 49–50). The speaker, like the cold day, is guarded and withdrawn at first:

> It was cold and windy, scarcely the day
> to take a walk on that long beach.
> Everything was withdrawn as far as possible,
> indrawn: the tide far out, the ocean shrunken,

seabirds in ones or twos.
The rackety, icy, offshore wind
numbed our faces on one side;
. . . .
Along the wet sand, in rubber boots, we followed
a track of big dog-prints (so big
they were more like lion-prints). Then we came on
lengths and lengths, endless, of wet white string,
looping up to the tide-line, down to the water,
over and over. Finally, they did end:
a thick white snarl, man-size, awash,
rising on every wave, a sodden ghost,
falling back, sodden, giving up the ghost. . . .
A kite string?—But no kite.
(ll. 1–7, 14–23; second ellipsis in original)

The "sodden ghost," led to by the giant footprints of the dog and the "lengths . . . of string," may recall the eerie "road home" in "Directive." It would be simplistic to equate the "sodden ghost" "rising on every wave" with Soares—whose birthday was March 15—but her death may haunt the poem (Bishop 25.11). Bishop seemed to feel guilt for Soares's death, as she wrote cryptically to Lowell in 1973, amid the controversy about his use of autobiography and his ex-wife's letters in *The Dolphin*: " 'We all have irreparable and awful actions on our consciences—that's really all I can say now. I do, I know. I just try to live without blaming myself for them <u>every</u> day, at least—every <u>day</u>, I should say—the nights take care of guilt sufficiently. (But for God's sake don't quote me!)' " (qtd. in Millier 485). Throughout the seventies Bishop tried and failed to complete an elegy for Soares ("Aubade and Elegy"; see Miller 538, *EAP* 149)—though "Crusoe in England" is, in its way, an extraordinary elegy for her. It is difficult to overemphasize the importance of the loss of Soares and Samambaia for Bishop; as she wrote to a friend in 1968:

> Can you imagine arriving at the only home (forgive me for being corny, but it is true) I have ever really had in this world and finding it not only not mine—I had agreed to all that [in the will of Soares]—but almost stripped bare? . . . . I'd give everything in this world—a foolish expression but I can't think what I'd give, but "everything" certainly—to have Lota back and *well*. (*OA* 490)

In "The End of March," the speaker turns away from the "sodden ghost" to describe her ideal destination, her dream-house. Speaking for many readers, Roger Gilbert asks, "Why is Bishop so attracted to this tiny, dilapidated house?" and notes that "'Proto-dream-house' suggests an archetype or original.... 'Crypto' moves us...to the enigmatic.... and...the hint that the house itself may be a crypt" (Gilbert 167–168). Indeed, this house evokes Bishop's archetypal dream-house, associated with Great Village, as well as a crypt:

> I wanted to get as far as my proto-dream-house,
> my crypto-dream-house, that crooked box
> set up on pilings, shingled green,
> a sort of artichoke of a house, but greener
> (boiled with bicarbonate of soda?),
> protected from spring tides by a palisade
> of—are they railroad ties?
> (Many things about this place are dubious.)
> I'd like to retire there and do *nothing*,
> or nothing much, forever, in two bare rooms:
> look through binoculars, read boring books,
> old, long, long books, and write down useless notes,
> talk to myself, and, foggy days,
> watch the droplets slipping, heavy with light.
> (ll. 24–37)

This fantasy of an ideally solitary existence is reminiscent of "The Sea & Its Shore," and the "railroad ties" remind us of the way to the hermit's cabin in "Chemin de Fer." In some ways, the "dream-house" can be read as a purely imaginative site, "hypothetical and obscure," where "the facts of the world no longer intrude at all" (Costello, *Questions of Mastery*, 170, 168). However, the fantasy of the "dream-house" also evokes the way Bishop tried to conduct her life in Key West, and in Samambaia—which reminded her of Great Village—she seemed to realize her fantasy. Her writer's studio there, set on the hill by itself, had a pointed roof, and the house itself was perched in a foggy atmosphere, as described in "Song for the Rainy Season." Like Frost on his Derry farm, Bishop found love and an ideal situation for reading and writing at Samambaia. In 1952, she had reported with delight, "it is so much easier to live exactly as one wants to here" (*OA* 247).

The desire to "retire" is significant, too. At Samambaia, Bishop did not have to teach for a living; in New England in the 1970s, she constantly wished to retire, but could not afford to do so. In "The End of March," her ideal day would end with a drink, of course, cooked over a gas stove:

> At night, a *grog à l'américaine*.
> I'd blaze it with a kitchen match

> and lovely diaphanous blue flame
> would waver, doubled in the window.
> There must be a stove; there *is* a chimney,
> askew, but braced with wires,
> and electricity, possibly
> —at least, at the back another wire
> limply leashes the whole affair
> to something off behind the dunes.
> A light to read by—perfect! But—impossible.
> (ll. 38–48)

In this peculiarly idyllic scene, the gas stove, the reflections in the dark window, and the primitive electricity, recall Great Village, as described in "Reminiscences of Great Village" and "Sestina," and also Samambaia, as she described it in 1952:

> I'm all alone for the time being in the large half-finished chilly house–with an oil lamp lit at 3 p.m. to keep me warm . . . a few friends make it up to the mountain over the weekends . . . but the rest of the time we go to bed to read at 9:30, surrounded by oil lamps, dogs, moths, mice, bloodsucking bats, etc. I like it so much that I keep thinking I have died and gone to heaven, completely undeservedly. (*OA* 248–249)

In "The End of March," however, the fantasy life of the "dream-house" is abruptly cut short—it is "perfect! But—impossible." But Bishop had lived such a life at Samambaia. Now the secluded, remote "dream-house" is inaccessible to her: "And that day the wind was much too cold / even to get that far, / and of course the house was boarded up" (ll. 49–51).

The journey, as it turns out, has taken place entirely in the imagination, as in "Directive." The "proto-dream-house" is so associated with loss by now that it also evokes a grave, a "crypto-dream-house." In "Directive," it is only in the imagination that the reader can follow the guide to visit "a farm that is no more a farm," "a house that is no more a house." And just as Frost's poem draws on his memories of the Derry farm, Bishop's ramshackle dream-house poem calls up memories of lost homes.

The retreat from the hope of reaching the idealized "dream-house" means turning back to face the reality of the cold day, to awareness of loss:

> On the way back our faces froze on the other side.
> The sun came out for just a minute.
> For just a minute, set in their bezels of sand,

> the drab, damp, scattered stones
> were multi-colored,
> and all those high enough threw out long shadows,
> individual shadows, then pulled them in again.
> They could have been teasing the lion sun,
> except that now he was behind them
> —a sun who'd walked the beach the last low tide,
> making those big, majestic paw-prints,
> who perhaps had batted a kite out of the sky to play with.
> (ll. 52–63)

The end of "The End of March," at the end of a winter day, is finally more somber than the end of "Directive." Frost leads his reader to the waters of "a house that is no more a house," to "[d]rink and be whole again beyond confusion." The fantasy is not suspended. Bishop's speaker, instead, turns back, however unwillingly, to face the loss embodied in the "sodden ghost," "perhaps" a kite batted out of the sky by a fateful force as indifferent as the sun. Bishop felt that her lover's depression and death were caused by a large-handed, arbitrary, and cruel fate, as in this letter she wrote shortly after she had finished dealing with lawyers and relatives of Soares in Rio in 1968: "It all seems like such a tragic waste to me—and I blame her stupid, incredibly cruel parents" (*OA* 491). The kite the "lion sun" played with ends up a "sodden ghost" of tangled string, drowned in the tide.

"The End of March" is also the end of the line, moving toward death—if it was once possible to try to reach the "dream-house," it is no longer. In the 1970s in New England, Bishop also wrote "One Art," her famous villanelle on "the art of losing"; among other major losses, the speaker tries to master the loss of "three loved houses" (*CP* 178). Although she did find another rural retreat at Sabine Farm on the island of North Haven, Maine, where she spent time in the summer from 1974 on (alone and with Methfessel, Frank Bidart, and others), she only rented the place. In 1975, she bought an apartment in Lewis Wharf on Boston Harbor (Millier 497). Her final meditations on dwelling, with which she closed *Geography III*, were "The End of March" and "Five Flights Up."

It was also in the 1970s that Bishop became friends with John Ashbery, who, as mentioned in the introduction, provided her with the epigraph and perhaps the inspiration for the title of *Geography III*, which would be Bishop's final volume of poems. That title implies, of course, that the poet had attempted or mastered advanced lessons in the study of landscape. Within the larger geographies of the book, "The End of March" and "One Art" chart the "confused migration" of Bishop's whole life, to quote "The Sandpiper," and express the deep appeal that the neglected rural house always had for her (*CP* 131). Bishop's life was unsettled to an extreme degree, yet this group of poems and prose evoking abandoned and neglected houses, from her earliest writing to her latest, resonates deeply with ubiquitous American experiences of displacement.

CHAPTER 3

John Ashbery: The Farm on the Lake at the End of the Mind

The old house guards its memories...

—"The Orioles," *Some Trees* (1956)

Growing up under the shade of friendly trees, with our brothers all around
....
But—and this is the gist of it—what if I dreamed it all,
The branches, the late afternoon sun,
The trusting camaraderie, the love that watered all,
Disappearing promptly down into the roots as it should?
For later in the vast gloom of cities, only there you learn
How the ideas were good only because they had to die,
Leaving you alone and skinless, a drawing by Vesalius.

—"Variations, Calypso and Fugue on a Theme of Ella Wheeler Wilcox," *The Double Dream of Spring* (1970)

What remote orchards reached by winding roads
Hides them? Where are these roots?

—"The One Thing That Can Save America," *Self-Portrait in a Convex Mirror* (1975)

there are some who leave regularly
For the patchwork landscape of childhood, north of here
....
'I was lost, but seemed to be coming home,

Through quincunxes of apple trees, but ever
As I drew closer, as in Zeno's paradox, the mirage
Of home withdrew and regrouped a little farther off.
....
And though I have been free ever since
To browse at will through my appetites, lingering
Over one that seemed special, the lamplight
Can never replace the sad light of early morning
Of the day I left'

—"A Wave," *A Wave* (1984)

I became very weepy for what had seemed
like the pleasant early years.

—"History of My Life," *Your Name Here* (2000)[1]

A Farmer's Son

Just as we now see through Frost's constructed, popular reputation as a farmer-poet to the facts of Frost's unsettled life, exemplified in the central image of the abandoned farmhouse in his poetry, so we should not think of Ashbery only as a New York City poet. If we do, we fail to notice the preoccupation in his poetry with his own and the larger American experience, in the twentieth century, of cheerfully leaving a rural childhood behind, expressing nostalgia for it, and, in the midst of displacements, making attempts to imagine or reconstruct a more settled life. Noticing this preoccupation in the poems, rather than adhering to a practically impossible anti-biographical stance, may help readers and critics to register and appreciate the emotional intensity of Ashbery's finest poetry.

As Ashbery stated matter-of-factly to me, "the first experiences in one's life tend to be the strongest ones, really" (MacArthur 193). Because some readers lack much knowledge of what those early experiences were for this poet, while others are reluctant to connect them to his poetry,[2] I offer here a closer look at his childhood and family background in "the holy land / of western New York State" (*SPCM* 6). That Ashbery emerged from this provincial world should make us all the more amazed by the poet he grew up to be.

On both sides of his family, John Lawrence Ashbery had deep roots in upstate New York, near Lake Ontario. His maternal grandfather,

Henry Lawrence, had grown up in the small town of Pultneyville, living in a small cabin constructed from the cabin of a ship that had belonged to his wealthy uncle, Captain Horatio Throop, who owned a whole fleet. Pultneyville was, Ashbery recalls, "before the railroads...an important lake port," and later became a summer resort (MacArthur 178).[3] As a teenager, Henry Lawrence worked as a cook on his uncle's ships. ("He had all these stories about lake voyages and terrible storms," Ashbery remembers.) After receiving a very basic education at the one-room schoolhouse in Pultneyville, he assiduously prepared himself to attend the University of Rochester, where he studied physics. Later he went on to do graduate work at New York University and Cornell University, and eventually he taught at the University of Rochester. In 1892, he married Adelaide Seeley, who was from Williamson, New York, near Pultneyville. At Rochester, Lawrence was chairman of the Physics Department for forty years, living in Rochester during the academic year and summering in Pultneyville with his wife Adelaide and daughters, Helen and Carol.

While Henry Lawrence had sought out a university education and a more urban, sophisticated lifestyle, Ashbery's paternal grandparents and father might be counted among the "disappointed, returning ones" in the poem "Pyrography," who leave the city to try the country again (*HD* 8). Chester Ashbery, the poet's father, had grown up in Buffalo, where his father had a rubber-stamp factory. But when Chester was a young man, his parents decided to move out into the country, at first to the village of Alden, east of Buffalo. Chester studied briefly at Cornell Agricultural College, and then moved with his parents to a farm outside Sodus in 1915, buying seventy-five acres of land on the advice of a friend, Arthur Boller, who already had a farm in the area. Although his paternal grandfather died when Ashbery was a just few months old, his paternal grandmother, Elizabeth Koehler Ashbery, lived with her son and daughter-in-law on the Sodus farm throughout Ashbery's childhood until her death in 1947. Living with this grandmother, Ashbery grew up hearing German: "She spoke German. I don't know if she was born in Germany or not, some of her siblings were. They would speak German when they came to stay at the farm [from Milwaukee and Chicago]" (MacArthur 178).

Ashbery's parents probably met at a dance in Pultneyville, perhaps through Arthur Boller, and they were married in 1925, at the relatively late ages of thirty-two and thirty-four. Ashbery describes his father as "very extroverted, he loved farm life," and his mother as "very shy and timid" and "very much the dutiful daughter"; she had taught high school biology before her marriage (MacArthur 180).

The poet, the couple's first child, was born July 28, 1927, in Rochester, New York.

Ashbery spent his childhood among three houses, in Rochester, Sodus, and Pultneyville, all of them deeply associated with immediate family and ancestors. His grandparents were very important figures in his childhood. For reasons he is not sure of, Ashbery spent much of his first seven years living with his mother and his maternal grandparents at their house in Rochester. He speculates: "it might have been because conditions on the farm were too harsh. I don't think my mother and my father's mother got along that well...she was very bossy [*laughs*]. I liked her, though. She was a wonderful cook and baker" (MacArthur 180). Henry Lawrence, who had studied Greek and Latin and possessed a great library, particularly doted on his grandson, and, unlike Chester Ashbery, encouraged his literary and artistic interests, as the poet explains:

> He also kind of took over my education, I think, displacing my father, which caused a certain amount of friction in the family...my father's interests didn't appeal to me very much; so it was nice to have an alternative. I obviously wasn't cut out to be a farm boy and Huck Finn type and neither of my parents read books, and I was something of an oddity in the family. (Labrie 29)

In his grandparents' large Victorian house in Rochester, near the university, Ashbery had access to his grandfather's library, where he read Shakespeare and the Victorian novelists, and also had many friends in the neighborhood.

At the age of seven, however, Ashbery moved to his father's farm outside Sodus, where he lived with his parents, his paternal grandmother, and his brother Richard, who was born in 1931. Compared to his maternal grandparents' Rochester house, the Ashbery farm was very isolated, and it was also dominated by his father's unpredictable, sometimes violent temper. (He was never an alcoholic, however, despite the claims of some scholars [MacArthur 189].) Although he shared a bedroom with his brother, Ashbery missed his friends from Rochester, especially, perhaps, because Richard "was more interested in athletics and the farm [than I was]...[though] we were basically very fond of each other. We used to sort of pummel each other, but it was just kid stuff." Showing me a photograph of Richard with the family dog, in which he wears a helmet and is about to throw a football, Ashbery commented, "I love this photograph because you can instantly tell what my brother was all about" (MacArthur 187).

Unenthusiastic as he was about farm life, Ashbery got to know it intimately as a child and teenager. Chester Ashbery, who died in 1964, still has a reputation in the Sodus area as a remarkably innovative and successful farmer, woodworker, blacksmith, and saddlesmith. (The present owner of the farmhouse, Jack Bopp, told me "*That's* who you should write your book about," when I visited in July 2003.) On the Sodus farm, Chester Ashbery was always experimenting, and grew many kinds of fruit:

> apples, cherries, peaches, plums, and for a while, grapes, I remember. He was always trying different things. He raised chickens at one point, at one point pigs, and turkeys.... When I was very young there was a barn with a horse and a cow in it.... My grandmother used to make butter and there were eggs from the chickens... I think there were two horses, actually, before my father got a tractor, and other farming machinery. (MacArthur 183)

This is the sort of farm life Frost tried out as a young man in the first decade of the twentieth century; Ashbery experienced it as a child in the 1930s and 1940s.

The Ashbery farmhouse, which the poet's mother sold in 1965, is two miles north of Sodus and one mile from Lake Ontario, at the crossroads of Maple and Lake Avenues. Today it is well kept, but it became rundown at some point after Ashbery's mother sold it. A large, squarish two-story white clapboard house with black shutters, a stone chimney, and stone front porch, it was built in 1826 and enlarged in 1875. As Ashbery explains, the area is "conducive to growing fruit. The Lake somehow warms the land in the winter" (MacArthur 182). Today the placid landscape is thoroughly planted in orchards, with some open meadows; "the white fence posts / Go on and on" ("Farm," *SPCM* 28). When Ashbery was growing up, the fruit farms were still being developed, particularly by a cooperative called the Sodus Fruit Farm. He remembers that "the land all around the farm was bare, you could see for miles and now it's all overgrown.... there were just fields then.... somehow these distant perspectives were very much in my memories of the place, rather than the way it looks now" (MacArthur 198). Jack Bopp does not farm and is not related to Ashbery, but has kept the handsome Ashbery Farm sign, made by the poet's father, which stands near the mailbox on Maple Avenue.

Luckily for the young Ashbery, who was very attached to his maternal grandparents, Henry Lawrence retired in 1934, and with his wife Adelaide, began to live year-round in Pultneyville, just six miles from the Ashbery farm. Their house there, a two-story white frame-house with a side porch, had previously been a summer home, which Henry inherited from a cousin, Sarah Miller, in 1915. Built by Ashbery's maternal great-uncle Samuel Throop in 1832, it always belonged to some member of Ashbery's maternal family. From 1934 on, Ashbery continued to spend a lot of time with his maternal grandparents, including most weekends and evenings, and "every summer, as much time...as possible," when his Rochester friends came to stay by the Lake (MacArthur 183).

At school in Sodus, Ashbery remembers that, unlike in Rochester, he "didn't really have any friends...I was sort of an outcast because I liked poetry and art. It was very rural" (Murphy 32). The farm was little better, especially in winter. When I asked Ashbery what his immediate family did for fun, he joked,

> I don't think they believed in fun [*laughs*]. Well, my mother would work with my grandmother all day, cooking and cleaning, and at night we'd just listen to the radio, and we'd go to movies sometimes, although the best movies were about 15 miles away. My father loved musicals, so we would go to see them in Newark, the largest town in Wayne County. And that was about it.
>
> Well, sometimes we'd play cards. Hearts, Rummy, stuff like that. (MacArthur 185)

Ashbery also regularly attended the Episcopalian Church in Sodus with his mother. In this quiet rural world—where a hobby such as pyrography might seem attractive—Ashbery and his family very much looked forward to weekly visits to Rochester.

The city had significant art and culture to offer. George Eastman of Eastman Kodak (who Ashbery probably met when he was four years old at a reception with his grandfather [Ford, *John Ashbery*, 4]) left a great deal of money and a strong collection of European and American paintings to the University of Rochester and its Memorial Art Gallery. Ashbery took art lessons there once a week from the age of eleven to fifteen:

> my father used deliver eggs to a restaurant there [in Rochester], and later turkeys as well on holidays, and everybody else always had things they wanted to do. After my art class, I would take a bus downtown and go to the library and take some books out, go to the big department store, usually buy some stamps for my stamp collection. Occasionally when I was older I went to a bookstore that had some "questionable" books, I remember standing reading all of Molly

> Bloom's soliloquy which I didn't dare take home. I didn't have the money to buy it either; it was a Modern Library giant. They also had some pseudo-porn. (MacArthur 186)

We can see here how Ashbery associated the city with cultural and sexual interests. (As a Harvard student, he wrote an enthusiastic analysis of Molly Bloom's soliloquy.)

In his first review for *Art News*, in 1957, Ashbery observes, "it took real guts to be an aesthete in America in the thirties" ("Refined Sensibility...," AM 6.31, Houghton Library.)[4] It must have been particularly awkward for the adolescent Ashbery, in the 1930s and the 1940s in rural Sodus, to be a precocious aesthete with incipient homosexual preferences. Ashbery said that his mother discovered he was gay "by accident" in June 1945 and "then I think she sort of suppressed it. And I never discussed it with my father, who never brought it up with me" (MacArthur 190, Shoptaw 362). Living on his father's farm, an hour's drive from Rochester, certainly limited the young Ashbery's pursuit of artistic, musical, literary, and sexual interests; the nostalgia expressed for this rural world in his later poetry might well surprise the child Ashbery, who seemed to feel so constrained by it.

Some of Ashbery's fondest childhood memories are of summers in Pultneyville, where his Rochester friends would come to stay at their families' summer cottages. They would spend much of the day swimming in the Lake, and playing in the woods behind his grandparents' house, along a creek:

> we'd play... games like Robin Hood, based on the Errol Flynn movie. And each one of us would have a castle in a willow tree or a different kind of tree.... And I would sort of make up games even by myself, playing there and also along the beach. I used to build sand castles, and villages with imaginary inhabitants. (MacArthur 184–185)

(This imaginative life recalls the work of outsider artist Henry Darger, which inspired Ashbery's *Girls on the Run.*) Because he had involuntarily moved to Sodus and left his friends in Rochester, Ashbery already had a sense of loss as a young child, but he could recover that little society of friends in the Pultneyville in the summer. But unexpectedly, he suffered a greater loss when his rural childhood was horribly changed by the tragic death of Ashbery's little brother in 1940.

Richard Ashbery died of leukemia at the age of nine on July 5, a few weeks before Ashbery's thirteenth birthday. Ashbery's parents did not tell him how sick his brother was, and during Richard's final illness, they sent Ashbery away from the farm to stay with family friends. Thus he was horribly surprised by the death, and had no chance to say goodbye:

> I remember going to see him once in the hospital and I was really shocked because he was obviously in a great deal of pain and could hardly talk, and I expected him to be glad to see me and I think he wasn't even really aware that I was there... of course, they [his parents] wanted to shield me from the fact that he was dying, and possibly they were hoping against hope that he would recover. I knew he had been very sick and then when he came home from the hospital, I sort of assumed he would be getting better, though they probably sent him home because there wasn't anything more that could be done for him. And so I really wasn't expecting it at all.... He loved the Fourth of July, and he somehow managed to survive until the day after. (MacArthur 187–188)

After Richard's death, Ashbery was left alone on the farm with his grandmother and his parents, who naturally grieved for a long time—"My father especially, I would imagine, because Richard would probably have carried on with the farm" (MacArthur 187). The poet showed me a photograph of his family from the summer of 1940 after Richard died, when Ashbery's great-aunt Carol and her family (next-door neighbors to his grandparents in Pultneyville) took Ashbery and his parents on a trip to "Blue Mountain, in the Adirondacks, I guess to sort of try and cheer up my parents a little, but my mother certainly doesn't look very cheerful there" (MacArthur 188). Neither does the young Ashbery.

Grieving the terrible and unexpected loss of his brother, Ashbery was further cut off from his Rochester friends because of his duties on his father's farm. While he was growing up, Ashbery helped harvest the fruit:

> In the summer I was expected to first pick cherries and then apples later on, although school would usually have started by the time the apples [came in]. And I really hated it because it ruined every summer, when I liked to spend as much time as possible in Pultneyville, where I had friends and I used to go swimming all day. But the cherry season would always arrive about July 20th and last until about August 15th. I never made any money doing this. I got paid, but only as much as I picked and I wasn't very good at it, I was very slow....
>
> [W]hen I was about 16, my father gave me the choice of working at a packing plant on the Sodus Fruit Farm, which... was about a mile

> from our house. So even though that was much harder work—we had to start around seven in the morning and work until ten at night during the season to get everything canned before it rotted—I got paid by the hour, so I ended up making some money before going back to school. (MacArthur 183–184)

Ashbery continued to work at the cannery in the summer during his college years. A line from a poem from 1995 suggests that Ashbery long remembered the way his tedious farm duties distracted him from artistic interests: "Well I can't be / picking apples and playing the piano simultaneously, / now, can I?" ("When All Her Neighbors Came," *CYHB* 160). He had begun taking piano lessons at the age of eight.

Given the death of Richard, and the conflict between Ashbery's artistic interests and his father's farming, it is understandable that he felt so lonely on his father's farm, as a child and adolescent. In his early years in Rochester, and with his grandfather's encouragement, he had already acquired some of the cosmopolitan tastes we associate with his poetry. Ashbery discovered the surrealists in *Life* magazine at the age of ten, and resolved to become a surrealist painter himself; in the same year, he fell in love with the work of Joseph Cornell. As he would write in a poem from *The Double Dream of Spring* (1970), "I voyaged to Paris at the age of ten / And met many prominent literary men" (*MSO* 239). Imaginatively, this is true of Ashbery's childhood, when, he said, "I did a great deal of reading and lived in a sort of fantasy world with what I read." In 1941, at the age of thirteen, Ashbery traveled with his mother and grandmother to Chicago as a contestant for the national radio program, "Quiz Kids," representing the Rochester region. His specialty was eighteenth-century French painting (Lehman 124, 122, 128).

A series of entertaining diary entries from Ashbery's adolescence in Sodus in the early 1940s evoke the development of his aesthetic interests on the farm. He records his discoveries in art, music, and literature alongside his tedious farm chores:

> [undated]
> Arose and mowed the rest of the lawn. This afternoon I'm selling peaches at the fruit stand.... I haven't sold many as yet. Some of the people were downright uppity so I was coldly sarcastic. Now I'm going to either read or write a short story.
>
> Friday—[18 of September]
> In Rochester today I got The Overture to Tannhauser and the Venusberg Music. It cost $5.25! I just love it! It's so beautiful. At the

library...I got a book called The Story of French Painteurs[.] [*sic*] Nana and Grampa are at Elmira, so of course I didn't stay there.

Saturday—This morning I got my hair cut. In the afternoon the lawn was partly mowed by me. My how I love Rachmaninoff's To the Children! I'm just hearing it now on the Bell Telephone hour, sung by Lawrence Tibbet. I love the announcer's voice also.

Well, anyway, the Ruperts were invited for the weekend and for supper we went down to Cohius[?] and had a picnic....Tonight I slept in the back room with the pouring rain and the murmuring wind.

Tuesday, Sept. 21, 1942
Arose and rode my bike to school through the chilly damp fog...When I got home I tried to get my lessons. Eventually I had to pick apples. Today I mailed $1.00 for a series of 50 French painting reproductions to The Geseles Publishing Co. Mamma don't know yet.

Thursday, Sept. 23, 1942
Arose, was taken to school on account of inclement weather. Inclement. What a word.
....
Picked apples all afternoon. Not much
today except that I may soon
be filling in as assistant librarian at town library
Particulars later.

Tuesday, October 6, 1942
After dinner I packed apples.

Wednesday [October 7, 1942]
Had to go to Geneva with Daddy and spent the afternoon in the truck, quietly bored.
("Diary—pre-Deerfield," AM 6.31, Houghton Library)

It is amusing to imagine the future experimental poet as an adolescent, "coldly sarcastic" at his father's fruit stand, confiding his delight in European culture to his diary.

Details associated with such tedious chores as picking apples, however, stuck in the poet's mind. Attuned to the fact that Ashbery helped with the fruit harvest throughout his youth, we more readily notice the richness of metaphor and imagery he gathered from the experience. The following are just a few instances of the apples and cherries scattered throughout his poetry, over nearly fifty years:

And that night you gaze moodily
At the moonlit apple-blossoms....
"The Orioles," *Some Trees* (1956)

Apples were made to be gathered, also the whole host of the world's ailments and troubles

"The Ecclesiast," *Rivers and Mountains* (1966)

getting out from under the major
weight of the thing
As it was being indoctrinated and dropped, heavy as a branch with apples,
And as it started to sigh, just before tumbling into your lap

"Sortes Vergilianae," *The Double Dream of Spring* (1970)

You know the sorrow of continually doing something that you cannot name, of producing automatically as an apple tree produces apples this thing there is no name for.

"The Recital," *Three Poems* (1972)

what tone of voice among the hedges
what tone under the apple trees
the numbered land stretches away
and your house is built in tomorrow

"As You Came from the Holy Land,"
Self-Portrait in a Convex Mirror (1975)

The twilight prayers begin to emerge on a country crossroads
Where no sea contends with the interest of the cherry trees.

"Variation on a Noel," *A Wave* (1984)

The orchard that was right for you has stiffened, another autumn is coming to place its hand across the sun

Flow Chart (1991)

before the apples rust
and the idea of winter takes over, to be followed in short order
by the real thing.

"Avant de Quitter Cex Lieux," *Hotel Lautréamont* (1992)

their reasons in the one
as in the other case remaining inscrutable even to apple-
scented mornings where the light seems newly washed, the gnarled trees in the prime
of youth, and the little house more sensible than ever before
as a boat passes,

"In My Way / On My Way," *Hotel Lautréamont*

Fifty years have passed
since I started living in those dark towns
I was telling you about.
Well, not much has changed...
....

Apple trees blossom in the cold, not from conviction,
and my hair is the color of dandelion fluff.

"The Problem of Anxiety,"
Can You Hear, Bird? (1995)

I remember the world of cherry blossoms looking up at the sun and wondering,
what have I done to deserve this or anything else?

"Vendanges," *Your Name Here*

Yet in time manure produces cherries
the clerk murmured.

"A Star Belched," *Your Name Here*

Hours later I stood with the good doctor
in a snow-encrusted orchard.

"Local Legend," *Chinese Whispers* (2002)

Human error caused a collision
of houndstooth check and puffs
of train smoke

and apple blossoms.
Here are blossoms for you—
you know, "habitat,"
and what to put into it
now.

"Echolalia Rag," *Chinese Whispers* (2002)

When we got back little cherubs were nesting
In the arbor, below the apple tree. We were incredulous,
And whistled.

"Involuntary Description,"
Where Shall I Wander (2005)[5]

The persistence of these images, likely acquired from the Sodus farm, begins to suggest the importance of this childhood landscape to Ashbery's poetry. Such imagery is drawn from different seasons and moods on the fruit farm, from the adolescent moodiness in "The Orioles" from Ashbery's first book, to a sense of overwhelming, fertile profusion in "Sortes Vergilianae" and "The Recital"—natural metaphors for the poet's prolific writing. In these two poems and also in "The Ecclesiast," coming to terms with difficulty is also figured as apple-gathering (perhaps, in the latter poem, by a pious parental figure), while in the other poems cited here, there is an increasingly elegiac tone associated with the landscape's seasonal transformations.

Some lines may point to the Ashbery farm itself or the house on the Lake in Pultneyville. Many of these poems concern departure, retrospection, harvest, return (as in "The Problem of Anxiety"), and a sense of loss.

As an adult, Ashbery has privately expressed mixed feelings about the world of his childhood. As he wrote to an old friend in 1979, "I felt much more exiled there in my home town [of Sodus] than I have ever felt anywhere since.... I'm glad we're both out of there[,] though I must say I rather enjoy going back to see my mother, who lives in Pultneyville, and driving through the countryside remembering those dim dopey days" ("Letter to Betsy Myers Exner," March 10, 1978, AM 6.23, Houghton Library). To another childhood friend, he commented wistfully, "that remote past when we knew each other is still very much alive for me" ("Letter to H. Ogden," October 30, 1977, AM 6.25, Houghton Library). In a poem "Has to Be Somewhere," published in 2000, he refers to "my so-called hometown, / where I had never felt at home, yet never dreamed / of wishing for another" (*YNH* 113).

Ashbery's move from Rochester to the remote farm outside Sodus, and his brother's death, partly account for the sense of loss associated with his childhood world in his poetry. Yet even while he wanted to escape Sodus, he found solace in the landscape: "I enjoyed very much the lake and the countryside. Somehow the lake[,] which was also close to where my parents lived, which I could see from my window, was a kind of soothing presence" (Herd, "Interview" 32). In his adult life, his attitude toward this world would shift more and more toward the elegiac, as Ashbery dwelt not only on displacement and loss, but on the pastoral beauty and close extended family of his irretrievable rural childhood.

Escape from Sodus and Early Nostalgia

In 1943, at the age of sixteen, Ashbery left the small world of Sodus and Pultneyville to attend Deerfield Academy in Massachusetts. In 1994 he remembered it as "a sort of a jock, upper-class WASP school which I didn't fit into at all" (Herd, "Interview" 32). Well aware of Ashbery's promise, his parents, and his grandfather especially, wanted him to have a better education than a rural high school could offer. A close family friend from Sodus, Mrs. Lynden Wells, paid his tuition to Deerfield, where he enjoyed the intellectual stimulation. But he was also homesick, apparently. In a letter, his doting grandfather wrote that he missed Ashbery, but also tried to reassure him:

> If you at times feel lonely I would not have it otherwise. It is a malady from which one recovers. I have had homesickness in its most violent form and have survived to have grandchildren. Do not feel urged to answer this but write when the spirit urges in this direction.
>
> With much love, your grandfather
>
> ("Letter from Henry Lawrence to John Ashbery," September 29, 1944, AM 6.11, Houghton Library)

While at Deerfield, Ashbery was already writing poems that were accepted for publication by *Poetry* magazine; the first were published in the fall of 1945 (Lehman 130). After Deerfield, the family had assumed that Ashbery would return home to study at the University of Rochester.

Instead, he followed the advice of a friend of his grandfather, the wife of a Rochester professor, who suggested he should apply to Harvard. At the time, Ashbery recalls, "I didn't think you could do that!" (MacArthur 189). But he applied, was accepted, and enrolled at Harvard in the fall of 1945. Though he eventually thrived there, he was intimidated at first by an impersonal and competitive environment, and perhaps felt homesick for the place he had been so eager to leave. His grandfather wrote him:

> I am much relieved that you are finding Cambridge more tolerable. We are trusting that you may be permitted to stay on till graduation.... Harvard is no mistake. Its only fault is largeness with correspondingly large competition. But it has correspondingly larger opportunities. It has the added minor advantage of easy access from Sodus. Trains from Newark go directly to Rochester. The rest is up to you. Go to it.
>
> ("Letter from Henry Lawrence to John Ashbery," November 2, 1945, AM 6.11, Houghton Library)

During his college years, Ashbery returned home frequently by train, for the Thanksgiving, Christmas, Easter, and summer holidays, and he worked at the cannery, preserving fruit from the Ashbery farm, in the summers following his sophomore and junior years. At Harvard, he majored in English and minored in art history.[6] He also joined the editorial board of the *Harvard Advocate*, though Kenneth Koch had to vouch that Ashbery was not homosexual in order to bring him on. When he graduated in 1949, he was elected Class Poet (Lehman 51).

During college, while Ashbery was developing his poetic voice and writing the poems that would appear in his first books, *Turandot and Other Poems* and *Some Trees*, he was reading deeply in Romantic and nature poetry. He also especially admired W.H. Auden, in part for "a kind of romantic tone which took abandoned mines and factory chimneys into account. There is perhaps a note of both childishness and sophistication which struck an answering chord in me" (Stitt 39).[7] In later years, Ashbery has said of his poetry, "the outlook is Romantic," and that "all my stuff is romantic poetry, rather than metaphysical or surrealist" (Kostelanetz 31, Bloom and Losada 30). He wrote in a retrospective poem, "Eternity Sings the Blues," "it was hard not to uproot the rancid / stalk of romanticism, so I left it there / as an experiment" (*CYHB* 40).

Harold Bloom has placed Ashbery firmly in the line of American Romanticism. It is clear from his college reading and adult tastes that Ashbery goes directly back to the English Romantics who inspired Emerson, Thoreau, and Dickinson. As Ashbery remarked to an English poet, "I was a snobbish child and read only English or French literature" ("Letter to John Ash," March 12, 1984, AM 6.31, Houghton Library).[8] Elaborating on the ways that his poetry is Romantic, Ashbery affirmed to me an association with childhood and landscape, emphasizing "the idea of nature being transcendental, and pointing to something beyond what we see, like Wordsworth, or the Hudson River Painters" (MacArthur 193).[9]

In an undergraduate essay evaluating Arthur Symons' *The Romantic Movement in English Poetry*, Ashbery enthusiastically agrees that the Romantic movement was an important "reawakening of the imagination."[10] While he identified with the Romantic poets, particularly Keats, in his studies Ashbery also contemplated natural and rural imagery (in Henry Vaughan and Andrew Marvell), which would dominate *Some Trees*.[11] Later he would discover affinities with the rural poetry of John Clare and Edward Thomas. Ashbery demonstrates his sympathy not only with the Romantic meditative mind—its "spiritual journey" and the Wordsworthian "serpentine sentence" that undulates in "overlapping, multilayered argumentation" (Perloff 194, Shoptaw 85)—but with the rural scenes and dwellings, tinged with loss and consolation, of Romantic landscape meditation.

Still, becoming a poet and a sophisticate meant, for Ashbery, trying to overcome his background. In the spring of his senior year at Harvard, in 1949, Ashbery met Frank O'Hara. The two young poets were initially charmed by each other partly because they were both trying to suppress their provincial roots. Ashbery recounts his fascination with O'Hara's rural accent, so similar to his own:

> Though we grew up in widely separated regions of the east, he in [Grafton,] Massachusetts and I in western New York state, we both inherited the same flat, nasal twang, a hick accent so out of keeping with the roles we were trying to play that it seems to me we probably exaggerated it, later on, in hopes of making it seem intentional. I don't know what the significance of this was, but it fascinated us and was doubtless a reason why we became friends so quickly after our first meeting. On the telephone, I was told, we were all but indistinguishable. Once when I was at Frank's apartment in New York I picked up the phone and impersonated Frank to Joe LeSueur, one of Frank's closest friends, pretending to pick a quarrel with him for several minutes during which he was entirely taken in. Another time when Frank came to visit my parents' farm in upstate New York he walked into the kitchen one evening when my mother was washing dishes and asked if he could help; without turning round from the sink my mother said, "No, John, go back in and talk with your friends." ("A Reminiscence" 20)

It took a long time for Ashbery to grow out of his self-conscious feeling about his rural accent. As late as 1985, he commented, "I don't really enjoy [poetry reading] because I'm very uncomfortable with the sound of my own voice, which perhaps to someone who's English sounds like any other American accent, but to Americans I have a kind of hayseed sound" (Appleyard 44A).

After Harvard, Ashbery "came to New York City with trepidation. . . . I didn't feel I was 'ready for' the big city (I had grown up in the country and at that point Boston seemed like metropolis enough)" ("Larry Rivers. Drawings and Digressions," AM 6.31, Houghton Library). There he entered the graduate program in English at Columbia University, eventually finishing an MA thesis on the novels of Henry Green (Lehman 81). It was during this period, of course—from 1949 until 1955—that he first became associated with New York City, though the term "New York School of Poetry" would not be coined until 1961, when he was living in France. He also did dull office work, including copyediting, and usually went home to his parents' farm for Christmas and summer visits. O'Hara and Koch (who helped Ashbery get settled in New York) and James Schuyler affectionately teased Ashbery about his farm past. One evening in Long Island in 1959, Schuyler and Koch wrote "A Poem in the Dark" to Ashbery in Paris:

> snow seemed to have covered the city with blue Ashbery footprints
> and anxious Sodus lights burned in every window
> beckoning the shy purveyor of apples to his windward house
> distantly Lake Erie ground its ice like teeth
>
> ("Letter from Kenneth Koch to John Ashbery," undated 1959, AM 6.11, Houghton Library)

His friends often wrote to him when he was home in Sodus. Schuyler, in particular, relished the apples Ashbery's parents would send to the city, which Ashbery himself had lost the taste for ("Letter from Schuyler to Ashbery," October 24, 1958, AM 6.25; "Letter from Helen Ashbery to John Ashbery," January 17, 1958, AM 6.2, Houghton Library).

In 1955, Ashbery realized his long-cherished dream of going to France when he won a Fulbright to teach and study there, first in Montpellier and Paris, and for a second year, at the University of Rennes (Lehman 146). He returned home in 1957, and departed again for Paris in the fall of 1958; he would not return to the United States for good until 1965. "In my early youth," Ashbery has said, "everyone wanted to get out of the country and the political environment here and I was only too delighted to leave for Paris when I was given a Fulbright scholarship" (Murphy 22). Enamored of French culture and literature, Ashbery may also have appreciated more liberal Parisian attitudes about homosexuality. Beginning in 1950, the U.S. government began to censure and fire thousands of allegedly homosexual civil servants, and "[t]hroughout the 1950s, and well into the 1960s, gay men and lesbians suffered from unpredictable, brutal crackdowns. Arrests were substantial in many cities" (D'Emilo and Freedman 293–294). Edmund White, who is younger than Ashbery but joined some of the same social and literary circles Ashbery belonged to, and also spent many years in France, remembers about the period: "[For] a homosexual growing up...in the 1950s, 'Europe' presented a benign and mysterious alternative to the beastly oppression we knew at home...we still could dimly hold out for 'tolerance' or even 'decadence,' and these qualities, piquant and somehow aristocratic, we located in 'Europe'" (White 174–175). Ashbery's relationship with Pierre Martory, a poet and novelist he had met at the Fiacre bar in Paris in 1956, provided a personal reason to stay in Paris (Lehman 154). During the early 1960s, Ashbery rarely visited the United States because of the expense; his parents wanted him home and would only pay for a one-way ticket (MacArthur 190). He did manage to visit New York and Sodus in the summers of 1963 and 1964.

Like Frost and Bishop in their nostalgia for Derry and Great Village, respectively, Ashbery turns to memories of Sodus and Pultneyville in his early work. While he was in France, *Some Trees* (1956) was published.[12] It had been selected by Auden for The Yale Younger Poets Series, and Ashbery dedicated the book to his parents. (His grandfather, who would have been so proud of Ashbery's achievement, had died in December 1954 [MacArthur 179].) These early poems, written at Harvard and in the early 1950s in New York, already express nostalgia for the poet's rural childhood, as well as relief at having escaped the limitations of that world.

The title *Some Trees* seems bland on first impression, but trees in these poems become, for the speaker, intensely beautiful figures, existing in relation, like lovers or members of the same family. The rhymed title poem, which Ashbery evidently wrote as a love poem for a Harvard classmate in 1948 (Shoptaw 22), suggests the orderly arrangement of trees in an orchard or a park:

> These are amazing: each
> Joining a neighbor, as though speech
> Were a still performance.
> ....
> you and I
> Are suddenly what the trees try
>
> To tell us we are:
> That their merely being there
> Means something; that soon
> We may touch, love, explain.
> (*MSO* 37)

Given that Ashbery had grown up on a fruit farm, it seems right that his speaker is so exquisitely sensitive to the trees' "comel[y]" and benevolent presence, as figures for human connection as well. Arboreal tropes, in his later work, become deeply associated with his childhood roots.

The first poem in *Some Trees* that quietly refers to the Sodus farm itself is "The Orioles" (*MSO* 27), in which "The old house guards its memories[.]" Orioles—voluble summer birds that are fond of fruit—did visit the Sodus farm, Ashbery says, where "they buil[t] these hanging nests. You don't see those anymore" (MacArthur 197). The poem describes the annual arrival and departure of the birds. Ashbery's mother, who wrote to her son constantly once he left home, sometimes reported the types of birds that were visiting the farm's "feeding station" ("Letter from Helen Ashbery to JA," February 3, 1958, AM 6.2, Houghton Library).

In the poem, the personified "old house" is wary and vulnerable, associated somehow with loss. Its inhabitants eagerly await the cheerful arrival of the orioles:

> What time the orioles came flying,
> Back to the homes...
> The sad spring melted at a leap,
> ....
> The old house guards its memories, the birds
> ....
> ...cluster at the feeding station, and rags of song
>
> Greet the neighbors. "Was that your voice?"
> And in spring the mad caroling continues long after daylight
> As each builds his hanging nest
> Of pliant twigs and the softest moss and grasses.
>
> But one morning you get up and the vermilion-colored
> Messenger is there, bigger than life at the window.
> "I take my leave of you; now I fly away
> To the sunny reeds and marshes of my winter home."
>
> And that night you gaze moodily
> At the moonlit apple-blossoms, for of course
> Horror and repulsion do exist! They do!
> ....
>
> And then some morning when the snow is flying
> Or it lines the black fir-trees, the light cries,
> The excited songs start up in the yard!
> The feeding station is glad to receive its guests,
>
> But how long can the stopover last?
> The cold begins when the last song retires,
> And even when they fly against the trees in bright formation
> You know the peace they brought was long overdue.
>
> (*MSO* 27–28)

The "old house" and its inhabitants are susceptible to sadness, in great need of the cheerful orioles; the otherwise sad atmosphere may remind us of the isolation Ashbery felt on the farm, especially after his brother died. The poem may faintly recall Frost's "The Need of Being Versed in Country Things," but the speaker establishes no distance from the sadness implied in the scene. The voluble birds may also be figures for Ashbery himself—admired for his lyrical poetry and his conversation—who was sorely missed by his family once he left; his summer visits, or "stopovers," were much anticipated.

If "Some Trees" and "The Orioles" tenderly evoke a rural landscape, "The Picture of Little J.A. in a Prospect of Flowers" (*MSO* 18–19) indicates impatience with rural childhood, and a hint of early loss. Written in Ashbery's first year out of college, and published in *Partisan Review* in the July/August issue of 1951, the poem echoes the title and themes of Marvell's "The Picture of Little T.C. in a Prospect of Flowers." The title may refer to Theophila Cornewall, whose family, like Ashbery's, suffered the death of children (*The Norton Anthology of Poetry* 342). Marvell's poem contrasts the "simplicity" with which "This nymph begins her golden days" against her future as a woman who will break hearts, and it ends in fear that the girl's life and promise could be cut off prematurely, like the buds of a flower. Ashbery's poem also meditates on the promise of his youthful self, with themes of longing for the future, and fear of it.

The epigraph to "The Picture of Little J.A...." is from Boris Pasternak's autobiographical sketch, *Safe Conduct*: "He was spoilt from childhood by the future, which he mastered rather early and apparently without great difficulty." This is apt for Ashbery, whose grandparents and mother doted on him, especially after the death of his brother.[13] At the same time, he dreamed of the future when he could leave his father's farm. In writing the poem, Ashbery says he had in mind a photograph of himself as a toddler, in a playpen outside on the grass one sunny day, about to push an object out of the pen (MacArthur 198). In the poem's third section, the speaker describes his youthful self, older than in the actual photo: "Yet I cannot escape the picture / Of my small self in that bank of flowers:.... / I had a hard stare, accepting / Everything, taking nothing," fearing that "the rolled-up future might stink / As loud as stood the sick moment / The shutter clicked" (*MSO* 19). Although the first section of the poem playfully recalls childhood games and fantasies, and the second apparently offers benevolent parental advice about the future (the voice almost seems modeled on Ashbery's grandfather), the third subverts the rural idyll evoked in Marvell's poem. The involuntary move to the Sodus farm from Rochester, the loss of his brother, and the rural isolation on the farm may infect Ashbery's poem with apprehension that his future may turn out no better, despite the assurances in the second section. The young, skeptical self passively absorbs experience, but refuses to seek it. Similar images of the lonely, guarded, shy young self would appear in later poems; here the speakers feels he is "not wrong / In calling this comic version of myself / The true one" (*MSO* 19).

In another poem from *Some Trees*, "And You Know," a youthful figure also dreams of escape from a dull world. Ashbery himself longed to travel in childhood: "Everything around me seemed dull and pedestrian, and I was always imagining that things were more interesting in Europe or somewhere else" (Labrie 29). The poem, which is reminiscent of Bishop, originally appeared in *Poetry* in December 1955; in the same issue, Howard Nemerov reviewed Bishop's *Poems: North & South—A Cold Spring*. "And You Know" describes a muggy schoolroom in summer, where students dream of voyages, touching a globe with the reverent curiosity of Bishop's speaker in "Map":

> It is the erratic path of time we trace
> On the globe, with moist fingertip, and surely, the globe stops;
> We are pointing to England, to Africa, to Nigeria;
> And we shall visit these places, you and I, and other places,
> . . . .
> Goodbye, old teacher, we must travel on, not to a better land,
>   perhaps,
> But to the England of the sonnets, Paris, Colombia,
>   and Switzerland
> And all the places with names, that we wish to visit—
> . . . .
> Out of the humid classroom, into the forever.
>
> (*MSO* 42–43)

As a child Ashbery wanted to venture beyond the limited rural world of Sodus and Pultneyville, and he wrote "And You Know" in New York in the summer of 1955 (Shoptaw 36, 357), shortly to leave for France. The poem bids a fond farewell to a childhood world, with its "summer light / Nauseous and damp" that some are "charmed by"—perhaps even the speaker, who is nevertheless ready to leave it for distant lands (*MSO* 42).

During his years in France, Ashbery's poetry often turned back to America, somewhat like Bishop rewrote her Nova Scotia childhood in Brazil. He became "nostalgic for American goodies" such as pumpkin pie, and had a hard time finding the ingredients for it in

Paris ("Letter to Fairfield Porter," October 19, 1959, AM 6.25, Houghton Library). Like many American writers living abroad, Ashbery came to appreciate his Americanness, and his roots, in a foreign context. "[T]hings that I had previously unwittingly appreciated, that were part of me when I was here [in the U.S.] without my even realizing it, suddenly presented themselves as very important to me" (Lehman 67).

When Ashbery thought and wrote about America, his childhood in Rochester, Sodus, and Pultneyville formed a large part of that vision—even in the highly experimental volume *The Tennis Court Oath* (1962), which Ashbery wrote partly by taking phrases from American magazines "in a sort of collage technique" ("Robert Frost Medal Address," *Selected Prose* 250). "'They Dream Only of America'" (*MSO* 63), a poem written in 1957 that appears second in the book (the first is the title poem) and helps to set its tone, is cited by Marjorie Perloff for its semantic inscrutability and lack of identifiable context (Perloff 192–193). The poem, whose title may refer to immigrant "dream[s] of America," was first published in *Partisan Review* in the summer of 1959; the same issue included Lionel Trilling's famous celebration of the dark side of Frost's poetry, "A Cultural Episode: A Speech on Robert Frost." It is strange to think of the careers of Frost and Ashbery overlapping at all, but, however disjointedly, Ashbery's poem evokes a kind of rural idyll that is almost recognizably Frostian, and more affirmative than the Frost poems Trilling had in mind. Ashbery might well be included here in "'They,'" thinking of scenes of his rural childhood:

> They dream only of America
> To be lost among the thirteen million pillars of grass:
> . . . .
>
> And hiding from darkness in barns
> They can be grownups now
> . . .
> The lake a lilac cube.
>
> . . . .
> He is thirty years old.
> That was before
>
> We could drive hundreds of miles
> At night through dandelions.
>
> (*MSO* 63)

In 1957, Ashbery was thirty years old, and when he returned in the summer to Sodus, he did so as a "[grownup] now," with a sense of freedom perhaps equivalent to being able to "drive hundreds of miles / At night" through the countryside. He had grown up among meadows and barns, and the Great Lakes can take on pastel colors in certain weathers. This poem sustains the theme of liberation from childhood that was hoped for in *Some Trees*, at the same time hinting at nostalgia, in the longing to be lost in a rural landscape.

Toward the end of his time in France, Ashbery wrote home asking his mother for some reminders of his childhood, including a picture of his father; she also sent an aerial photo of the farm ("Letter from Helen Ashbery to JA," November 27, 1964, AM 6.25, Houghton Library). At the time, he was writing some of the poems that would appear in *Rivers and Mountains* (1966). The first poem in that volume, "These Lacustrine Cities," in which "the past is already here" (*MSO* 163), may refer to Rochester and the village of Pultneyville on the shore of Lake Ontario. The longest poem, "The Skaters," published in *Art and Literature* in the Autumn/Winter issue of 1964, was inspired by a children's book Ashbery found in Paris, *Three Hundred Things a Bright Boy Can Do*, which reminded him of an illustrated encyclopedia he read in childhood, and of his lonely childhood on the farm (Lehman 121). Ashbery has called "The Skaters" (*MSO* 194–223) "a meditation on my childhood" (Bloom and Losada 20). In it, the poet seems to contrast his lonely, repressive youth on his father's farm on Lake Ontario, and the drudgery of office work in New York City in the early fifties, with the rather hedonistic, rich cultural and social life he led in Paris, in the poem's second and third sections:

> Yet I shall never return to the past, that attic,
> Its sailboats are perhaps more beautiful than these, . . .
> . . . .
>
> But once more, office desks, radiators—No! That is behind me.
> No more dullness, only movies and love and laughter, sex and fun.
> . . . .
>
> Looking out over the whole darn countryside, a beacon
>   of satisfaction
> I am. I'll not trade places with a king. . . .
> . . . .
>   . . . . I am happier now than I ever
>   dared believe
> Anyone could be. . . .
> . . . .

> . . . . I am happy once again,
> Walking among these phenomena that seem familiar to me from my earliest childhood.
>
> (*MSO* 204, 205, 214)

In Sodus, Ashbery certainly could not indulge much in "movies . . . sex and fun," and 1950s New York, with its police raids on gay bars, was perhaps not ideal either, when he was working full-time in a dreary office, such as the one he evokes in the Bishop-like fantasy of travel, "The Instruction Manual" (*MSO* 8). Painter Nell Blaine, a frequent hostess to the New York poets, remembered that Ashbery seemed unhappy about " 'his love life' " and rather " 'lonely' " in New York in the early 1950s (qtd. in Lehman 64). In France, Ashbery could further escape the limitations of his rural childhood world. At the same time, he imaginatively revisited his childhood, "happy once again" among such memories in France. It is also remotely possible that Ashbery associated slightly more tolerant attitudes to homosexuality with his childhood world and his own family, unlike New York in the 1950s. Ashbery recalls that one of the lakeshore houses in Pultneyville, a cobblestone built by his prosperous uncle, Captain Horatio Throop, was inherited by a cousin of Henry Lawrence, Paul Holling: "Cousin Paul was gay and inherited enough money to live comfortably with his sister Lilly, Cousin Lilly, and they went to live in Europe about 1910, I think. They would come back occasionally, and Paul had a Cockney boyfriend Pat who was quite flamboyant, especially for that little town [*laughs*], although no one seemed to take it too much amiss" (MacArthur 184). Like "Cousin Paul," Ashbery seemed more comfortable in Europe than at home, but enjoyed visiting; later when Pierre Martory would join him on visits home, he was warmly welcomed by Ashbery's family, even if, as Ashbery suggests, his mother avoided the question of her son's sexuality.

The longer Ashbery stayed in France, the more his mother and grandmother pleaded with him to return. Their frequent letters begging for news of Ashbery echo Henry James's novel *The Ambassadors*, in which Chad Newsome's mother fears that her son has been so charmed by France that he may never come home. At one point, Ashbery's mother feared he would lose his U.S. citizenship if he did not return soon, and she tried to get indirect news of him from cousins and friends of the family who were traveling to France. In 1963, she wrote, "I was about to write to Pierre [Martory] to ask if you were alive" ("Letters from Helen Ashbery to JA," August 12, 1962 and November 7, 1963, AM 6.25, Houghton Library).

While the poet's mind was already on his native landscape, judging from some of the poems he was writing, letters from home would also have vividly recalled Sodus and Pultneyville, full as they were of news of the weather, the fruit harvest, church picnics, sailboat regattas, and reports of Lake conditions. Throughout these years, the poet depended partly on his parents' income from the farm's fruit harvests to live in Paris. As James Schuyler wrote to him in September 1958: "I am happy for you that you can stay longer where you want to be. Paris. Really, you are lucky. Did you astutely wait until the fruit was picked to ask your family for more cashola?" (*Just the Thing* 87). Happy as Ashbery was to be in Paris, the poems he wrote there often looked homeward.

Pulled Home

Ashbery was abruptly and painfully drawn back to Sodus when, on December 1, 1964, his father died. (His death occurred just a few days after his mother had replied to Ashbery's request for a picture of him.) As the poet recalls, the death was completely unexpected:

> No one is sure [of the cause], whether it was a stroke or what. At the time the hospital in Sodus was a really primitive place. He had had some kind of seizure and was taken in the ambulance to the hospital. My mother didn't want to go in the ambulance. She wanted to pack some clothing for him and probably change her own clothes, so as a result she went later and went in the room and he had just died, which was a horrible shock for her. Just the next year they opened a new hospital about a mile from where we lived, just on the top of that hill, which might have made the difference. (MacArthur 191)

His father's sudden death, which Ashbery said "destroyed [his mother's] life," had dramatic effects on the poet and his poetry.[14] Ten years later he wrote sympathetically to a friend who had just lost his own father: "I have been through that and 'know the feeling,' an unexpected and very disquieting aspect of which is suddenly being yanked back into one's childhood" ("Letter to Charles Newman," [dated] Twelfth Night 1976, AM 6.25, Houghton Library). The death of Chester Ashbery brought his son back to New York for good, as the poet felt a strong sense of filial duty toward his widowed mother (MacArthur 191). Taking a jet plane for the first time—he was afraid of flying—he flew home for the funeral, returned to France, and moved back to New York City in the fall of 1965. Ashbery was on good terms with his father when he died, having spent a "very pleasant" month with his parents in the summer of 1964. "My father, I think, was getting ready to retire.... They always wanted to move to Florida, like everybody else" (MacArthur 190–191).

After her husband's death, Helen Ashbery quickly sold the farm, throwing out many of her son's papers in the process.

> My mother was probably sort of hysterical while that was going on. I should have come over for it, but I didn't have the money and didn't want to fly. My aunt saved a few collages that I had done, and those things were all in the closet of my room. I guess she saved drafts of early poems, most of which I destroyed later. (MacArthur 192)

Helen Ashbery then moved in with her own mother in Pultneyville; she would live there until her death in 1987. From this point on, Ashbery felt deeply responsible for his mother, and his childhood landscape became further associated with sudden loss.

While he was at home on the Sodus farm for his father's funeral in 1964, Ashbery began the poem "Fragment" (*MSO* 290–305), conscious that "these were the last days I'd ever live in our house, where I'd grown up" (Ford, *John Ashbery*, 51). The poem, written in ten-line stanzas, is partly a meditation on pictures from childhood and his childhood landscape. It was published in *Poetry* in February of 1966, and included in *The Double Dream of Spring* (1970). In "Fragment"—whose title literally means a piece broken off from something that was once whole—Ashbery may contemplate the return home from "abroad," and register the loss of his father, which pushed his childhood world irretrievably into the past, as it called up memories:

> Our daily imaginings are swiftly tilted down to
> Death in its various forms. We cannot keep the peace
> At home, and at the same time be winning wars abroad.
> And the great flower of what we have been twists
> On its stem of earth, for not being
> What we are to become, fated to live in
> Intimidated solitude and isolation. No brother
> Bearing the notion of responsibility of self
> To the surrounding neighborhood lost out of being.
> (*MSO* 292)

The speaker's thoughts involuntarily turn to death, and apparently to home; the reference to the proverbial impossibility of "keep[ing] the peace / At home, and...winning wars abroad" suggests the necessity of Ashbery's return to the United States after his father's death, and perhaps the loneliness he anticipated in leaving Martory in Paris. The trope of roots, as unbreakable connections between the solitary present and the past, is emphasized here. "The surrounding neighborhood lost of being" could refer to the Sodus farm itself, after Chester Ashbery's death and the sale of the farm. Since the death of Richard Ashbery, the poet had had "[n]o brother" to help him bear family responsibilities and expectations, and the death of his father may have revived his grief for Richard.

Yet the beauty of the childhood landscape is evoked throughout the poem. The Sodus farm is perhaps among the personified farms that wait, wary of impending change, as "we," teary at times, contemplate the new isolation, and find solace in photographs from a rural childhood. The entire landscape seems suffused with the speaker's mood

> . . . . The farms
> Knew it, that is why they stood so still.
> The gold might reverse them to fields
> Of flowering sand or black, ancient and intimate.
> . . . .
> Our habits ask us for instructions.
> (*MSO* 294, 295)

It is not clear how to go on; habits, useless once an entire mode of life has changed, apparently are at a loss to help. The following passage recalls the sort of photographs Ashbery had asked his mother to send him in France, as "we" look at pictures from all four seasons:

> The pictures were really pictures
> Of loving and small things . . . .
> . . . .
> Near [autumn] was spring, a girl in green draperies
> Half sitting, half standing near the trunk of an old tree.
> Summer was a band of nondescript children
> Bordering the picture of winter, which was indistinct
> And gray like the sky of a winter afternoon.
> The other pictures told in an infinity of tiny ways
>
> Stories of the past: separate incidents
> Recounted in touching detail, or vast histories
> Murmured confusingly, as though the speaker
> Were choked by sighs and tears, and had forgotten
> The reason why he was telling the story.
> It was these finally that made the strongest

> Impression, they shook you like wind
> Roaring through branches with no leaves left on them.
> (*MSO* 295)

These "pictures" may evoke summers in Pultneyville, when Ashbery's childhood friends from Rochester would come to stay. The "old tree" and wintry gray landscapes are "nondescript," like the children, unremarkable perhaps to anyone but the speaker, who is choked up at the sight of them, almost rendered speechless by the "Stories of the past" they bring back to life. As in *Some Trees*, the tree here seems a benevolent guardian; Ashbery would later use tree-climbing, and the family tree, as elaborate tropes for growing up and for the generations of a family in "Whatever It Is, Wherever You Are." The final trope here, however, involves a simile comparing the speaker's distraught state to the leafless branches in autumn, with their deathly associations. A cold wind keeps buffeting the trees that have nothing left to lose. As in later poems, the shifting pronouns are not immediately personal; they also universalize the experience of sadly contemplating the photographs; "you," "we," "he," etc., may include the reader and the speaker both.

In "Fragment," Ashbery may also contemplate the grief of his mother. Set in relief against the landscape of the farm, a loss makes life seem not worth living:

> All space was to be shut out. Now there was no
> Earthly reason for living; solitude proceeded
> From want of money, her quincunxes standing
> To protect the stillness of the air. Darkness
> Intruded everywhere. This was the first day
> Of the new experience. The familiar brown trees
> Stirred indifferent at their roots, deeply transformed.
> . . . .
> An orchard diminishes the already tiny
> Notion of abstract good and bad qualities
> Pod of darkness which goes vociferating early
> Unchangeables that in time's mire have hid weapons.
> (*MSO* 298)

"[T]he new experience" is typically impersonal for Ashbery, a phrase onto which any reader may project his or her own transforming experience. Yet "the familiar brown trees" and "orchard" may be autobiographical, as metaphors drawn from the farm landscape, for those affected by the loss of Chester Ashbery, the farmer. The term "quincunxes" will turn up again in "A Wave," describing the arrangement of apple trees in an orchard. The "Pod of darkness," perhaps the seed of death itself at the heart of every living thing, pronounces what cannot be changed, the dangers that lurk in time; this irrevocable feeling is connected to forgetting "good and bad qualities," as one does in simply grieving the death of a beloved person.

The future will inevitably be inflected by the lost past, associated with "parental concern":

> Out of this intolerant swarm of freedom as it
> Is called in your press, the future, an open
> Structure, is rising even now, to be invaded by the present
> As the past stands to one side, dark and theoretical
> Yet most important of all....
> ....
> But a clear moonlit night in which distant
> Masses are traced with parental concern.
>
> (*MSO* 301)

Again, the sense of almost too much freedom in the present and future is opposed to the meaningful, constraining, overwhelming past.

As Ashbery continued to absorb the fact of his father's death, in the spring of 1965, he wrote the poem "Clepsydra," which announces a return to the past (*MSO* 186–193, Shoptaw 83). The sense of a manifestly present past bears on the poem, which was included in *Rivers and Mountains* (1966). A clepsydra, a water clock, was formerly used to mark the passage of time by the draining of water. "Clepsydra" is preoccupied with the feeling of time passing, which the death of Chester Ashbery made his son feel so deeply, and it prefigures water imagery related to Lake Ontario and perhaps to Ashbery's voyages to France, culminating later in *A Wave*. With elaboration of similes, here the remote and dreamlike past seems to press on the present:

> There where the tiny figures halt as darkness comes on,
> Beside some loud torrent in an empty yet personal
> Landscape, which has the further advantage of being
> What surrounds without insisting, the very breath so
> Honorably offered, and accepted in the same spirit.
> There was in fact pleasure in those high walls.
> Each moment seemed to bore back into the centuries
> For profit and manners, and an old way of looking that

Continually shaped those lips into a smile. Or it was
Like standing at the edge of a harbor early on a summer morning
With the discreet shadows cast by the water all around
And a feeling, again, of emptiness, but of richness in the way
The whole thing is organized, on what a miraculous scale,
Really what is meant by a human level....

(*MSO* 189)

In the "empty yet personal / Landscape," a retrospective look admits that "there was pleasure" in an old-fashioned and limited life (high-walled like a convent or monastery), which was also rooted and enjoyed a sense of history and tradition. A specific site in that landscape could be Pultneyville harbor, where one might stand with a sense of restrained, peaceful appreciation of the whole scene—or we might think of a New York harbor, from which Ashbery would have departed for France. A page later, the poem announces "a feeling of well-being":

But its fierceness was still acquiescence
To the nature of this goodness already past
And it was a kind of sweet acknowledgment of how
The past is yours, to keep invisible if you wish
But also to make absurd elaborations with
And in this way prolong your dance of non-discovery
In brittle, useless architecture that is nevertheless
The map of your desires, irreproachable, beyond
Madness and the toe of approaching night, if only
You desire to approach it that way.

(*MSO* 190–191)

This passage may suggest the benevolent associations Ashbery would develop with his rural childhood—as the loss of his father somehow brought its idyllic moments into relief—and the free use he would make of it in his poetry.

It seemed he had been repeating the same stupid phrase
Over and over throughout his life; meanwhile,
Infant destinies had suavely matured;....
....
                There should be an invariable balance of
Contentment to hold everything in place, ministering
To stunted memories, helping them stand alone
And return into the world, without ever looking back at
What they might have become, even though in doing so they

Might just once have been the truth that, invisible,
Still surrounds us like the air and is the dividing force
Between our slightest steps and the notes taken on them.
It is because everything is relative
That we shall never see in that sphere of pure wisdom and

Entertainment much more than groping shadows of an incomplete
Former existence so close it burns like the mouth that
Closes down over all your effort like the moment
Of death, but stays, raging and burning the design of
Its intentions into the house of your brain, until
You wake up alone, the certainty that it
Wasn't a dream your only clue to why the walls
Are turning on you and why the windows no longer speak
Of time but are themselves, transparent guardians you
Invented for what there was to hide. Which was now
Grown up, or moved away, as a jewel
Exists when there is no one to look at it, and this
Existence saps your own.

(*MSO* 192)

Here, inside "the house of your brain," awakened from a dream and looking out the windows, we seem concerned with coming to terms with the sense that the past self overwhelms the present self, indeed saps the latter's energy. But at the poem's conclusion, the present self is reconciled to the past on equal terms:

. . . . What is meant is that this distant
Image of you, the way you really are, is the test
Of how you see yourself, and regardless of whether or not
You hesitate, it may be assumed that you have won, that this
Wooden and external representation
Returns the full echo of what you meant
With nothing left over, from that circumference now alight
With ex-possibilities become present fact, and you
Must wear them like clothing, moving in the shadow of
Your single and twin existence, waking in intact
Appreciation of it, while morning is still and before the body
Is changed by the faces of evening.

(*MSO* 193)

Chester Ashbery's death, an "ex-possibilit[y] become present fact" as much as the "[i]nfant destinies" realized in Ashbery's success as a poet and art critic, had also brought Ashbery extremely "close" to his "incomplete / former existence" in childhood. Here he may echo

Wallace Stevens' poem "The Dwarf": "Now it is September and the web is woven. / The web is woven and you have to wear it. // The winter is made and you have to bear it" (ll. 1–3). "Clepsydra" concludes with an image of the self that is reminiscent of "the comic version of myself" from "The Picture of Little J.A. in a Prospect of Flowers." The past self is fiercely reasserted, as a measure for judging the present self, as he will be again in "Whatever It Is, Wherever You Are" in *A Wave*. The past is irrevocable, but manifestly present, as "Your single and twin existence" apparently conflates the adult and child self.

Other poems from *The Double Dream of Spring*, a collection that is remarkable for the frequent evocation of the rural, continue to be concerned with themes of loss, while explicitly contemplating childhood in a rural landscape. This was the first book of poems Ashbery wrote mostly after his return from France in 1965; once he returned to New York, Ashbery made regular visits to see his mother in Pultneyville. We might interpret the book's title—reflecting on de Chirico's painting of an unfinished drawing amid a realistically depicted landscape—as expressing youthful desire for a rapturous future that would involve both art and experience. Indeed, the title poem anticipates departures into the future, by "rowboat" and train and "sidewalk," to get "lost in millions of tree-analogies" that Ashbery likely gained from his childhood landscape; the exaggeration of the number of arboreal tropes registers the poet's awareness, perhaps, of the poetic wealth of his rural childhood (*MSO* 254).

The poem "Soonest Mended," which takes its title from the expression "least said, soonest mended," reminds us of Ashbery's attribution of his reticence in his poetry to his childhood upbringing, mentioned in the Introduction. Ashbery has "often called [the poem] my 'One-size-fits-all confessional poem,' which is about my youth and maturing but also about anybody else's" (Murphy 32). The famous closing lines, which provide the title for the collection of his first five books—"Making ready to forget, and always coming back / To the mooring of starting out, that day so long ago"—imply a paradox, of course (*MSO* 233). Though we prepare to forget the past, we are always returning to it, as the gesture of leaving it behind is contradicted by the figure of mooring, securing a ship or boat in a particular place; the day of "starting out" is where we are moored. For Ashbery, "starting out" could mean leaving for Cambridge, New York, and France, while he felt the opposing pull of his rural past, on the shores of Lake Ontario.

"Variations, Calypso and Fugue on a Theme of Ella Wheeler Wilcox," whose title refers to a prolific sentimental poet and songwriter of the late nineteenth and early twentieth centuries, enacts an imaginative return to the childhood landscape. The poem begins by quoting Wilcox's poem, "Wishing," which instructs the reader to "make the world better" by "scatter[ing] seeds of kindness;" Ashbery quotes the last four lines, "'For the pleasures of the many / May be ofttimes traced to one / As the hand that plants an acorn / Shelters armies from the sun'" (*MSO* 238). This is the sort of poetry that Ashbery's parents and grandparents likely appreciated far better than the poet's, and it may embody their kind of advice, to do good selflessly for others. It is shortly followed by the opening line of Schumann's *Dichterliebe*, Opus 48, after the poems of Heinrich Heine, *Im wunderschönen Monat Mai* (In the lovely month of May). Near the beginning of "Variations," the childhood landscape is tenderly evoked by a speaker who begins to doubt that the distant past, so vastly different from his present urban life, really happened:

> The feeling is of never wanting to leave the tree,
> Of predominantly peace and relaxation.
> ....
> Insecurity be damned! There is something to all this, that will not
> elude us:
> Growing up under the shade of friendly trees, with our brothers all
> around.
> And, truly, young adulthood was never like this:
> Such delight, such consideration, such affirmation in the way the
> day goes 'round together.
>
> ....
> But all good things must come to an end, and so one must move
> forward
> Into the space left by one's conclusions. Is this growing old?
> ....
> But—and this is the gist of it—what if I dreamed it all,
> The branches, the late afternoon sun,
> The trusting camaraderie, the love that watered all,
> Disappearing promptly down into the roots as it should?
> For later in the vast gloom of cities, only there you learn
> How the ideas were good only because they had to die,
> Leaving you alone and skinless, a drawing by Vesalius.
> (*MSO* 238–239)

Among the benevolent trees—figures for family—the youthful self was watered with love, basking in the sun and familial closeness; these lines may also refer to Ashbery's brother Richard and his friends from

Rochester. Such rural scenes of youth are reevaluated and newly appreciated, however, from the perspective of adult life, in "the vast gloom of cities." Here the "you" is vulnerable, stripped of "ideas" of "trusting camaraderie," somewhat like the drawings of Vesalius, the sixteenth-century artist of human anatomy, revealed the structure of muscles, tissue, and bones underlying the protective skin.

In the poem's "Calypso" section (a popular, often satirical, West Indian ballad form), a self-mocking, comic tone is taken toward nostalgia for the childhood home:

> So my youth was spent, underneath the trees
> I always moved around with perfect ease
>
> I voyaged to Paris at the age of ten
> And met many prominent literary men
>
> . . . .
>
> But of all the sights that were seen by me
> In the East or West, on land or sea,
> The best was the place that is spelled H-O-M-E.
>
> Now that once again I have achieved home
> I shall forbear all further urge to roam
>
> (*MSO* 239–240)

Ashbery had certainly not been able to "move around with perfect ease" in youth, living, against his cultural and sociable inclinations, on his father's farm. Thus the comic verses seem apt, in their tidy idealization of the past and dutiful resolution to stay home. In 1965, as we have seen, Ashbery would, in a sense, "forbear all further urge to roam" when he moved back to New York for good, out of obligation to his mother.

Perhaps "Evening in the Country" (*MSO* 247–248) grew out of one of the long weekends Ashbery spent visiting his mother in Pultneyville in the late 1960s. The speaker reconsiders a familiar rural landscape in a detached, nostalgic manner:

> Now as my questioning but admiring gaze expands
> To magnificent outposts, I am not so much at home
> With these memorabilia of vision as on a tour
> Of my remotest properties, and the eidolon
> Sinks into the effective "being" of each thing,
> Stump or shrub[.]
>
> (*MSO* 247)

The apparition or phantom of the past is becoming part of the diminished landscape, sinking in.

In *The Double Dream of Spring*, Ashbery also declares his fondness for rural poetry, in part for its obsessive nostalgia for a kind of childhood innocence. He had first started reading John Clare in the early 1950s; James Schuyler had probably introduced him to it (MacArthur 194). The short prose poem "For John Clare" (*MSO* 249–250) evokes Clare's exquisite, painful sensitivity to the phenomenal, natural world, first apprehended in childhood: "There is so much to be seen everywhere that it's like not getting used to it, only there is so much it never feels new, never any different." Clare never lost a childlike perspective, which would seem to be part of his appeal for Ashbery.

Ashbery outlined his affinities with Romantic and rural poetry more explicitly in 1989 in one of his Norton lectures. Later published as *Other Traditions* (2000), the Norton lectures are among the few pieces of literary criticism Ashbery has written on poetry in English since he was an undergraduate at Harvard. In his first lecture, Ashbery retells Clare's biography with sensitivity to the sense of loss associated with his childhood landscape. The great fact of Clare's life was his

> removal from Helpstone to the nearby village of Northborough... though his new home was only three miles from the far more primitive cottage where he had been born and raised, it was a new world for him and a strange one. The sense of loss, linked with an automatic, unreflecting joy in nature, had been the dominant note in his poetry from the beginning.... Enclosure arrived at Helpstone in 1809, in Clare's sixteenth year: after that his landscape was never the same, its fens drained, its lovely waste places deforested, ploughed, and fenced off. (*Other Traditions* 11)[15]

Ashbery admires Clare's rural poetry as "a distillation of the natural world with all its beauty and pointlessness, its salient and boring features preserved intact" (*OT* 11).[16] In his own poetry of rural landscapes, Ashbery also acknowledges the tedium of rural life as well as the beauty. The sense of loss Ashbery associates with the Sodus farm, first with his involuntary move there from Rochester, and later with the death of his brother and his father, and with the sale of the farm, also imply that "his [own native] landscape was never the same." Ashbery apparently identifies with Clare, and his poetic sensibility finally suits Ashbery better than Wordsworth's, for its refusal of transcendence:

> Unlike Wordsworth's exalted rambles in "The Prelude," there is no indication...that the result will be an enriching vision, a placing of

> man in harmonious relation to his God-created surroundings.... Clare...com[es] full circle again and again, with the same traveling companions—birds, insects, flowers, occasionally a passing ploughman or a band of gypsies, but essentially alone, mourning the loss of childhood felicity. (*OT* 17)

Making sense of his taste for both rural and highly sophisticated poetry, Ashbery comments that, "my own [poetry] has swung–on its own, I might add–always between the poles of Clare's lumpy poetry of mud and muck and [Thomas Lovell] Beddoes's perfumed and poisonous artifice" (35).

Mud is often a hint of Clare's spirit in Ashbery's later poems such as "Crazy Weather," a phrase Ashbery recalls overhearing his mother say to his grandmother when he was four or five years old, from *Houseboat Days* (1977):

> It's this crazy weather we've been having:
> ....
> You are wearing a text. The lines
> Droop to your shoelaces and I shall never want or need
> Any other literature than this poetry of mud
> And ambitious reminiscences of times when it came easily
> Through the then woods and ploughed fields and had
> A simple unconscious dignity we can never hope to
> Approximate now except in narrow ravines nobody
> Will inspect where some late sample of the rare,
> Uninteresting specimen might still be putting out shoots,
> for all we know.
>
> (*HD* 21)

A poet of "ambitious reminiscence," Ashbery himself is such a specimen, still putting out shoots from his transformed childhood landscape, though we would not call him uninteresting.

Another poem from *The Double Dream of Spring*, "Rural Objects" (*MSO* 256–258), makes an argument about the relationship between the youthful and adult self that is very similar to the earlier passage in "Variations," yet with a greater sense of attachment and obligation to the past:

> Wasn't there some way in which you too understood
> About being there in the time as it was then?
> A golden moment, full of life and health?
> Why can't this moment be enough for us as we have become?

Is it because it was mostly made up of understanding
How the future would behave when we had moved on
To other lands, other suns, to say all there is time for
Because time is just what this instant is?

. . . .

And now you are this thing that is outside me,
And how I in token of it am like you is
In place. In between are the bits of information
That circulate around you, all that ancient stuff,

Brought here, reassembled, carted off again
Into the back yard of your dream . . . .

. . . .

As you are older and in a dream touch bottom.
The laburnum darkened, denser at the deserted lake;
Mountain ash mindlessly dropping berries: to whom is all this?
I tell you, we are being called back

For having forgotten these names
For forgetting our proper names, for falling like nameless things
On unfamiliar slopes. To be seen again, churlishly into life,
Returning, as to the scene of a crime.

. . . .

The mind of our birth. It was all sad and real.

(*MSO* 256–257)

The sense of the past as a "golden moment" depended on the expectation of escape into the future—which has now become a present in which the past reasserts itself. It reemerges in the dream-life of the speaker, with details drawn from Ashbery's own childhood landscape: a dense cluster of small trees, "the deserted lake," the fertile ash tree, which is perhaps a pun on Ashbery's name and his poetic productivity (his nickname among the New York School was Ashes). The guilty speaker insists that the past, and his or our or your rural roots and family origins, reproach us for forgetting them, for settling in new places as though we had no past. There is also greater consciousness of the landscape's dreamlike nature, and of the poetic quality of these "Rural Objects." In the 1970s, Ashbery would turn his imaginative gaze more directly to his rural childhood, enacting and questioning nostalgia and embracing a rural poetics.

The poet's next book and his own favorite, the long prose work *Three Poems* (1972), initially seems to depart from such guardedly personal reminiscences. But as we have seen in earlier poems, in which shifting pronouns may include the reader and the speaker both, *Three Poems* is, in an Ashberyian manner, quite personal. It also contains some of Ashbery's most moving poetry. Ambitious to write a long work, but afraid he would have "nothing to say," Ashbery wrote the book while thinking of, at his psychoanalyst's suggestion, "various people whom I was in love with and my dead brother and my parents, and so on" (Koethe 180). *Three Poems*, the first of the poet's books dedicated to Ashbery's long-time partner David Kermani, whom he met in New York after his return from France, is full of affection that gathers around old photographs and details that may be drawn from the Sodus-Pultneyville landscape.

The first poem, "The New Spirit," promptly introduces images that seem to be of the dead, perhaps of family members standing near Lake Ontario:

> There are some old photographs which show the event. It makes sense to stand there, passing. The people who are there—few, against this side of the air. They made a sign, were making a sign.
>
> ....
>
> This is shaped in the new merging, like ancestral smiles, common memories, remembering how the light stood on the water that time. (*Three Poems*, 4, 5)[17]

Generously inclusive in its abstract impersonality, the first sentence quoted invites the reader to project his or her own experience onto the poem. Surely we all have "old photographs which show [an] event," picturing many who are now dead, and have longed to know the thoughts of the photograph's subjects. The speaker imagines that the dead ancestors may have had advice on how to live, as he will in "Whatever It Is, Wherever You Are." "The light...on the water" could be anywhere; in Ashbery's poetry, ancestors and memories are often associated with Lake Ontario, and the lakefront house in Pultneyville where he spent so much time as a child, and where his widowed mother was living when he wrote "The New Spirit." The memories seem painful too, as the speaker contemplates "all the unwanted memories" (7). A moment of revelation is brought on by "assum[ing] the idea of choosing" (8), as though a privileged child were trying to find his way among an overwhelming array of choices.

And then, a benevolent landscape opens up, a scene that recalls the fruit farms on Lake Ontario and the Land of Beulah from

The Pilgrim's Progress. It turns out to be the speaker's interior vision:

> Only then will the point of not having everything become apparent, and it will flash on you with such dexterity and such terribleness that you will wonder how you lived before—as though a valley hundreds of miles in length and full of orchards and all sorts of benevolent irregularities of landscape were suddenly to open at your feet, just as you told yourself you could not climb a step higher.
>
> ....
>
> I'm sorry–in staring too long out over this elaborate view one begins to forget that one is looking inside, taking in the familiar interior which has always been there, reciting the only alphabet one knows. (*TP* 9, 11)

The past leaves "time-inflicted lesions," yet this rural landscape has become "the only alphabet one knows," recited with a renewed sense of wonder for the same old nostalgic feelings and hopes for the future that emerge from such a "familiar interior" of memories (9). If this landscape of the past is the persistent essence of the self, it is associated with pain but it is also wonderfully sufficient, as its rich variety becomes an objective correlative, paradoxically, for "the point of not having everything." These sentences may suggest Ashbery's renewed appreciation of his childhood world, as he contemplated "[his] brother and [his] parents and so on," against the sense of limitations that he felt growing up there, when he longed to leave it for everything that was not to be found there—"movies...sex and fun," for example (*MSO* 204).

Further into the constantly renewed quest of "The New Spirit," however, the speaker chastises the self for such nostalgic retrospect: "There must be nothing resembling nostalgia for a past which in any case never existed. It is like standing up because you've been sitting all day and are tired of it" (*TP* 19). Ashbery undercuts any consolation founded on an idealized version of the past. Longing for home can falsely idealize it, as the appreciation of the past depends on the perspective of the present. But this is not the last word.

The oddly harmonious dialectic between nostalgia and mistrust of it also characterizes the second of the *Three Poems*, "The System," which begins: "The system was breaking down" (53). The "system," from the late 1960s into the present, of course, could refer to the military-industrial complex and the whole social system of inequality and repression, which must either be fixed or avoided. In "The System," " 'a house by the side of the road[,]' " as an appealing resting place, is considered and dismissed, and the questing speaker contemplates the seductive power of the past, which is likened to "the unearthly weirdness of an old photograph" (*TP* 64, 96). This quality of old photographs is associated with the ancestral dead, as in "The New Spirit," and the speaker replays the past like a movie, reciting "the only alphabet one knows":

> The sadness that infected us as children and stayed on through adulthood has healed, and there can be no other way except this way of health we are taking, silent as it is. But it lets us look back on those other, seemingly spoiled days and re-evaluate them: actually they were too well-rounded, each bore its share of happiness and grief and finished its tale just as twilight was descending; those days are now an inseparable part of our story despite their air of tentativeness and immaturity: they have the freshness of early works which may be wrongly discarded later. Nor is today really any different: we are as childish as ever, it turns out, only perhaps a little better at disguising it, but we still want what we want when we want it and no power on earth is strong enough to deny it to us.
>
> . . . .
>
> This was the message of that day in the street when you first perceived that conventional happiness would not do for you and decided to opt for the erratic kind despite the dangers that its need for continual growth and expansion exposed it to. This started you on your way, although it often seemed as though your feet had struck roots into the ground and you were doomed to grow and decay like a tree.
>
> . . . .
>
> It isn't wrong to look at things in this way—how else could we live in the present knowing it was the present except in the context of the important things that have already happened? No, one must treasure each moment of the past, get the same thrill out of it that one gets from watching each moment of an old movie.
>
> . . . .
>
> And it is here that I am quite ready to admit that I am alone, that the film I have been watching all this time may be only a mirror, with all the characters including that of the old aunt played by me in different disguises. (*TP* 99–100, 102, 105)

The "sadness that infected us as children," though again the reader may project any cause that comes to mind, may arise in Ashbery's case from the move to the Sodus farm and the loss of his brother Richard. From the present, we can "look back" on the past that seemed partly spoiled, and now recognize that there was a fullness to those days. The adult self has remained like the strong-willed child; the desire for an "erratic kind" of happiness we might read as an early rejection of, for instance, a "conventional" heterosexual lifestyle. His desires took

Ashbery far from the limited rural world of his childhood, but roots in the original past are strong, both sustaining and constraining, as such organic and arboreal metaphors, which are used as figures for the self here, remind us. The present grows out of the past. As in "Fragment," the speaker alerts us to how idealized memories have become. As the figures from the past begin to disappear, presumably dying, he must play all the roles of the dead himself to relive the past, just as all figures in a dream are supposed to be aspects of the self.[18] After the death of Chester Ashbery, and as Helen Ashbery began to sink into senility, the poet was virtually the lone member of his immediately family left.

Toward the end of the last of the *Three Poems*, "The Recital," in which the speaker recites what he has learned from his imaginative quest, he compares his retrospective attitude to that of Wordsworth in Book I of "The Prelude": "days... past / In contradiction... / with no skill to part / Vague longing, haply bred by want of power, / From paramount impulse not to be withstood, / A timorous capacity, from prudence, / From circumspection, from infinite delay" (ll. 238–242). In Wordsworth's poem, the child self has a "timorous capacity" to wait for the anticipated future, which is slightly stronger than his "vague longing." Grounded in the present in Ashbery's poem, the self faces an unpredicted future that makes him turn back toward the past: "[Now] always presents itself as the turning point, the bridge leading from prudence to 'a timorous capacity,' in Wordsworth's phrase, but the bridge is a Bridge of Sighs the next moment, leading back into the tired regions from which it sprang. It seems as though every day is arranged this way" (*TP* 115). As earlier in *Three Poems*, no "definite break with the past" seems possible short of death. How to relate to the past is the persistent question as the speaker ages—his age metaphorically suggested by the invasion of dusk into his room (116).

Moving from the somewhat abstract contemplation of the past in *Three Poems*, a number of poems from *Self-Portrait in a Convex Mirror* (1975) identify and contemplate the specific landscape that represented the past for Ashbery. Sometimes these poems include details linking them to the Sodus farm and to the family's lakeshore house in Pultneyville. In these years, Ashbery also began to entertain the idea of buying a country house in upstate New York for himself ("Guest Speaker: The Poet's Hudson River Restoration" 44).

The most familiar poem that refers to Ashbery's native region is "As You Came from the Holy Land" (*SPCM* 6–7). The poem's title is only partly ironic about the sacredness of the poet's roots, not, apparently, questioning their sacredness, but the speaker's self-importance, as he chastises the self-aggrandizing self, or "you," who has recently left home again, for imagining that something would depend on what "you" have grown up to do:

> As you came from the holy land
> of western New York state
> were the graves all right in their bushings
> . . . .
>
> you reading there so accurately
> sitting not wanting to be disturbed
> as you came from that holy land
> what other signs of earth's dependency were upon you
> what fixed sign at the crossroads
> what lethargy in the avenues
> where all is said in a whisper
> what tone of voice among the hedges
> what tone under the apple trees
> the numbered land stretches away
> and your house is built in tomorrow
> but surely not before the examination
> of what is right and will befall
> not before the census
> and the writing down of names
> remember you are free to wander away
> as from other times other scenes that were taking place
> the history of someone who came too late
> (*SPCM* 6–7)

The speaker seems to ask the self, almost accusingly: Was everything in order at home when you left? What is the state of the graves left behind there? Have you fulfilled expectations? "[A]t the crossroads" of Maple and Lake Avenues, there is a "fixed sign" for the Ashbery Farm, and the apple and cherry orchards and the plotted farmland mark the childhood landscape in which Ashbery imagined his future elsewhere; of course "fixed sign" also indicates some certain prediction of the future. As "you" left home, the speaker asks, what did you take from there? "[Y]ou" cannot avoid reckoning with the past, with its tense or secretive conversations among the hedges and apple trees. Perhaps the self is also chastised for wandering away, though "you" were free to do so, and for returning home "too late." As in *Three Poems*, the past can only be understood, however inaccurately, out of a sense of emptiness and loss, from the perspective of the present:

> out of night the token emerges
> its leaves like birds alighting all at once under a tree

taken up and shaken again
put down in weak rage
knowing as the brain does it can never come about
not here not yesterday in the past
only in the gap of today filling itself
as emptiness is distributed
in the idea of what time it is
when that time is already past

(*SPCM* 7)

The birds beneath the tree and the tree shaken "in a weak rage" recall the lonely trees left behind by "The Orioles," and the leafless tree of "Fragment," in which "stories of the past . . . shook you like wind / Roaring through branches with no leaves left on them."

Just "what time it is" in this landscape becomes slightly more evident in "Voyage in the Blue" (*SPCM* 25–27), which immediately precedes the series of "Farm," "Farm II" and "Farm III" poems in *Self-Portrait in a Convex Mirror.* Turning our attention toward rural traditions, "As on a festal day in early spring[,]" we see that the landscape has been abandoned, but is no less beloved to the speaker: "But what of / Houses, standing ruined, desolate just now: / Is this not also beautiful and wonderful? / For where a mirage has once been, life must be" (*SPCM* 25). The ruins of the houses, no longer whole yet not wholly desolate, are imagined to contain life still. Once such ruined houses embodied hopeful visions of the future, like the Ashbery farm when Chester Ashbery established it in 1915. Though the Sodus farmhouse was not a ruined house, it did become very run down at a certain point, and after Helen Ashbery sold it, it may have seemed both desolate and beautiful to Ashbery.

Ashbery's "Version of America"

In several poems from the 1970s, Ashbery generalizes about his rural past to link it with the national past, notably in "The One Thing That Can Save America" from *Self-Portrait in a Convex Mirror* (1975), "Pyrography" from *Houseboat Days* (1977), and "Litany" and "Haunted Landscape" from *As We Know* (1978). These are as close as Ashbery gets to Frost's commentary on colonial history and U.S. land policy, "The Gift Outright"—though predictably, Ashbery casts doubt on myths of American origins more directly, and approaches them more often through particularism.

The title, "The One Thing That Can Save America" (*SPCM* 44–45), is reminiscent of political speeches suggesting that America needs saving, and ridiculously half-promising that one thing could do it, but the poem is not entirely ironic. Originally published in *The New York Review of Books* on November 28, 1974 (in an issue that featured a long review-essay by Alexander Cockburn on Watergate), the poem apparently addresses itself to a slightly different question: what is central to our dispersed, postmodern America?

> Is anything central?
> The orchards flung out on the land,
> Urban forests, rustic plantations, knee-high hills?
> Are place names central?
> Elm Grove, Adcock Corner, Story Book Farm?
> As they concur with a rush at eye level
> Beating themselves into eyes which have had enough
> Thank you, no more thank you.
> And they come on like scenery mingled with darkness
> The damp plains, overgrown suburbs,
> Places of known civic pride, civic obscurity.
> These are connected to my version of America
> But the juice is elsewhere.
>
> (*SPCM* 44)

The fast-paced imagery suggests a speaker is driving through the countryside, passing signs that announce the names of obscure towns and villages, none of which is, of course, central, except to itself; every locale is a "plac[e] of known civic pride, civic obscurity." The signs, orchards and "knee-high hills" and "damp plains" could point to places such as Sodus. "These are connected to my version of America." But where is the juice of America, then?

Leading up to the question of his own "roots," the speaker then advances self-accusations of obscurity and deflects them. He hints that he may reveal sources of the private self that will make sense to the larger public, transfigured in poems that will ring out over a city:

> I know that I braid too much of my own
> Snapped-off perceptions of things as they come to me.
> They are private and always will be.
> Where then are the private turns of event
> Destined to boom later like golden chimes
> Released over a city from a highest tower?
> The quirky things that happen to me, and I tell you,
> And you instantly know what I mean?

What remote orchards reached by winding roads
Hides them? Where are these roots?
(*SPCM* 44–45)

The "roots" of this poet can, of course, be found among "remote orchards," but the poem is not sure if anything of his personal background, with its obscure rural origins, can speak to others. It is hard to remember that, when Ashbery wrote this poem, he was fairly obscure outside poetic circles, until *Self-Portrait in a Convex Mirror* won the Pulitzer Prize, The National Book Award, and The National Book Critics Circle Award in 1976. Like Frost, Ashbery had almost despaired of reaching a large readership, but persisted in writing anyway.

As "The One Thing That Can Save America" continues to wonder whether the speaker's fate can prove "exemplary," it points back to the rural American landscape as a source of common meaning and reference:

It is the lumps and trials
That tell us whether we shall be known
And whether our fate can be exemplary, like a star.
All the rest is waiting
For a letter that never arrives,
Day after day, the exasperation
Until finally you have ripped it open not knowing what it is,
. . . .
The message was wise, and seemingly
Dictated a long time ago.
Its truth is timeless, but its time has still
Not arrived, telling of danger, and the mostly limited
Steps that can be taken against danger
Now and in the future, in cool yards,
In quiet small houses in the country,
Our country, in fenced areas, in cool shady streets.
(*SPCM* 45)

In closing, the poem returns to the question of what can save America; the wise old message could be the founding documents of the nation—the Declaration of Independence, the Constitution—that speak especially to a small rural country, "In quiet small houses in the country." Such a message could express Jeffersonian ideals, which, as Frost also indicated in the closing lines of "The Gift Outright," we have failed to fully realize ("its time has still / Not arrived"), and the related idea that America's strength is in its agricultural life. Oddly enough that landscape is where this New York poet has his roots, where the speaker may find something private that he can express to a wide American audience, who will understand such rural background as a shared realm of experience.

The occasional poem "Pyrography" (*HD* 8–10), which Ashbery wrote for a traveling exhibition of American landscape painting marking the U.S. bicentennial in 1976, clearly typifies his own and the nation's history of leaving the country for the city, and having second thoughts. The title refers to "A method of wood-carving by means of heated metallic plates or cylinders in relief, by which the design is burned into the substance of the wood" (*Oxford English Dictionary*). In writing it, Ashbery said he was thinking "about [the] American landscape and my childhood and my past. And pyrography was an old-fashioned hobby even when I was a child, something that people used to do to pass the time....in the very different America that I grew up in" (MacArthur 194–195). "Pyrography" opens with the line: "Out here on Cottage Grove it matters[,]" "it" referring to the hobby of pyrography. Ashbery also explained that he was "thinking of Cottage Grove Avenue in Chicago....a long thoroughfare...[that] sort of stretches out into.... the street car suburbs, as they used to call them, the first suburbs....They were sort of co-existing with the farmland" (MacArthur 195). Though he is not sure he ever saw Cottage Grove Avenue, Ashbery recalls that a similar trolley line, which his parents used to take until it was suspended in 1929, once ran all the way from Rochester to Sodus Point, not far from his parents' farm.

"Pyrography" pictures an escape from the tedium of small towns, which nevertheless have real charms—close community, fresh air, a lovely landscape, even leisure to take up a quaint hobby like pyrography, "colloquial greetings like golden / Pollen sinking on the afternoon breeze." In the poem, the escape from the country is not a one-way journey, as some return from the cities and suburbs, hopes dashed:

> If this is the way it is let's leave,
> They agree, and soon the slow boxcar journey begins,
> Gradually accelerating until the gyrating fans of suburbs
> Enfolding the darkness of cities are remembered
> Only as a recurring tic. And midway
> We meet the disappointed, returning ones, without its
> Being able to stop us in the headlong night
> Toward the nothing of the coast.
>
> (*HD* 8)

This is partly an accelerated narration of internal migration in America, from east to west, from rural to urban and suburban areas, not only for economic reasons but out of boredom: "if this is the way it is let's leave." The journey begins by train; fans of suburbs proliferate, surround the cities and are almost forgotten, and some people return to the countryside, as others leave it for the first time. The impulse to move is irresistible, especially westward, "Toward the nothing of the coast." As Bonnie Costello notes, Ashbery is part of the "meditative tradition of landscape reverie and allegory from Dante to Stevens," but in Ashbery's landscapes, "temporality is dramatized rather than suppressed" (Costello, "John Ashbery's Landscapes" 61). That is certainly the case here, as Ashbery dramatizes internal migration, rather than meditating on a single rural scene with a pretense of rooted stability.

In "Pyrography," abandoned structures and unfinished projects are scattered all over the American landscape, attempting to civilize the country, perhaps with the European-style "ivied ruins" that Henry James missed in America. From a colonial perspective, especially in the early years of the nation, the landscape seemed unfinished, in need of development:

> The land wasn't immediately appealing; we built it
> Partly over with fake ruins in the image of ourselves:
> An arch that terminates in mid-keystone, a crumbling stone pier
> For laundresses, an open-air theater, never completed
> And only partially designed. How are we to inhabit
> This space from which the fourth wall is invariably missing,
> As in a stage-set or a dollhouse, except by staying as we are,
> In lost profile, facing the stars, with dozens of as yet
> Unrealized projects, and a strict sense
> Of time running out, of evening presenting
> The tactfully folded-over bill? And we fit
> Rather too easily into it, become transparent,
> Almost ghosts. One day
> The birds and animals in the pasture have absorbed
> The color, the density of the surroundings,
> The leaves are alive, and too heavy with life.
>
> (*HD* 9)

There is a sense here of the overwhelming size and potential of the American continent, in which individual ambitions and "Unrealized projects" are prized and easily lost; here we ourselves can get lost, "become transparent, / Almost ghosts." But gradually, the landscape, and the homes and settlements, acquired a sense of reality, a nation that can be apprehended as a coherent, if loose, totality. And then,

> A long period of adjustment followed.
> In the cities at the turn of the century they knew about it
> . . . .
> The children under the trees knew about it,
> But all the fathers returning home
> On streetcars after a satisfying day at the office undid it:
> The climate was still floral and all the wallpaper
> In a million homes all over the land conspired to hide it.
> One day we thought of painted furniture, of how
> It just slightly changes everything in the room
> And in the yard outside, and how, if we were going
> To be able to write the history of our time, starting with today,
> It would be necessary to model all these unimportant details
> . . . .
> otherwise the narrative
> Would have that flat, sandpapered look the sky gets
> Out in the middle west toward the end of the summer,
> The look of wanting to back out before the argument
> Has been resolved. . . .
>
> . . . .
> That way, maybe the feeble lakes and swamps
> Of the back country will get plugged into the circuit
> (*HD* 9)

The Whitmanian ambition "to write the history of our time" entails "model[ing] all these unimportant details" that evoke the settlement and development of the American landscape, and the vague but intense desire to strike out in a different direction. What is it that those in the cities, and the children, knew? That finally we had a history, an identity that constrained us, or that maybe there were more exciting lives going on elsewhere? "It" may be a dawning sense of national identity and history, which only arises out of these "unimportant details" of the "back country," marginal to the centers of American culture and power, literally not "plugged into the circuit" if they lacked electricity, as many rural areas did well into the twentieth century.

The end of the poem insists on the persistent significance of the rural American landscape, and predicts that our restless internal migrations will continue:

> The land
> Is pulling away from the magic, glittering coastal towns
> To an aforementioned rendezvous with August and December.
> The hunch is it will always be this way,
> . . . .
> No sighs like Russian music, only a vast unravelling
> Out toward the junctions and to the darkness beyond
> To these bare fields, built at today's expense.
>
> (*HD* 10)

"Pyrography" ends not in the cities and suburbs, where the majority of the American population moved in the twentieth century, but out in the "bare fields"—and the last line hints, like Frost's "The Gift Outright," at the destruction that created them—"built at today's expense." The "bare fields" are like those that surrounded the Ashbery fruit farm outside Sodus, where the poet, as a child, witnessed the transformation of fields into orchards. Another sense of "pyrography," in reference to firearms, may resonate here, as the craft involves wood and fire; the American landscape was cleared violently, and we now recognize the "expense" and consequences of having destroyed so much wilderness and having decimated and displaced Native American populations. The poem also leaves the unsettled reader, then, in a rural landscape that is the site of America's ideas and false ideals of its origins, to which the nation imaginatively and actually returns—restoring country homes, for instance, and trying to recover rural life.

In 1979, Ashbery bought his house in Hudson—a Victorian, built in 1894, with Richardsonian, Colonial Revival, and Queen Anne touches. The house, Ashbery said, "so strongly reminds me of my grandparents' house [in Rochester] that I must have carried with me the desire to recreate it." (In a pun on the desire of antique collectors to recreate the past, one of the larger antique shops in Hudson is called Historical Materialism.) He was pleased that "it had remained unscathed since 1894," and that "The owners apparently never threw anything away[.]" Like his grandparents' Pultneyville house, "the house had passed down through several generations, always on the female side of the family." He explained why he feels so at home there:

> Upstate New York is where I was born and raised, and though that part of it is two hundred and fifty miles west of where I am now, there is something about the land and the cadence of people's voices that

> perhaps amounts to "roots." And New York City, where I wanted to be when I was growing up and where I'm still based . . . isn't far away. So I feel I've successfully collaged two nostalgias—that of the metropolis I never knew until I was an adult and that of the country where I spent my childhood. And nostalgia, if it isn't good for anything else, seems to elicit poetry. ("The Poet's Hudson River Restoration" 36, 40, 44)

Hudson, once a whaling town populated by Nantucket families who moved inland after the American Revolution partly because they still feared British attacks, is now a rather schizophrenic town. Renowned for the flourishing antique stores on Warren Street, its outskirts are dominated by big box superstores. Its inhabitants include not only wealthy New York weekenders, artists, and writers, but also drug dealers and bored, underprivileged teenagers. In Hudson, Ashbery rediscovered the "cozy gloom" he associates with his maternal grandparents' homes, where it was "very quiet and warm, and I didn't have to be on guard from my father's explosive temper. It [the sense of nostalgia] probably has a lot to do with that, the feeling of being secure" (MacArthur 199–200).

The occasion for which Ashbery wrote "Pyrography" foregrounds the poem's concern with the history of the American landscape. We are less likely to perceive that the experimental poem, "Litany," also deals with the larger cultural relevance of abandoned or ruined houses and of rural America. "Litany" is written in two columns, with the instruction that they "are meant to be read as simultaneous but independent monologues," imitating the way we often try to listen to two conversations at once—in a bar, for instance. "Litany" appears in *As We Know* (1978),[19] whose title makes readers question what knowledge and experience we assume and share with the poet. The title "Litany" suggests a sacred community ritual that is repeated, whose words should somehow be familiar to the reader. In the poem, recurrent experiences of ennui, and frustrations in love, are expressed. Among these experiences, perhaps because of the common American preoccupation with leaving and losing and finding homes, familiar images of rural landscape are introduced, and they persist:

> *Now houses have been razed*
> *Where once fields of vegetables*
> *Stood; nothing's there*
> *That cannot truly be*
> *And was all along*
> *Yet never was for the seeing,*
> (*AWK* 17, 19, his italics)

(The italicized passages—which we may think of as one half of a conversation in which two speakers often talk over each other—appear in the right-hand column of the poem.) Land once cleared for farming has been cleared again, this time by destroying houses for an unstated reason, and thus the American landscape reveals itself as endless transformation. As in "Pyrography," decades, even centuries, of change are condensed into a few lines.

Amid such restless change, memories of relatives and ancestors are vague because some of them have, as in "Pyrography," migrated west:

> *Bells were rung*
> *For some members of the family only,*
> *These relatives like scarlet trees who infested*
> *The background but were not much more than*
> *The dust as it is seen*
> *In folds of the furniture,*
> *They were the ones who were always*
> *Pushing out toward the Pacific coast—what*
> *A time we all had of it, but all that part*
> *Is over, in a chapter*
> *That somehow passed us by. And yet, I wonder.*
> (*AWK* 27, his italics)

The vastness of the American landscape is suggested, as some relatives are nearly forgotten when they move far away. A hint of nostalgia for the era of early migration is extended in a memory that concludes the first section of "Litany":

> *Sometimes*
> *We would all sing together*
> *And at night people would take leave of each other*
> *And go into their houses, singing.*
> ....
> *A time*
> *of reading and listening to the wireless.*
> *We never should have parted, you and me.*
> (*AWK* 31, his italics)

These lines evoke something of the charm of quiet rural America in the first half of the twentieth century, the world in which Ashbery grew up.

As the poem reaches a peak of intensity in its contemplation of landscape, the voice in the left hand column (unitalicized) takes up the theme that the second speaker has emphasized. We seem to be staring at an abandoned house in a transformed landscape, toward the end of the poem's second section:

> That house
> Grew all alone in a desolate avenue
> (Avenue so shady)
> That people began to forget coming to
> Long before its present state
> Of patched-up oblivion, and even
> In those days were those who remembered back
> To what seemed a state of true freedom:
> Bopping down the valleys wild, beaks
> Tearing the invisible ear to shreds
> But was actually a rudimentary stage
> Of serfdom dating from the Silver Age.
> Now, however, that house was as it was
> Never going to be: a modest yet firmly
> Rooted pure excrescence, a spiritual
> Rubber plant:
> A grave no one wanted to visit
> Which remained popular and holy down to the present afternoon,
> Something which nobody in particular
> Was interested in, yet which mattered more
> To the earth's population in general
> Than practically anything they could think of.
> It was history just as it disappears in the
> Twilight of yesterday and before it
> Materializes today as everything that is
> Fresh, young, and strange, and almost
> Out of the house and halfway down the street—
> An index, in other words, of everything
> That is not going to and is going to happen
> To us once we forget about its progress
> And actually begin to feel better
> For having done so.
>
> (*AWK* 106, 108)

Again, in a relatively short passage, we move back and forth between almost-forgotten history and the present. The lonely house is a sort of ghost of the past, which never intended to be discarded. But its original construction is forgotten, and in its present state of ruin it is disregarded. The speaker recalls those who remembered the early days in such a landscape, before there were houses, as a time of playful, childlike innocence, perhaps of the individual and of the nation (in the reference to Blake's "piping down the valleys wild" from *Songs of Innocence*). But actually, the early years were falsely idealized, "a rudimentary stage / Of serfdom"—perhaps referring to indentured servitude and slavery in early American history. Nostalgia for earlier eras is not to be trusted.

This remote, decaying house that has apparently lasted, almost invisibly, through several phases of American history becomes a forgotten emblem of that history, and of our future; no one notices it, as indeed it is hard to pause to notice in the poem, because of the hypnotic momentum that propels a reading of "Litany." But the poem is slowed down here, by the emphatic language (and a few particularly short lines) that the speaker uses to call attention to the ruin, as Frost does in "Directive." It is a grave, idealized and sacred in the imagination, but ignored and neglected in actuality. Such abandoned dwellings ought not to be ignored, the speaker forcefully asserts; they are the material remains of history, and "[matter] more / To the earth's population in general / Than practically anything [else] they could think of."

In ranging over the American landscape, Ashbery's poems often return to this kind of scene, trying to reach the past through contemplation of an abandoned rural landscape or neglected house, once left behind but now drawing our attention. Such a ghostly scene appears in another poem from *As We Know*, "Haunted Landscape" (*AWK* 150–153). Here Ashbery seems to meditate on someone's initial hopes for starting a farm, contemplating a rural landscape haunted by those who have died or abandoned it. In Ashbery's own family history, this poem might recall the decision of the poet's paternal grandparents and father to move to the Sodus farm in 1915, where his mother joined them when she married Chester Ashbery. Yet the narrative could also describe the appeal of rural America for many people, sometimes as a retreat from the city, as it was for the Ashberys an escape from Buffalo:

> Something brought them here. It was an outcropping of peace
> In the blurred afternoon slope on which so many picnickers
> had left no trace....
> ....
>
> There were no
> People now but everywhere signs of their recent audible passage.
>
> She had preferred to sidle through the cane and he
> To hoe the land in the hope that some day they would grow happy
> Contemplating the result: so much fruitfulness. A legend.
>
> (*AWK* 150)

This could become a family legend about starting out on a farm. But as the poem continues, an assumption develops that the lifespan of any farm or human habitation is limited, as a geological sense of time, and geological forces, threaten the landscape (Ashbery studied geology with considerable interest at Harvard):

> They were thinking, too, that this was the right way to begin
> A farm that would later have to be uprooted to make way
> For the new plains and mountains that would follow after
> To be extinguished in turn as the ocean takes over
>
> Where the glacier leaves off....
> ....
>
> and now it has happened
> And we have to look at it, and have to look at it
> For the good it now possesses which has shrunk from the
> Outline surrounding it to a little heap or handful near the center.
> (*AWK* 151)

The catastrophic forces that threaten the farm are disproportionate; this is not the degree of change experienced in human time, except, perhaps, as a trope of the intense psychological effects of change. We might recall here that the Ashbery farm is on Lake Ontario, which, like the other Great Lakes, was formed by glaciers. The Lake has eaten away at the shoreline in Pultneyville over the past two hundred years; Ashbery can remember dramatic annual variations in the water level during his childhood (MacArthur 179).

An exaggerated sense of natural destruction here may also come, as I have suggested, from an extreme sense of loss, and from awareness that in the United States, farms have often been abandoned quickly and landscapes transformed drastically. Metaphorically, the accelerated geological destruction of the farm reduces the past to an isolated pile of—soil? ashes? Whatever it is, it demands our attention. Its original goodness is shrunken down and simplified, into the meager substance of memory. Later poems also describe the past as a diminished, shrunken substance.

In the remainder of "Haunted Landscape," a stranger politely tells the "you" that it is time to leave the house, but he also says "you may stay / If you wish":

> You reply that it is one and the same to you.
> It was only later, after the house had materialized elsewhere,

That you realize you forgot to ask him what form the change
would take.
But it is probably better that way. Now time and the land are
identical,

Linked forever.

(*AWK* 153)

The echoes of failed, abandoned, or unrealistic dreams ring over "[t]he phantom village" and the house, which will "materializ[e] elsewhere," perhaps in memory. Both seem to become ghosts, as the landscape becomes an enduring, reflexive emblem of the past, and "you" may continue to dwell in the idea of it; it is not clear what the response to the man's offer was, but the idea of the landscape remains even if "you" leave the actual place. Left behind, the farm is only accessible as a precious memory, as an idea and ideal of starting out. If there is any autobiographical significance here, it may be relevant that, after the Sodus farm was sold in 1965 after Chester Ashbery's death, Ashbery did not re-enter the farmhouse until a visit in the fall of 2003 (MacArthur 182). It must have been strange for the poet, visiting his mother in Pultneyville often in the 1970s and 1980s, to pass near the farm where he had grown up, which had become inaccessible to him.

The End of the Ashbery Line

As he has lost members of his family, Ashbery seems to have become ever more attached to the houses and landscapes he associates with them, in his poetry and in his own life. As his mother's health continued to decline, the world of his childhood would have felt ever more remote to Ashbery, even as he continued to visit Pultneyville. In poems from *A Wave* (1984), and in *Flow Chart* (1991), the poet creates extended elegies of a sort for his father and mother, and for his childhood landscape.

In the opening poem from *A Wave*, the beautiful "At North Farm," "Somewhere someone is traveling furiously toward you[.]" The "you" seems to inhabit "North Farm," which is paradoxically barren and fruitful:

Hardly anything grows here,
Yet the granaries are bursting with meal,
The sacks of meal piled high to the rafters.
The streams run with sweetness, fattening fish;

> Birds darken the sky. Is it enough
> that the dish of milk is set out at night,
> That we think of him sometimes,
> Sometimes and always, with mixed feelings?
> (*AW* 1)

Several interpretations arise, in addition to the more familiar point that Ashbery found his form and title for the poem in the Finnish epic *Kalevala* (Shoptaw 12). The adult self could be "traveling furiously" toward the farm and the childhood self there, who may not yet realize the poetic richness of his home. Or, a beloved may be hurrying towards "you." Or, to make a connection to the title poem, which is concerned with Ashbery's father, toward whom his son apparently had "mixed feelings," perhaps he is returning to the farm.

Ashbery wrote much of *A Wave* in his first years in the house in Hudson, which, as it reminded him powerfully of his grandparents' homes, seemed to turn his mind again to his childhood landscape. In many poems in *A Wave*, as in the title poem, "past experience matters again" (*AW* 69). The occasion for "Purists Will Object" is houses changing hands, which suggests the poet's awareness of the widespread trend in America of housing restoration, as people return to once-abandoned rural areas and small towns to find and fix up country homes: "On the day someone sells an old house / And someone else begins to add on to his" (*AW* 17). Another poem from *A Wave*, "Variation on a Noel" includes an epigraph from the Christmas carol "Noel," "...when the snow lay round about, / deep and crisp and even..." (ellipses in original); the Great Lakes region where Ashbery grew up is known as the snowbelt. This poem may point directly to the Sodus farm, situated at a country crossroads near the lake: "The twilight prayers begin to emerge on a country crossroads / Where no sea contends with the interest of the cherry trees" (*AW* 45). And "The Path to the White Moon" depicts a familiar rural scene:

> There were little farmhouses there they
> Looked like farmhouses yes without very much land
> And trees, too many trees and a mistake
> Built into each thing rather charmingly
> But once you have seen a thing you have to move on
> (*AW* 31)

In his affectionate portrayal of the diminutive houses, the speaker is charmed by their idiosyncrasies, their "too many trees," and perhaps by their attempt to look like farmhouses, with architectural idiosyncrasies, and without the land to be farms.

The effort to universalize a rural childhood landscape, with an ancestral house at the center, is embodied in one of several prose poems in *A Wave*, "Whatever It Is, Wherever You Are" (63–65). Like *Three Poems* in its fluent meditative style and Wordsworthian tenderness toward the childhood self, "Whatever It Is..." is imbued with the presence of benevolent ancestors and their homes, which Ashbery said he had in mind in writing it (MacArthur 197). The poet, as he pointed out to me, is "the end of the [Ashbery] line" (MacArthur 178). I do not know if he has ever wanted to have children, but like Bishop, Ashbery's lack of descendants may strengthen his attachment to his own childhood world, and encourage a longing to recreate it or find a comparably secure home. In "Whatever It Is..." he seems to imagine how benevolent ancestors would want their offspring to live, evoking the landscape and the atmosphere of the family homes in which he grew up:

> The cross-hatching technique which allowed our ancestors to exchange certain genetic traits for others, in order to provide their offspring with a way of life at once more variegated and more secure than their own, has just about run out of steam and has left us wondering, once more, what there is about this plush solitude that makes us think we will ever get out, or even want to.... If only we could go out back, as when we were kids, and smoke and fool around and just stay out of the way, for a little while. But that's just it—don't you see? We are "out in back." No one has ever used the front door.... When we were children it seemed that adulthood would be like climbing a tree, that there would be a view from there, breathtaking because slightly more elusive. But now we can only see down, first down through the branches and further down the surprisingly steep grass patch that slopes away from the base of the tree. It certainly is a different view, but not the one we expected. (*AW* 63)

As in many poems from *Some Trees* onward, arboreal tropes are comfortingly associated with childhood and also with the contradictions of growing up and still feeling rooted in childhood. The family tree metaphor is also elaborated in the genetic tropes that open the poem; as our ancestors' descendants enjoying a "more variegated" lifestyle, we wonder:

> What did *they* want us to do? Stand around this way, monitoring every breath, checking each impulse for the return address, wondering

> constantly about evil until necessarily we fall into a state of torpor that is probably the worst sin of all? To what purpose did they cross-hatch so effectively, so that the luminous surface that was underneath is transformed into another, also luminous but so shifting and so alive with suggestiveness that it is like quicksand, to take a step there would be to fall through the fragile net of uncertainties into the bog of certainty, otherwise known as the Slough of Despond? (*AW* 63)

As in *Three Poems*, we are touring an allegorical landscape akin to *Pilgrim's Progress*, and one sin to be avoided is certainty of our destination. The tree may recall those that Ashbery climbed, with his brother and friends, behind his grandparents' house in Pultneyville; each child imagined that his or her tree was a castle (MacArthur 184–185). Here we seem to be in the tree, looking fearfully "down" at adulthood and wondering how to proceed.

> Probably they meant for us to enjoy the things they enjoyed, like late summer evenings, and hoped that we'd find others and thank them for providing us with the wherewithal to find and enjoy them. Singing the way they did, in the old time, we can sometimes see through the tissues and tracings the genetic process has laid down between us and them. The tendrils can suggest a hand.... Yet still in the old time, in those faraway summer evenings, they must have had a word for this, or known that we would someday need one, and wished to help. (*AW* 63–64)

The effort to imaginatively connect with ancestors across the years is full of pathos. The childhood illusion that someone older can tell us *exactly* how to live is lost when we reach adulthood, just as we learn that "[n]o one has ever used the front door." The speaker imagines the ancestors' offering vague good wishes, hoping that their descendants will "enjoy...late summer evenings" and singing[20] and "whatever [else] it is" they might discover as pleasurable. Certainly Ashbery wanted to explore and pursue his own desires when he left Sodus, and he would likely have felt grateful to his parents for helping to support him in Paris, where he pursued literary, artistic and sexual interests they did not in the least understand. Yet the pleasures and freedoms of adulthood, as in earlier poems, have not trumped the beloved rural childhood.

The poem closes with a description of a photograph reminiscent of "The Picture of Little J.A. in a Prospect of Flowers":

> It must be an old photograph of you, out in the yard, looking almost afraid in the crisp, raking light that afternoons in the city held in those days, unappeased, not accepting anything from anybody. So what else

> is new? I'll tell you what is: you are accepting this now from the invisible, unknown sender, and the light that was intended, you thought, only to rake or glance is now directed full in your face, as it in fact always was.... The point is that you are accepting it and holding on to it, like love from someone you always thought you couldn't stand, and who you now recognize as a brother, an equal. Someone whose face is the same as yours in the photograph but who is someone else, all of whose thoughts and feelings are directed at you, falling like a gentle slab of light that will ultimately loosen and dissolve the crusted suspicion, the timely self-hatred, the efficient cold directness, the horrible good manners, the sensible resolves and the senseless nights spent waiting in utter abandon, that have grown up to be you in a tree with no view; and place you firmly in the good-natured circle of your ancestors' games and entertainments. (*AW* 64–65)

Here the adult self becomes a sort of ancestor-parent to the childhood self, aligning his voice with the benevolent ancestors, claiming continuity with the "faraway summer evenings" they enjoyed and addressing the same youthful self, remembering his suffering. The childhood self, in turn, was always directed toward imagining who he would grow up to be. This sense of continuity, and the surrounding familial love, seem especially poignant if we recall that Ashbery's mother was the poet's only living elder relative when he wrote "Whatever It Is..." As in "Variations, Calypso and Fugue on a Theme of Ella Wheeler Wilcox," the "you" has accepted that he is himself a branch of the family tree, unlike in "The System," in which "it often seemed as though your feet had struck roots into the ground and you were doomed to grow and decay like a tree" (*TP* 100).

In 1982, Ashbery wrote the long title poem of *A Wave* after coming close to death, when he suffered an epidural abscess in the spine, which is usually fatal. Emergency surgery saved him. He was in the hospital for seven weeks, and unable to walk for a month after that ("Letter to John Ash," March 12, 1984, Am 6.31, Houghton Library). This experience obviously sharpened his sense of his own mortality, and turned his mind to memories of his father, who had died so suddenly in 1964. Many signs of the poet's native landscape on Lake Ontario appear in "A Wave."

In writing "A Wave," Ashbery said, "I was thinking about my father, you could probably tell that from the poem, and people I knew in New York in the early fifties for some reason, and somebody I had an affair with, who shall be nameless" (MacArthur 195). This complex of emotions and situations is typical of a long Ashbery poem, into which many aspects of personal experience make their way, however indirectly. In

"A Wave," we seem to be partly in the landscape of the Sodus farm, where the Lake, which Ashbery could see from his bedroom window as a child, "was a kind of soothing presence" in the household dominated by his father's temper (Herd, "Interview" 32). The poem begins with a hint of Ashbery's illness, and a miraculous sense of survival:

> To pass through pain and not know it,
> A car door slamming in the night.
> To emerge on an invisible terrain.
>
> So the luck of speaking out
> A little too late came to be worshipped in various guises:
> . . .
> And our landscape came to be as it is today:
> Partially out of focus, some of it too near, the middle distance
> A haven of serenity and unreachable, with all kinds of nice
> People and plants waking and stretching, calling
> Attention to themselves with every artifice of which the human
> Genre is capable. And they called it our home.
> . . . .
> In the haunted house no quarter is given: in that respect
> It's very much business as usual. . . .
> . . . .
> There will be no getting away from the prospector's
> Hunch; past experience matters again; the tale will stretch on
> For miles before it is done.
>
> (*AW* 68–69)

If the landscape becomes a figure for time itself, recalling the end of "Haunted Landscape," the middle distance would seem to be somewhere in the near future, where "our home" is located, "A haven of serenity and unreachable." But we are now in the "haunted house" where we either cannot stay or hide, and where the past is making demands for our attention. The poem promises a long consideration of "past experience," with a faint echo of Frost's "Stopping by Woods on a Snowy Evening": "But I have promises to keep, / And miles to go before I sleep" (*CPPP* 207).

We might well associate the "haunted house" with the Sodus farmhouse and the house in Pultneyville. Here Ashbery's early childhood, when his father raised chickens, may flicker into focus, as we make our way into a house "deep in the country," and perhaps turn back to Rochester as well, "the city of our starting out":

> All those days had a dumb clarity that was about getting out
> Into a remembered environment. . . .
> . . . .

While awaiting further orders that must materialize soon
Whether in the sand-pit with frightened chickens running around
Or on a large table in a house deep in the country with messages
Pinned to the walls and a sense of plainness quite unlike
Any other waiting. I am prepared to deal with this
While putting together notes related to the question of love
For the many, for two people at once, and for myself
In a time of need unlike those that have arisen so far.
. . . .
Meanwhile I have turned back
Into that dream of rubble that was the city of our starting out.
No one advises me;
(*AW* 72–74)

Once we arrive in the past, what is remembered is a child's unreflective sense of well being:

We had, though, a feeling of security
But we weren't aware of it: that's
How secure we were. Now, in the dungeon of Better Living,
It seems we may be called back and interrogated about it
Which would be unfortunate, since only the absence of memory
Animates us as we walk briskly back and forth
At one with the soulless, restless crowd on the somber avenue.
(*AW* 75)

The familiarity of the past environment is comforting and simplifying here. A "feeling of being secure" is just what Ashbery identifies with old family homes (MacArthur 200). Despite the denial of memory, as in "Variations, Calypso and Fugue on a Theme of Ella Wheeler Wilcox," the past in the country is considered from the present in a city, and the great security of childhood is understood only from the perspective of adulthood among, perhaps, strangers on the streets of New York. Mockingly, amid the present adult life, with its modern conveniences, freedoms and advantages as a "dungeon of Better Living," the speaker seems to call himself back to be interrogated about the past. Of course Ashbery, who continued to visit his mother in Pultneyville in the 1980s, can be counted among those

who leave regularly
For the patchwork landscape of childhood, north of here,
. . . .

Acres of bushes, treetops;
Orchards where the quince and apple seem to come and go
Mysteriously over long periods of time; . . .
. . . .

Only the way we feel about the everything
And not the feeling itself is strange, strange to us, who live
And want to go on living under the same myopic stars we have
known
Since childhood, when, looking out a window, we saw them
And immediately liked them.

And we can get back to the raw state
Of feeling, so long deemed
Inconsequential and therefore appropriate to our later musings
About religion, about migrations. What is restored
Becomes stronger than the loss as it is remembered;
Is a new, separate life of its own.

(*AW* 76–77)

The speaker's mysterious attachment to the "raw state of feeling," the complacently secure perspective of childhood, seemingly arises from this rural landscape. That state is frankly sought out and revived, as the proper orientation toward religious questions, questions "about migrations," perhaps the transmigration of the soul after death, as well as movement from one home to another. What can be salvaged or "restored" from this perspective offers much consolation for loss—loss, perhaps, of Ashbery's father, of the whole world of childhood—as well as the poet's fresh sense of his own mortality.

The solitary speaker, eventually, returns imaginatively to the farm itself, through "A landscape stippled by frequent glacial interventions" (an apt description of the Great Lakes region and the Finger Lakes of upstate New York), and encounters the hitherto avoided "past self" on the way:

nothing is any longer a secret
And one can live alone rejoicing in this:
That the years of war are far off in the past or the future,
That memory contains everything. And you see slipping
down a hallway
The past self you decided not to have anything to do with any more
And it is a more comfortable you, dishonest perhaps,
But alive. Wanting you to know what you're losing.

(*AW* 79)

The partial consolation of memory is in its capacity to recreate the past and imagine a dialogue with it. Meeting and making peace with the past self, the present self more deeply recognizes the value of what he left behind in the childhood landscape. In a characteristic distancing gesture, the poet puts quotation marks around one of the most moving and apparently personal passages of "A Wave," as "the opposing view" that "sounds better in translation / Which is the only language you will read it in[.]" The passage may be a dreamlike encounter with Ashbery's father on the farm:

> "I was lost, but seemed to be coming home,
> Through quincunxes of apple trees, but ever
> As I drew closer, as in Zeno's paradox, the mirage
> Of home withdrew and regrouped a little farther off.
> I could see white curtains fluttering at the windows
> And in the garden under a big brass-tinted apple tree
> The old man had removed his hat and was gazing at the grass
> As though in sorrow, sorrow for what I had done.
> Realizing it was now or never, I lurched
> With one supreme last effort out of the dream
> Onto the couch-grass behind the little red-painted palings:
> I was here! But it all seemed so lonesome. I was welcomed
> Without enthusiasm. My room had been kept as it was
> But the windows were closed, there was the smell of a closed room.
> And though I have been free ever since
> To browse at will through my appetites, lingering
> Over one that seemed special, the lamplight
> Can never replace the sad light of early morning
> Of the day I left, convinced (as indeed I am today)
> Of the logic of my search, yet all unprepared
> To look into the practical aspects, the whys and wherefores,
> And so never know, eventually, whether I have accomplished
> My end, or merely returned, another leaf that falls."
>
> (*AW* 85–86)

The dream of a return home to the fruit farm, and to "the old man," perhaps his father, is so desired that the speaker "lurche[s]" to attain it. Somehow he arrives home, apparently in a dream, but the scene is lonely, though little had really changed—his "room had been kept" as a sort of timeless memorial to his departure, a sort of crypt for the past. The speaker has somehow failed or disappointed those he left behind at home, perhaps by leaving, perhaps in other ways. The "'sad light of early morning / Of the day I left'" may refer to Ashbery's departures for Deerfield, or Harvard, or New York, or France. The "'appetites'" may be his various cultural and social interests, reasons for wanting to live in New York City, the "'special'" one his homosexual desires or his poetic interests, which he could hardly pursue on the farm. Yet there is some feeling that the security, simplicity and natural beauty of this rural home could never be replaced by a freer life, as the speaker wonders whether he has "'merely returned'" to the idea of home, to die, as from the family tree, "'another leaf that falls.'" Also characteristically, the next lines attempt to undercut the "histrionics / And . . . the rigorous logic with which the enemy / Deploys his message[,]" yet the intense pathos of the quoted passage has its effect: "There is still the breached sense of your own being / To live with, to nurse back to plenitude" (*AW* 86).

The force of nostalgia here, which brings the childhood landscape to life momentarily in the present, only to lose it again, is reminiscent of Wordsworth's Book I of "The Prelude":

> need I dread from thee
> Harsh judgments, if the song be loth to quit
> Those recollected hours that have the charm
> Of visionary things, those lovely forms
> And sweet sensations that throw back our life,
> And almost make remotest infancy
> A visible scene, on which the sun is shining?
> (ll. 632–636)

Like Wordsworth, Ashbery recreates the scene of his childhood through the force of imaginative longing.

The Wordsworthian sense of loss of the childhood world is elaborated as "A Wave" continues:

> To be always articulating these preludes, there seems to be no
> Sense in it, if it is going to be perpetually five o'clock
> . . . .
> But it says more
> About us. When they finally come
> With much laborious jangling of keys to unlock your cell
> You can tell them yourself what it is,
> Who you are, and how you happened to turn out this way,
> And how they made you, for better or for worse, what you are now,
> And how you seem to be, neither humble nor proud, *frei aber einsam.*
> (*AW* 86–87)

The departure from home implied in the poem, and perhaps the loss of his father and Ashbery's own illness, have left the self "free but alone"—the German phrase, which appears first in "The Skaters," is the title of an 1853 sonata by Johannes Brahms, Robert Schumann, and Albert Dietrich (*MSO* 213). It is repeated in the face of death and loss, and if nothing else, the speaker now understands his past and how it brought him to this present. Though there is no way to recover the lightness of childhood, rehearsing "these preludes" to adulthood (showing Ashbery's awareness of his tendency to do so) proves worthwhile:

> Flares are launched out over the late disturbed landscape
> Of items written down only to be forgotten once more,
> forever this time.
> . . . .
>
> And perhaps it's too late for anything like the overhaul
> That seemed called for, earlier, but whose initiative
> Was it after all? I mean I don't mind staying here
> A little longer, sitting quietly under a tree, if all this
> Is going to clear up by itself anyway.
>
> There is no indication this will happen,
> But I don't mind. I feel at peace with the parts of myself
> That questioned this other, easygoing side, chafed it
> To a knotted rope of guesswork looming out of storms
> And darkness and proceeding on its way into nowhere
> Barely muttering.
>
> (*AW* 88–89)

Indeed, the other voice, which spoke the dream reverie of return to the farm, is revealed to be part of the self, and now, the present and past selves have been reconciled; the speaker is prepared to abide in the childhood landscape a while, contented and not hopeless, if not hopeful. In "A Wave," Ashbery indulges in Wordsworthian nostalgia as he had not since *The Double Dream of Spring*. No final resolution has been reached, but in "A Wave," as in Frost's "Directive" and to a lesser degree in Bishop's "The End of March," we come very close to transcendence of loss through meditation on the landscape of a lost home.

Three years after Ashbery published *A Wave*, in January of 1987, his mother died. This was after "slowly sinking into senility for the past 20 years, since my father died," as he wrote to a friend, John Lenton, in response to his condolences:

> It is a bit hard to he orphaned when one is approaching 60! On the other hand, the person I knew as my mother actually disappeared

> some years ago; I'm not quite certain when. In the past several years it was really painful for everybody, especially her, since she (I think) hated the way she was and didn't want to live.
>
> So it was a great relief, although unexpected: true, she was 93 but had been chronically ailing for years, so one half expected her to go on indefinitely. It happened too suddenly for me to get there: her home is about an hour by plane from New York. The nurse called me that afternoon and said I should come, and I was going the next day, but she died very quickly that evening.
>
> ("Letter to John Lenton," March 31, 1987, AM 6.24, Houghton Library)

Helen Ashbery had been living with a paid companion since 1966, and was diagnosed with Parkinson's in 1976 ("Letter to Dean Anne Ludlow," September 11, 1976, AM 6.24, Houghton Library). Her last years, as Ashbery makes clear, had been sad ones.

The poet then had the task of cleaning out and selling the house in Pultneyville, which had been in the family since it was built in 1832. He explained to Lenton in the same letter:

> I also have to sell the house and move everything out of it or sell it, so that a great deal of to-ing and fro-ing is in the works. . . . it has always belonged to some member of my family, so in a way I hate to see it go, but it now has so many sad associations for me, what with one close relative or another wasting away there and dying, that I'm just as happy to walk away from it.

Ashbery probably refers also to his beloved maternal grandparents, who had lived in the Pultneyville house when he was a child.

Almost a year after his mother died, in December of 1987, Ashbery began to write what became the longest meditative poem of his career—*Flow Chart*—partly at Trevor Winkfield's suggestion that he write a long poem about his mother (Shoptaw 302). Early on, he writes, "So my old mother has become a niche in time" (*FC* 30). Ashbery wrote most of the poem in the spring of 1988 (MacArthur 196), after he had completed the task of cleaning out the house in Pultneyville. The neglected house evoked in the poem has a creepy, mournful atmosphere, more so than the ruined, haunted, or abandoned houses that stand as beautiful remnants of the past in previous poems. Tonally, the house described in *Flow Chart* echoes the ghostliness of the farm in Frost's "Directive" and of the uninhabitable beach shack in Bishop's "The End of March." In *Flow Chart*, Ashbery directly associates the abandonment or ruin of buildings with death: "The generations collapse like floors / in a burning building, and it will all somehow be . . . *appropriate*. Er, yes" (*FC* 203, italics and ellipsis in original).

Section IV of *Flow Chart* begins with the lines, "I had / many ties to the region. And yes, life has a way of sidling on in rain-slick afternoons / like this as though nothing were amiss" (*FC* 103). The section particularly relates to the painful process, for Ashbery, of seeing the lakeshore house pass out of the family, as the speaker keeps returning to a "haunted house":

> It was the cutest darn haunted house you ever saw. . . .
> . . . .
> Inside everything was clean and neat.
> But haunted houses are like whores—there's no such thing as a nice one, no matter
> how prim they act, or how the spotted sun greets them as the warm morning is painted.
> And then such a one, some other one, would want to know why in the name of thunder
> these repairs were necessary. After all, the place looked all right. Even the bailiff
> who lived next door said so. In the event of a storm or flood, the door
> could be shut, and there was an end to it.
> . . . .
> At
> midnight the door slowly opened a crack: "Who's there?" Who wants to know?
> It would be better if you returned to whatever kingdom you came from.
> . . . .
> the clipclopping door falls silent
> again. Inside the place reeked of mildew and decay though it looked pretty tidy
> considering no one had set foot there for twenty years.
> . . . .
> Presently they began the rudimentary preparations for the raindance
> everyone knew was to follow in order for the séance to take place.
> (*FC* 111, 112)

Here a jocular tone blends with lyrical sadness, characteristic of Ashbery's modulating manner and humorous deflection of sentiment; one tone does not contradict another. Indeed there is nothing "nice" about the eerie desolation of the house, in which the sound of the door like footfalls only emphasizes its loneliness, and the very smells evoke abandonment. Even the sun cannot cheer the haunted scene.

In writing this part of *Flow Chart*, Ashbery confirmed that he "was particularly thinking of the house in Pultneyville, the back room, where I had all of my stuff, including John's Report Cards, my mother would have these labeled boxes of things of mine" (MacArthur 196). These carefully arranged materials sadly call up the past and emphasize its irretrievable nature, its missed opportunities, and the absence of the people the speaker shared it with, except as ghosts:

> signs of haste in the form of bitten fingernails
> and scribbled messages were everywhere apparent, and I have
> this thing
> I must do without knowing what it is or whether anyone
> will be helped or offended by it. Should I do it? And there,
> it was gone.
> It will never be printed on a banner in a political demonstration
> or fed to rabbits first to see whether they die, and as I live
> in a house,
> am so bound to its principles, in the corners, that coming and going
> are very much the same thing to me. . . .
> Oh,
> the good old days! If only we could have received permission to
> stay a little longer!
> But it wasn't to be. So, sadly, I changed into my plain woollen suit
> and moved off toward the crest, attitude upgraded. It was a kind
> of lumber
> room, full of boxes of papers ("John's report cards") and branches
> of artificial holly from Christmases past. It seemed the ghosts
> had taken a particular dislike to this room; it felt colder than the
> others,
> though the cold was the result of natural causes. Sunlight, however,
> warmed the sill.
> And I thought of all my lost days and how much more I could have
> done with them
> if I had known what I was doing. But does one ever? Perhaps
> it's best
> this way, and a riper, more rounded you could only be
> the product
> of so much inefficiency, hence these pear-shaped tones;
> conversely,

too much planning could have produced a meticulous but
   dry outline
of what my speech sketches in the rooms, ghost-like, like clouds
   of steam
on a day of bitter cold[.]

(*FC* 114)

At first the speaker is preoccupied with some activity, perhaps with writing the poem itself, whose effect is anticipated to be slight—of no political or scientific value, but not harmful, at least. Donning the "plain woollen suit" like a mourning costume, he readies himself for the sad task at hand. The house's former inhabitants and the poet's speech alike have become ghostly, in the desolate atmosphere that is heavy with the unchangeable past. The speaker tries not to have regrets, reasoning that if "you" wasted opportunities in the past, no other life could have made you who you are. But it is an effort to be cheerful, in the cold, ghostly isolation of the old house.

The familiar equation of a house with a grave is evident on the next page of *Flow Chart*, when we return to the refuge of a house, "the beloved home." Welcoming at first, the walls of a house threaten to close in and trap the speaker ("immured" shares a root with the French *mur* for wall):

Who, indeed, would want to know what could have been if one
   had made the slightest
exertion in another direction? So it is always a relief to come back
to the beloved home with its misted windows, its teakettle, its
   worn places on the ceiling,
for better or worse,
. . . .
                              Just as one longs for a solitary hole to call one's own,
so one is horrified at the prospect of being immured in it: that,
   at any rate,
was my take on the setup this winter.
. . . .
                                                            and there
was nothing to think about except one's bowels and the miserable
   climate.
Breakfasts were consumed; houses were put up for sale; and the
   whole sad, bad shimmer of it
charmed viewers the way a cobra is mesmerized

(*FC* 115, 116)

At first, domestic comfort transforms into a crypt, and then "one" is almost immured in the house, as the dull quotidian activities go on—evoking perhaps the quiet life that Ashbery, aging himself, sometimes leads in his house in Hudson. Sad fatigue is connected with putting up houses for sale, as though each sale might signify a death; to find any of this charming is to be creepily distracted by it, then transfixed.

As *Flow Chart* continues, the poet may then dwell on his mother and his visits to her in Pultneyville. As Helen Ashbery's mind had atrophied in later years, the following lines may refer to her sad life as an aging widow, long after she had sold her husband's farm and moved to Pultneyville:

> The orchard that was right for you has stiffened, another autumn
> is coming
> to place its hand across the sun ; geese ruffle their feathers and
> there are whitecaps on the pond
> and daybreak still eludes us. What could be the point of counting, or
> counting on anything?
> ....
> In some way the woman knew she was the pivot here, yet it was
> enough just
> being adorable in the sun. A memory of a wish would pass over, but
> it was a bird-shadow,
> giving way to frank sunlight the next moment, wholesome in its
> steady decline
> as all things that seek a way out must be—
>
> (*FC* 117–118)

The "you" no longer has any claim to the orchard, which is dead or heading into winter, as a rough wind ruffles the body of water. The "adorable" woman is only half-conscious of herself and her importance to the speaker. The "wholesome...steady decline" may reflect the poet's respect and understanding for his mother's perpetual mourning of his father's death, which sent her into a long decline.

These last few lines could almost be spoken by Helen Ashbery, as her son could visit her in her "small house," but could barely lessen her suffering, and thus found her death to be something of a relief. The last lines also seem to cast a glance at the Sodus farm; someone has stepped outside, perhaps to check on the orchard, and been told that it is still cold and the fruit is unripe.

> My fear is like a small house: you can come visit me
> but it will not go away, or will itself into an education; the bonds
>   are loosed,
> the pattern lost....
> ....
>   Go back inside;
> it's still chilly out here; the fruit is unripe, and no one knows
>   what time it is.
>
> (*FC* 119)

At moments in Section V of *Flow Chart*, the poet may reflect obliquely on a final break with his childhood, perhaps the experience of cleaning out and selling the Pultneyville house. Early the speaker announces: "All my links with a certain past were severed" (*FC* 165). Nostalgia for a former life is expressed, not at a single time appointed for it—"Old Home Week," as in Frost's "The Generations of Men"—but much of the time:

>   Not quite late-twentieth-century panic, but
>   sobering in its
> simple difference which can scarcely be demonstrated. All the people
>   we knew and the songs
> we sang are on our side, sinking imperceptibly
> along with us into Old Home Week. Except it's not. And we
>   cannot see the bottom
> of these issues; they have outgrown us; which made the eye in
>   the church shine even brighter
> when it finally opened. Meanwhile, over the scruffy skies of
>   New York, a doubt hangs
> like a jewel, a melancholy melon-color that could be the
>   correct shade of mourning
> in heaven, pitting all that we said against us.
> ....
>   every place seems as mortally insipid
> as every other place, and I've got used to living, like a toothache;
>   I can stand
> what's coming, but that doesn't mean I don't have to like it.
>
> (*FC* 173–174)

Everyone is sinking into death or nostalgia, it seems, haunted by reproachful ancestors. From the perspective of late-twentieth-century

New York, the deep attachment to the particular haunted house is strange; places have become less meaningful, even as the speaker is nostalgic for Old Home Week. As further death and loss approach, the speaker accommodates himself to them with rueful determination, a manner that persists in later poetry. He *does* "have to like" "what's coming," or learn to do so, somehow, to live on. Yet the abandoned house functions as a simile for the speaker's recurrent sadness and sense of irrelevance: "Like a home that must be abandoned quickly, whose carpets and wallpaper get that faintly distressed look, earth would go on without us" (*FC* 182). Perhaps Helen Ashbery is put to rest on the final page of the poem: "Yet once the funeral herbs were strewn there was peace of a sort" (*FC* 216).

Since *Flow Chart*, Ashbery has written no long poems of such fullness. Yet many of the shorter lyrics in recent books cast longing, intermittent glances back to the Sodus and Pultneyville landscape, with self-mocking, gloomy nostalgia. "By Forced Marches," for instance, from *Hotel Lautréamont* (1992), takes us to a native lakeshore landscape where the speaker frankly pronounces his fearful isolation:

> the prodigal returns—....
> ....
> Now the links we had left behind
> must be reassembled, since this is the land we came from.
> It is no place for the squeamish....
> ....
> I am all I have. I am afraid. I am left alone.
> ....
> And the old sense of a fullness
> is here, though only lightly sketched in.
>
> (*HL* 31–32)

It is not clear why this native land, which retains some "sense of a fullness," is not "for the squeamish"; it may call up painful memories of loss for the returning "prodigal." The touching poem "How to Continue" closes the same volume, and evokes a sort of summer resort like Pultneyville (Ashbery said at a 2006 reading that he wrote it after visiting Dingle harbor in Ireland), as though the memories themselves can sustain the reader who tries to continue through difficult times. When the resort's heyday is over, death seems imminent:

> And then one day the ship sailed away
> There were no more dreamers just sleepers
> in heavy attitudes on the dock

moving as if they knew how
. . . .
and a gale came and said
it is time to take all of you away
from the tops of the trees to the little houses
on little paths so startled

And when it became time to go
they none of them would leave without the other
for they said we are all one here
and if one of us goes the other will not go
and the wind whispered it to the stars
the people all got up to go
and looked back on love

(*HL* 156–157)

This is the end of an idyll, and as "the little houses" are threatened, everyone sticks together as they depart, perhaps for the afterlife.

In *And the Stars Were Shining* (1994), painful memories are attached to the loss of a house in "Coventry":

There was one who was put out of his house
. . . .
And now, he said, please deny there was ever a house.
But there was one and you were my mirror in it.
These lines almost convey the comfort of it,
. . . .
Just stay out in the country a lot.
You have no house.

(*ATSWS* 74, his italics)

Coventry, of course, was bombed brutally during WWII; the title suggests the pathos of that city's destroyed houses. In later books, hints of Ashbery's house in Hudson also begin to appear more often. The title poem of *And the Stars Were Shining* may refer to the Hudson house, which in 1979 Ashbery bought rather cheaply and in disrepair:

My shanty
looks okay to me now, I can live with it
if not in it,
who had the prescience—the prescience of mind
to buy a part of New York
while it was still a logo on someone's umbrella,
a rococo convict from the Laocoön tableau.

(*ATSWS* 87)

The title poignantly refers to an aria from Puccini's *Tosca*, "E lucevan le stelle," in which the painter Cavaradossi, condemned to death and imprisoned n a cell, sings his heart out for love.

In "Three Dusks" from *Can You Hear, Bird?* (1995), the isolated speaker says that "I think it's nice of me / to admire this coastline / of small houses: / .... // No one ought to know / what I was thought to know / for many years, among cherries / and without[,]" perhaps in reference to Pultneyville harbor and the Sodus fruit farm. What is worth expressing one could "whisper to a little brother" (*CYHB* 131–132). In "Tuesday Evening," the precious past becomes more and more remote, as in the late Wallace Stevens: "You see, the past / never happened. Nothing can survive long in its heady / embrace. Our memories are a simulcast / of lost conventions, already // drowning in their sleep" (*CYHB* 139).

We seem to be in the house in Hudson again in the title poem of *Wakefulness* (1998), which reminds Ashbery so much of his grandparents' houses—"Everything was spotless in the little house of our desire, / the clock ticked on and on, happy about / being apprenticed to eternity..../ Everything was as though / it had happened long ago" (*W* 3)—and in "Palindrome of Evening": "In my second house rare footage / of metempsychosis plays endlessly, like a tune / variously tooted" (*W* 6). Another poem from that volume, "The Last Romantic," may refer to Ashbery's quiet house, which faces a courtyard: "Say, I had a great / idea and now it's gone off and become useless. / So may I someday, sitting at play in my little unknown courtyard" (*W* 32). In "Bogus Inspections," the speaker pronounces, "A man is his house" (*W* 43). In "Autumn in the Long Avenue," the past and everyone who shared it have apparently died, and the speaker is urged to follow: "Once upon a time everybody was here. / Then the pellets started to go. / They move and move little, / like my brother or childhood..../ to tell you, go through, go through now, / die and formally die" (*W* 70).

Of Ashbery's recent volumes, one of the richest is *Your Name Here*, with its invitation to the reader (as in "Whatever It Is, Wherever You Are") to assume the experience of the poems as one's own. It is full of tears, and the book is dedicated to Pierre Martory, who died in 1998. Here again we may be in Hudson, in "Another Aardvark": "There was a party last night but I didn't go, / couldn't stand the ruckus, the questions / people put to you: How do you like living / in your new house? Fine. I moved there twenty-five / years ago, but it all still seems new to me" (*YNH* 112). Several poems refer to his childhood, as in "They Don't Just Go Away, Either," which evokes cozily boring winter afternoons playing cards—"games like Authors and Old Maid"—like those Ashbery spent as a child on the Sodus farm with "Father" and "Mama" (*YNH* 64). And in "The Impure," we are presented with "This gray October day // that no one could have imagined, save Mama and Papa / sitting on their porch, having doubts about the weather. / When they go inside, / it will all be over" (*YNH* 119). In "The Fortune Cookie Crumbles," the poet seems to register how persistently he has returned to his childhood as a poetic theme, when he writes: "Your past is all used up now, anyway" (*YNH* 44). This theme reappears in *Chinese Whispers* (2002), in a poem that seems to hint at preparing for death, "The Business of Falling Asleep." In the poem, an image from "Haunted Landscape" seems to return: "It's amazing how the past shrinks down to the size of your palm, forced to hold all that now." In "Lost Profile," in which "I am a Chinese monk / chasing after his temple[,]" the conclusion echoes Bishop's "The End of March": "It seems we were so happy once, just for a minute. / Then the sky got clouded" (*CW* 82–83).

Your Name Here also contains "History of My Life," an unusual declarative poem that sounds more like Louise Glück than Ashbery:

> Once upon a time there were two brothers.
> Then there was only one: myself.
>
> I grew up fast, before learning to drive,
> even. There was I: a stinking adult.
>
> I thought of developing interests
> someone might take an interest in. No soap.
>
> I became very weepy for what had seemed
> like the pleasant early years. As I aged
>
> increasingly, I also grew more charitable
> with regard to my thoughts and ideas,
>
> thinking them at least as good as the next man's.
> Then a great devouring cloud
>
> came and loitered on the horizon, drinking
> it up, for what seemed like months or years.
>
> (*YNH* 31)

The first and fourth couplets of this poem and its last three lines—referring, respectively, to his childhood and the loss of his brother, his nostalgia for an idealized childhood and youth, and the deaths and the passage of time that made the beloved past ever more remote and idealized—suggest not only a history of Ashbery's life, but some of the most persistent and moving themes of his poetry.

In *Where Shall I Wander* (2005), several poems reflect on the poet's childhood landscape and register the range of approaches to which Ashbery's poetry is susceptible. "Involuntary Description" begins:

> That his landscape could have been the one you meant,
> that it meant much to you, I never doubted,
> even at the time. How many signifiers have you?
> Good, I have two. I took my worries on the road
> for a while. When we got back little cherubs were nesting
> in the arbor, below the apple tree. We were incredulous,
> and whistled.
>
> (*WSIW* 16)

The landscape and the poem can signify a range of meanings for readers, and adorable little boys are to be found near the apple trees. In the poem "In Those Days," Ashbery seems to address his critics as they apprehend the various tones and themes of his poetry:

> We see a few feet into our future
> of shrouded lots and ditches.
> Surely that way was the long one
> to have come. Yet nobody
>
> sees anything wrong with what we're doing,
> how we came to discuss it, here, with the wind
> and the sun sometimes slanting.
> You have arrived at this step, and the way down
>
> is paralyzing, though this is the lost
> youth I remember as being okay, once.
> Got to shuffle, even if it's only the sarcasm
> of speech that gets lost, while the blessed
> sense of it bleeds through,
>
> open to all kinds of interpretations.
>
> (*WSIW* 13)

The poem suggest that many readers now accept Ashbery, and the way his poetry meditates upon process, as he returns to a perennial subject, his "lost / youth[.]" Sarcasm is sometimes lost and a sense of blessedness "bleeds through / open to all kinds of interpretations," like the inexhaustible fact of Ashbery's poetic oeuvre, as its rich variety and rapid shifts in tone so accurately mimic the experience of consciousness unfolding in time, reflecting on memory in the present, looking into the hazy future. All the same, throughout his career, moments of deepest pathos and lyric intensity often resurrect the rural landscapes of Ashbery's childhood, standing out among the equivocal, bewildered and amused tones that we already apprehend and appreciate so much. Our appreciation of Ashbery deepens, I think, when we learn to feel the significance of his "early years" and "roots" in rural America, as much as the poet himself has.

Notes

Introduction

1. See James 43, Jarrell 80, and Auden 360–361.
2. See Critchfield.
3. In 1932 and 1933, interestingly, a spike in migration to farms occurred, as some of the urban homeless and unemployed returned in desperation to the country. See *Historical Statistics of the United States* (Carter et al. 1–492).
4. Lionel Trilling famously called for a shift in perceptions of Frost in 1959: "The manifest America of Mr. Frost's poems may be pastoral; the actual America is tragic . . . when ever have people been so isolated, so lightning-blasted, so tried down and calcined by life, so reduced . . . to some last irreducible core of being" (Trilling 448, 451).
5. The Robert Frost Stone House Museum in South Shaftsbury, VT; the Robert Frost Farm in Derry and the Frost Place in Franconia, NH; and the Robert Frost Cottage at 410 Caroline Street in Key West, FL.
6. In 1905, he took up teaching, while continuing to live at the farmhouse until 1909. See Thompson, *The Early Years.*
7. While Thompson does not give a balanced portrait of Frost in his three-volume biography, some of his work is quite valuable because, as the poet's official biographer, Thompson was provided with direct access to Frost for more than twenty years. Some of the most insightful passages in the biography read like transcriptions of dictation from Frost.
8. In the promisingly titled *Abandoned New England. Landscape in the Works of Homer, Frost, Hopper, Wyeth and Bishop* (2003), Priscilla Paton does not discuss the abandoned house in her chapter on Frost. In a later chapter, aptly titled "The Vernacular Ruin and the Ghost of Self-Reliance," she touches briefly on "The Black Cottage" and "Directive."
9. The house belonged to Marshall Merriam, "who owned almost all of the land which later became the Frost farm[.]" After a fire destroyed this house, Merriam moved back from the turnpike and built another there. See Lesley Frost Francis, Notes I, 19, 4–5.
10. John Ashbery, *Flow Chart,* hereafter cited as *FC.*
11. Many authors preceded Frost in touring rural New England, including Hawthorne, Emerson, Thoreau, and the Fireside Poets, among others. See Brown 41—74, and Kilcup.

12. Roger Gilbert concludes *Walks in the World. Representation and Experience in Modern American Poetry* (1991) with an analysis of the guided walk to the cellar hole of an abandoned house in "Directive."
13. In an early guidebook, *Little Journeys to the Homes of Good Men and Great* (1895), Elbert Hubbard guides the reader to the homes of twelve authors, including Dove Cottage, where Wordsworth lived from 1799 to 1808. Just as Frost's homes have become tourist sites that idealize the poet's life as settled, Dove Cottage is idealized as Wordsworth's long-time rural retreat.
14. See Sayer.
15. The poem "In the Home Stretch," from *Mountain Interval* (1916), apparently describes Frost's frequent experience of moving with his wife.
16. Helen Vendler and others have considered the ambivalent relation to domesticity evident in Bishop's poetry, and various critics, including biographer Brett Millier, have noted "the poet's lifelong preoccupation with places of refuge, shelters, and solitary retreats" (Millier 492). See Vendler, "Domestication," Bromwich, Goldensohn, Laskin, and McCabe.
17. Thomas Travisano argues that Frost is an important model for Bishop, Lowell, and Jarrell in *Midcentury Quartet*. Roger Gilbert suggests that, for Roethke, Bishop, Penn Warren, and Lowell, "Frost provided . . . the clearest paradigm for the poetic fusion of experience and wisdom" (Gilbert 149).
18. She seemed, perhaps jocularly, to fear his influence on "The Fish" in 1940. In 1953 she called him a "malicious old bore," though in 1959 she gleefully quoted a catty remark he made about a fellow poet (Bishop, *One Art. Letters* 276, 378; this will be cited hereafter as *OA*).
19. Three drafts of the poem exist. See Bishop 66.10 and 73.9 in the Elizabeth Bishop Papers, Vassar Special Collections Library, as well as the version in *Edgar Allan Poe & the Juke Box*, hereafter referred to as *EAP*.
20. See von Hallberg.
21. "Foreign-Domestic" and "Gypsophilia," published in *EAP*, also seem to evoke the atmosphere at Samambaia.
22. See Axelrod.
23. Not long before deciding to sell the Ouro Prêto house in 1972, Bishop wrote, "I get homesick for O.P. but know that soon after I get there I'll be bogged down in housekeeping and maintenance, and also dying of isolation and boredom and finding it hard to work—this is what seems to happen there" (*OA* 555).
24. The label was coined in 1961 by the curator John Myers, who ran the Tibor de Naghy gallery and generously brought out the first chapbooks by these poets (John Ashbery, Frank O'Hara, Kenneth Koch, and James Schuyler). He wanted to capitalize on their friendship with

the New York School of Painters, the Abstract Expressionists. Ashbery in particular resists the label, because he lived in France for most of the decade (1955–1965) considered the heyday of the New York School of Poets (Lehman 20).

25. O'Hara and Koch were the most devoted New Yorkers. Schuyler, as Vendler calls him in *Soul Says. On Recent Poetry*, is "New York Pastoral." For all four poets (including Ashbery), country retreats—in Long Island, upstate New York, and New England—have probably been as important in their work as New York City.
26. See Gangel. Because Ashbery has generously given so many interviews, I cite them by the last name of the interviewer.
27. *A Wave*, hereafter referred to as *AW.*
28. This point seemed rather obvious to Ashbery, when I asked: "Do you think that nostalgia for the country can be representative for American readers? It's just so common in your poetry, but your poetry isn't very autobiographical. I wonder if you think that your readers will automatically have a feeling for that." He answered, "Well, yes, I suppose so. . . . the American landscape is certainly common to our American experience" (MacArthur 199).
29. Sentiment is often read only as ironic cliché in Ashbery, as Andrew Ross puts it: "the cliché of sentiment *and* the ironic knowledge of its contrived articulation" (176).
30. *Houseboat Days*, hereafter cited as *HD.*

1 Robert Frost: "The Ruined Cottage" in America

1. See Frost, *The Collected Poems, Prose & Plays,* hereafter cited as *CPPP,* 16, 341. Lesley Frost is quoted in the New Hampshire State Parks pamphlet, "Robert Frost Farm," available at the farmhouse in Derry.
2. Peter Giles reminds us that "Frost was always older than one thinks: although he has become closely identified with the twentieth century, his intellectual roots lay further back" (713). See Thompson, *Early Years,* for Frost's early literary tastes, especially Chapters 25 and 28 for texts the poet taught before he went to England, including Milton's *Comus* and Yeats's *Cathleen ni Houliban.*
3. Hereafter I refer to these letters as *LRFLU.*
4. I counted up the number of Frost's homes, until his move to Derry, noted in Thompson's biography. In later years, he became an almost itinerant lecturer and reader at times, and rented homes frequently in New England and Florida.
5. The White Mountains had long been a literary tourist attraction when Frost discovered them; Brown notes the growth of health tourism there for sufferers of "maladies like hay fever and consumption" (41–74, 146).

6. In his lecture on the poet at Cornell University in 1950, Frost recited a number of poems from memory. See "A Tribute to Wordsworth."
7. The other two were "The Death of the Hired Man" and "The Housekeeper."
8. The title "refers to the repeated phrase in Genesis 'These are the generations of men[,]'" as Robert Faggen observes; Frost's poem ironizes any sense of providential genealogy (*Robert Frost and the Challenge of Darwin*, 237).
9. Perhaps Frost had in mind the Old Man of the Mountain, a profile in granite in Franconia Notch, a tourist attraction since at least 1830. "[W]hen the face showed signs of crumbling in the late 1920s, the state [of New Hampshire]...had its rocks bolted and chained in place" (Brown 68). Despite these efforts, the profile crumbled in a rockslide in 2003.
10. I tend to see Frost's relationship to early female New England poets, including Dickinson and Robinson, as suggested in this poem, more affirmatively than Karen Kilcup. See Kilcup 159–163.
11. *Harper's Magazine* 7.12 (December 1920).
12. Major articles included "The Future of Industrial Man" by Peter Drucker, "Axis Prose" by Gilbert Highest, "The War and the Humanities" by Stuart Gerry Brown, "The War and the Future" by Helen Hill, and "Remaking Europe" by Joseph Reither (*The Virginia Quarterly Review* 18.2 [Spring 1942]).
13. Many thanks to Faggen for sharing this recent unpublished research.
14. See also Thompson, *Later Years* 84, and Porter.
15. Even in the otherwise laudatory *Homage to Robert Frost* (1996), Nobel Laureate Derek Walcott reiterates the standard reading of "The Gift Outright," and also points out an apparently egregious racist statement made by Frost in a 1934 letter to his daughter on modernism (*CPPP* 735–736). Frost certainly overlooks the malicious racism of the source he read on Stein in repeating it; his point, however, is that the source did not expect Stein to make much sense—it is "a thing that can be reported without malice" toward Stein, not toward blacks.
16. See Jeff Westover's thoughtful discussion of "The Vanishing Red," "Genealogical," "A Cabin in the Clearing," and "The Gift Outright." See also a dialogue from Frost's Notebook 34—titled "What is your attitude toward our having robbed the Indians of the American Continent?"—which I discuss in my review of the *Notebooks*, "Talking Points." Frost wrote, "The first poem I ever wrote, La Noche Triste still extant deals would shows where my sympathies lie and so also would several later" (*NBRF* 564).
17. "Letter to the Amherst Student," published in the *Amherst Student* newspaper on March 25, 1935, was almost certainly written in Key West. See *NBRF* 388, *CPPP* 739–740.

18. I have retained Faggen's use of ampersands to indicate words written above lines.
19. Critics of FERA's activities in Key West were also alarmed at perceived corruption; "the *Sarasota Tribune* mockingly called for a 'regular department of NCER—Night Club Emergency Relief,' in reference to the revelation that Stone had made FERA money available to two Key West nightclubs" (Boulard 124).
20. *The Virginia Quarterly Review* 22:1 (Winter 1946).
21. See Robert Faggen, "Frost and the Question of Pastoral" 68–69; Lentricchia 34; Parker 192–193; and Richardson 238–239.
22. Frost's descendants also cherished the memory of Derry. See *New Hampshire's Child. The Derry Journals of Lesley Frost* (1969), and Lesley Lee Francis, *The Frost's Family Adventure in Poetry. Sheer Morning Gladness at the Brim* (1994).
23. As Parker notes, "'ladder road' is a Vermont idiom for country road" (189).
24. See Poirier 83.

2 Elizabeth Bishop: Incarnations of the "Crypto-Dream-House"

1. These epigraphs are taken from Elizabeth Bishop, *The Complete Prose*, 171–172 (cited as *CPr* in the text); *The Complete Poems: 1927–1979*, 34, 112, 178, 179 (cited as *CP*); and *Edgar Allan Poe & the Juke-Box. Uncollected Poems, Drafts and Fragments*, 166 (cited as *EAP*).
2. William T. Bishop died at the age of thirty-nine of Bright's Disease. He was then "vice-president of his father's highly successful contracting firm, the J.W. Bishop Company, builders of such noted Boston Landmarks as the Public Library, the Museum of Fine Arts, and the old Charlestown jail." His own father had grown up on a farm on Prince Edward Island; his mother was a Massachusetts native (Millier 2–3).
3. Bishop's mother grew up in Great Village, Nova Scotia. The Boomers had had farms in New York state, and, as Tories during the Revolutionary War, received land grants in Nova Scotia from George III, where they had a tannery and did small-scale farming. As sailors, some of the family traveled widely, and three great-uncles went to India as Baptist missionaries. For their honeymoon in 1907, William and Gertrude Bishop visited Jamaica and Panama before settling in Worcester (Millier 2–3).
4. In 1964, Bishop wrote to Anne Stevenson, "Like most poets, I have a really morbid total recall of certain periods and I could go on for hours—but I won't!" ("Answers to your questions of March 6th," Elizabeth Bishop Papers, Washington University Libraries, Department of Special Collections).

5. Perhaps the title of the Hopkins poem reminded Bishop of the portraits of her mother and her uncle Arthur, which hung in the parlor in Great Village and which her aunt Grace sent to her in Brazil in 1957 (*OA* 349).
6. This light bulb attracted large moths, which Bishop closely observed and described in this piece; she may have drawn on "Reminiscences" in composing her poem "The Man-Moth."
7. Joanne Feit Diehl has made a similar argument about the narrator's "attentiveness to the external world" in Bishop's autobiographical story "In the Village" (Diehl 105).
8. For other references to Hansel and Gretel in Bishop's notebooks, see Alice Quinn's notes to "A lovely finish I have seen" and to *Three Poems* (*EAP* 249–250, 253–254).
9. I owe this insight to Alice Quinn.
10. On the symbolist and surrealist in Bishop, see, for instance, the insightful work of Mark Ford, in *Poetry and the Sense of Panic*, and Richard Mullen, "Elizabeth Bishop's Surrealist Inheritance."
11. Recent innovative work revisits the relationship between modernist aesthetics and the political climate of the 1930s, notably Michael Szalay's *New Deal Modernism*. Bishop is unfortunately absent from this study.
12. See "Mechanics of Pretence: Remarks on W.H. Auden" (*EAP* 183–185), and Costello, "A Whole Climate of Opinion: Auden's Influence on Bishop."
13. She wrote to her friend T.C. Wilson, a poet, critic, and committed communist, in March 1938: "I have just seen Muriel [Rukeyser]'s Silicosis poem in 'Life and Letters' and I think it's awful" (qtd. in Javadizadeh 13).
14. Longenbach notes that it was "reprinted in *The Magazine* (beside work by William Carlos Williams and Janet Lewis) the following year" (470).
15. In the 1930s, schemes for the redistribution of wealth were seriously discussed. See McElvaine 207.
16. Other hints of homosexual license appear in the story. The use of a male narrator, sometimes with a suggestion of homosexuality, occurs often in Bishop's prose and poetry; e.g., "In Prison" and "Crusoe in England." In her notebook in the 1930s, Bishop wrote: "The chief trouble with writing novels, etc., about homosexuals seems to be the difficulty of handling the pronouns: One always runs into things like, 'He took him in his arms & he..' etc." (Bishop 77A).
17. See also Mullen.
18. My article, "'In a Room': Elizabeth Bishop in Europe, 1935–37," appears in *Texas Studies in Literature and Language* 50.4 (Winter 2008).
19. In the summer of 1934, fresh out of Vassar, Bishop was charmed by her Thoreauvian landlord on Cuttyhunk Island who "wanted to 'simplify

life' all the time" and by the "'Robinson Crusoe atmosphere; making this do for that, and contriving and inventing.... A poem should be made about making things in a pinch–& how sad it looks when the emergency is over'" (qtd. in Millier 62–63). Bishop would explore these ideas most obviously in her late poem "Crusoe in England."

20. The poem was originally titled "José's House," and it is possible that the final name refers to the Jeronymites, hermits affiliated with St. Jerome; Bishop was fascinated with hermits and isolated characters. Jerónimo, however, is obviously not a hermit.
21. Many thanks to Steinshouer for permission to cite her unpublished paper, "Bishop and Place: Florida."
22. Millier believes that "It Is Marvellous to Wake Up Together" is about Stevens (*EAP* 44). During their relationship of five years, Bishop continued to spend some of her time in New York. When she split up with Stevens, Bishop stayed with Pauline Hemingway for a few months in Key West and later stayed in rented rooms around town. Like Frost with his respiratory problems, Bishop also frequently traveled because of her asthma (Millier 165, 195, 180, 75).
23. The European travels Wordsworth recounts in his narrative poem "Descriptive Sketches" are also only loosely related, though unlike Bishop he tries to connect them with pastoral and political reflections.
24. Bishop eventually published the poem as a children's book (Travisano 162).
25. Travisano also links the burglar to "the American gangster films of the thirties, in which a deadly outlaw emerges as the inevitable product of a flawed society" (163).
26. It is impossible to reproduce the disorganized arrangement of lines exactly here, but I try to match it closely.

3 John Ashbery: The Farm on the Lake at the End of the Mind

1. *The Mooring of Starting Out: The First Five Books of Poetry*, 27, 238–239; *Self-Portrait in a Convex Mirror*, 35; *A Wave*, 76, 85; and *Your Name Here*, 31. Hereafter these books will be cited as *MSO*, *SPCM*, *AW*, and *YNH*.
2. Good general accounts of Ashbery's youth appear in David Lehman's *The Last Avant-Garde*, 120–130, and in the book-length interview *John Ashbery in Conversation with Mark Ford*.
3. As a sign near the little Pultneyville harbor remarks, "The sophisticated architectural styles [in the area] reflect the prosperity of this Great Lakes shipping port."
4. This piece on Bradley Walker Tomlin was revised slightly and published in *Reported Sightings*, 191–194.

5. See *MSO* 27, 178, 288, 378; *SPCM* 6; *AW* 45; *FC* 116; *HL* 50, 134; *CYHB* 121: *YNH* 107, 117; *CW* 44, 51; *WSIW* 16.
6. Ashbery once dreamt that he was "changing [his] major from English to Comparative Religions," a reminder, perhaps, of the spiritual aspect of his poetry; he has attended Episcopalian church as an adult ("Dreams," July 4, 1947, AM 6.31, Houghton Library).
7. His senior thesis, "The Poetic Medium of W.H. Auden," would earn him the honor of graduating Cum Laude in 1949 (AM 6.31, Houghton Library).
8. At the time Ashbery was reading *Huckleberry Finn* "for the first time. It's actually quite good, besides laying down the lines along which American closeted homophilia would evolve for the next century"
9. In a 1997 piece on Frederic Church's fantastic estate, Olana, not far from Ashbery's own house in Hudson, the poet also evinces great feeling for the American landscape and especially the Hudson River Valley, and sounds almost nostalgic for Manifest Destiny's spiritual relationship to landscape, if not for its politics:

   > Those were the years [the antebellum nineteenth century] of Manifest Destiny, when the lush, sparsely peopled landscapes of America were taken as a sign of God's special benevolence toward the fledgling nation and as a symbol of the spiritual and material blessings about to fall like manna on its people....
   >
   > Olana still raises its proud, but not haughty, bulk high above the admittedly grander spectacle of the great river that inspired Church and his fellow artists, in the halcyon days when nature could still be read as a message of hope set down in God's cursive, unwavering hand. ("Frederic Church at Olana" 62, 64, 68)

10. Ashbery praises Symons' "most brilliant inspiration [that] prompted him to include" a famous passage from Keats that "I think...almost sums up the romantic movement in England," and that Ashbery obviously identifies with: " 'A poet is the most unpoetical of anything in existence, because he has no identity; he is continually infor[ming], and filling, some other body. The sun, the moon, the sea, and men and women, who are creatures of impulse are poetical, and have about them an unchangeable attribute, the poet has none, no identity....' " ("College Paper: Arthur Symons' 'The Romantic Movement in English Poetry,' " Undated, AM 6.31, Houghton Library).
11. "College Paper: Nature Imagery in the Poetry of Vaughan and Marvell" (Undated, AM 6.31, Houghton Library).
12. His first book, *Turandot and Other Poems*, was published by the Tibor de Naghy Gallery in 1953, with illustrations by Jane Freilicher. All but two of these poems appeared in *Some Trees*.
13. "Hotel Dauphin," also from *Some Trees*, would seem to refer to a young heir; the bored, precocious Ashbery started studying French at a young age, and liked to escape to his grandparents' house near the

Pultneyville harbor: "Winter boats // Are visible in the harbor. A child writes / 'La pluie' " (*MSO* 38).

14. This quotation is taken from the slightly longer, unpublished version of my 2003 interview with Ashbery.
15. *Other Traditions*, hereafter cited as *OT*.
16. Angus Fletcher offers new insights into Clare's appeal for Ashbery in *A New Theory for American Poetry*.
17. "Three Poems," hereafter cited as *TP*.
18. At Deerfield, Ashbery played an aunt in a performance of "Arsenic and Old Lace," with great success ("Letter from Frank Boyden to Chester Ashbery," January 3, 1944, AM 6.25, Houghton Library).
19. *As We Know*, hereafter cited as *AWK*.
20. During my interview with Ashbery, he sang some lyrics from "Love's Old Sweet Song," which he quotes in *Flow Chart* and said it was "The sort of thing you would find in your grandmother's piano bench" (MacArthur 196).

Bibliography

Adorno, Theodor. *Minima Moralia. Reflections from Damaged Life.* New York: Verso, 2000.

Agamben, Giorgo. *Homo Sacer. Sovereign Power and Bare Life.* Trans. Daniel Heller-Roazen. Palo Alto: Stanford UP, 1998.

Allison, Alexander W., ed. *The Norton Anthology of Poetry.* 3rd edition. New York: W.W. Norton, 1983.

Altieri, Charles. *Self and Sensibility in Contemporary American Poetry.* New York: Cambridge UP, 1984.

Ashbery, John. *And the Stars Were Shining.* New York: Farrar, Straus and Giroux, 1994.

———. *As We Know.* New York: Viking, 1979.

———. *Can You Hear, Bird?* New York: Farrar, Straus and Giroux, 1995.

———. *Chinese Whispers.* New York: Farrar, Straus and Giroux, 2002.

———. "Craft Interview." By Janet Bloom and Robert Losada. *The Craft of Poetry: Interviews from the New York Quarterly.* Ed. William Packard. Garden City: Doubleday, 1974: 11–33.

———. "The Experience of Experience: A Conversation with John Ashbery." By A. Poulin. *Michigan Quarterly Review* 20:3 (Summer 1981): 232–255.

———. *Flow Chart.* New York: Knopf, 1991.

———. "Frederic Church at Olana. An Artist's Fantasy on the Hudson River." *Architectural Digest* (June 1997): 60–68.

———. *Hotel Lautréamont.* New York: Knopf, 1992.

———. *Houseboat Days.* New York: Viking, 1977.

———. "How to Be a Difficult Poet." An Interview with John Ashbery. By Richard Kostelanetz. *The New York Times Magazine.* May 23, 1976: 18–33.

———. Interview. By Sue Gangel. *American Poetry Observed: Poets on Their Work.* Joe David Bellamy, ed. Urbana: U Illinois P, 1984: 9–20.

———. Interview with Brian Appleyard. *The London Sunday Times* June 16, 1985: 44A.

———. Interview with David Herd. *PN Review* 99: 22.1 (September–October 1994): 32–37.

———. An Interview by John Koethe. *Sub-Stance* 37/38 (1983): 178–186.

———. An Interview by Ross Labrie. *The American Poetry Review* (May/June 1984): 29–33.

———. Interview by Marit MacArthur. *LIT* 12 (Spring 2007): 177–200.

Ashbery, John. An Interview with John Murphy. *Poetry Review* 75:2 (August 1985): 20–25.

———. Interview by Peter A. Stitt. "The Art of Poetry No. 33." *The Paris Review* 90 (Winter 1983): 30–60.

———. *John Ashbery in Conversation with Mark Ford.* Chester Springs: Dufour Editions, 2003.

———. *Other Traditions.* Cambridge, MA: Harvard UP, 2000.

———. Papers, ca. 1927–1987. Houghton Library. Harvard University. Cambridge, MA.

———. "The Poet's Hudson River Restoration." *Architectural Digest.* June 1994: 36–44.

———. "A Reminiscence." *Homage to Frank O'Hara.* Berkeley: Creative Arts Book, 1980: 20–22.

———. *Reported Sightings: Art Chronicles 1957–1987.* Cambridge, MA: Harvard UP, 1991.

———. *Rivers and Mountains.* New York: Holt, Rinehart and Winston, 1966.

———. *Selected Prose.* Ed. Eugene Richie. Ann Arbor: U of Michigan P, 2004.

———. *Self-Portrait in a Convex Mirror.* New York: Penguin, 1976.

———. *Three Poems.* New York: Ecco, 1972.

———. *A Wave.* New York: Viking, 1984.

———. *Where Shall I Wander.* New York: Ecco, 2005.

———. *Your Name Here.* New York: Farrar, Straus and Giroux, 2000.

Auden, W.H. *The Dyer's Hand and Other Essays.* New York: Random House, 1962.

Axelrod, Steven Gould. "Elizabeth Bishop: Nova Scotia in Brazil." *Papers on Language & Literature* 37:3 (Summer 2001): 279–292.

Bachelard, Gaston. *The Poetics of Space.* New York: Orion, 1964.

Bishop, Elizabeth. *The Collected Prose.* Ed. Robert Giroux. New York: Farrar, Straus and Giroux, 1984.

———. *The Complete Poems: 1927–1979.* New York: Farrar, Straus and Giroux/Noonday, 1983.

———. *Edgar Allan Poe & the Juke-Box. Uncollected Poems, Drafts and Fragments.* Ed. Alice Quinn. New York: Farrar, Straus and Giroux, 2006.

———. Elizabeth Bishop Papers. Vassar College Special Collections Library. Vassar College. Poughkeepsie, NY.

———. Elizabeth Bishop Papers. Washington University in St. Louis. St. Louis, Missouri.

———. *North & South.* Boston: Houghton Mifflin, 1946.

———. *One Art. Letters. Elizabeth Bishop.* Ed. Robert Giroux. New York: Farrar, Straus and Giroux, 1994.

Bishop, Elizabeth and Editors. *Brazil.* New York: Time-Life Books: 1967.

Bloom, Harold, ed. *John Ashbery. Modern Critical Views.* New York: Chelsea House, 1985.

———, ed. *Elizabeth Bishop. Modern Critical Views.* New York: Chelsea House, 1985.

———, ed. *Robert Frost. Modern Critical Views.* New York: Chelsea House, 1986.

Boulard, Garry. "'State of Emergency': Key West in the Great Depression." *Hope Restored. How the New Deal Worked in Town and Country.* Ed. Bernard Sternsher. Chicago: Ivan R. Dee, 1999: 115–130.

Brendon, Piers. *The Dark Valley. A Panorama of the 1930s.* London: Jonathan Cape, 2000.

Bromwich, David. "Elizabeth Bishop's Dream-Houses." *Elizabeth Bishop. Modern Critical Views.* New York: Chelsea House, 1985: 159–173.

Brose, Eric Dorne. *A History of Europe in the Twentieth Century.* New York: Oxford UP, 2005.

Brower, Reuben. *The Poetry of Robert Frost.* New York: Oxford UP, 1963.

Brown, Ashley. "An Interview with Elizabeth Bishop." *Elizabeth Bishop and Her Art.* Ed. Lloyd Schwartz and Sybil P. Estess. Ann Arbor: U of Michigan P, 1983: 289–302.

Brown, Dee. *Bury My Heart at Wounded Knee.* New York: Owl Books/ Henry Holt, 2001.

Brown, Dona. *Inventing New England. Regional Tourism in the Nineteenth Century.* Washington, DC: Smithsonian, 1995.

Buell, Lawrence. "Frost as a New England Poet." *The Cambridge Companion to Robert Frost.* Ed. Robert Faggen. New York: Cambridge UP, 2001.

Carter, Susan B., Scott Sigmund Gartner, Michael R. Haines, Alan L. Olmstead, Richard Sutch, Gavin Wright, eds. *Historical Statistics of the United States. Earliest Times to the Present.* Millennial edition. Vol. 1. Part A. Population. New York: Cambridge UP, 2006.

Crase, Douglas. "The Prophetic Ashbery." *Beyond Amazement.* Ed. David Lehman. Ithaca: Cornell UP, 1980: 32–65.

Crawford, Robert. *Identifying Poets: Self and Territory in Twentieth Century Poetry.* Edinburgh: Edinburgh UP, 1993.

Critchfield, Richard. *The Villagers. Changed Values, Altered Lives: The Closing of the Urban-Rural Gap.* New York: Anchor, 1994.

Conrat, Maisie and Conrat, Richard. *American Farm.* San Francisco/ Boston: California Historical Society/Houghton Mifflin, 1977.

Costello, Bonnie. *Elizabeth Bishop. Questions of Mastery.* Cambridge, MA: Harvard UP, 1991.

———. "John Ashbery's Landscapes." *The Tribe of John: Ashbery and Contemporary Poetry.* Ed. Susan M. Schultz. Tuscaloosa: U of Alabama, 1995.

———. "A Whole Climate of Opinion: Auden's Influence on Bishop." *Literary Imagination* 5:1 (2003): 19–41.

Cramer, Jeffrey S. *Robert Frost among His Poems: A Literary Companion to the Poet's Own Biographical Contexts and Associations.* Jefferson: McFarland, 1996.

D'Emilio, John and Estelle B. Freedman. *Intimate Matters. A History of Sexuality in America.* 2nd edition. Chicago: U of Chicago P, 1997.

Diehl, Joanne Feit. *Elizabeth Bishop and Marianne Moore: The Psychodynamics of Creativity.* Princeton: Princeton UP, 1993.

Erkkila, Betsy. "Elizabeth Bishop, Modernism, and the Left." *American Literary History* 8:2 (1996): 284–310.

Faggen, Robert. *Robert Frost and the Challenge of Darwin.* Ann Arbor: U of Michigan P, 1997.

———. "Frost and the Question of Pastoral." *The Cambridge Companion to Robert Frost.* Ed. Robert Faggen. New York: Cambridge UP, 2001.

Floyd, Margaret H. *Robert Frost Homestead. Derry, New Hampshire. Architectural-Historical Analysis.* February 15, 1972. Rauner Special Collections Library. Dartmouth College. Hanover, NH.

Fletcher, Angus. *A New Theory for American Poetry: Democracy, the Environment, and the Future of Imagination.* Cambridge, MA: Harvard UP, 2004.

Foss, Christopher F., ed. *The Encyclopedia of Tanks and Armored Fighting Vehicles. A Comprehensive Guide to over 900 Armored Fighting Vehicles from 1915 to the Present Day.* San Diego: Thunder Bay Press, 2002.

Francis, Lesley Lee. *The Frost Family Adventure in Poetry. Sheer Morning Gladness at the Brim.* Columbia: U of Missouri P, 1994.

Frost, Lesley. *New Hampshire's Child. The Derry Journals of Lesley Frost.* Albany: State U of New York P, 1969.

Frost, Robert. *Collected Poems, Prose, & Plays.* New York: Library of America, 1995.

———. *Interviews with Robert Frost.* Ed. Edward Connery Lathem. New York: Holt, Rinehart & Winston, 1966.

———. *The Letters of Robert Frost to Louis Untermeyer.* New York: Holt, Rinehart & Winston, 1963.

———. *The Notebooks of Robert Frost.* Ed. Robert Faggen. Cambridge, MA: Belknap/Harvard UP, 2006.

———. *Selected Letters of Robert Frost.* Ed. Lawrance Thompson. New York: Holt, Rinehart, & Winston, 1964.

———. "A Tribute to Wordsworth." *The Cornell Library Journal* 11 (Spring 1970): 77–99.

Gilbert, Roger. *Walks in the World. Representation and Experience in Modern American Poetry.* Princeton: Princeton UP, 1991.

Giles, Peter. "From Decadent Aesthetics to Political Fetishism: The 'Oracle Effect' of Robert Frost's Poetry." *American Literary History* 12:4 (2000): 713–744.

Goldensohn, Lorrie. *Elizabeth Bishop. The Biography of a Poetry.* New York: Columbia UP, 1992.

Hall, Michael C. and Dieter K. Müller, eds. *Tourism, Mobility and Second Homes. Between Elite Landscape and Common Ground.* Clevedon: Channel View, 2004.

Harrison, Robert Pogue. *The Dominion of the Dead.* Chicago: U of Chicago P, 2003.

Harrison, Victoria. *Elizabeth Bishop's Poetics of Intimacy.* New York: Cambridge UP, 1993.

Hartman, Geoffrey. "Romantic Poetry and the Genius Loci." *Beyond Formalism. Literary Essays 1958–1970.* New Haven: Yale UP, 1970: 311–336.

———. *The Unremarkable Wordsworth.* Minneapolis: U of Minnesota P, 1987.

Herd, David. *John Ashbery and American Poetry.* New York: Palgrave Macmillan, 2001.

Herring, Robert and Petrie Townsend, eds. "Notes on contributors from United Kingdom Dominions, United States, Irish Free State, Union Soviet Socialist Republics, France, Austria, Greece, India, China, Japan, Palestine, Iceland, Scandinavia, Switzerland, Etc., etc." *Life and Letters To-Day.* 1936. Harry Ransom Center. University of Texas, Austin.

Hoffman, Frederick J., Charles Allen, and Carolyn F. Ulrich. *The Little Magazine. A History and a Bibliography.* Princeton: Princeton UP, 1946.

"The Homestead Act." National Park Service. <http://www.nps.gov/home/homestead_act.html>

Hopkins, Gerard Manley. *Poems and Prose of Gerard Manley Hopkins.* Ed. W.H. Gardner. Baltimore: Penguin Books, 1963.

Hubbard, Elbert. *Little Journeys to the Homes of Good Men and Great.* New York: Putman, 1895.

James, Henry. *Hawthorne.* New York: Harper & Brothers, 1879.

Jarrell, Randall. *No Other Book. Selected Essays.* Ed. Brad Leithauser. New York: HarperCollins, 1999.

Javadizadeh, Kamran. "Elizabeth Bishop. Letters to T.C. Wilson." *The Yale Review* 93:4 (October 2004): 20–50.

Kalstone, David. *Becoming a Poet. Elizabeth Bishop with Marianne Moore and Robert Lowell.* New York: Farrar, Straus and Giroux, 1989.

Kelly, Lionel, ed. *Poetry and the Sense of Panic. Critical Essays on Elizabeth Bishop and John Ashbery.* Atlanta: Rodopi, 2000.

Kilcup, Karen. *Robert Frost and Feminine Literary Tradition.* Ann Arbor: U of Michigan P, 1998.

Kniffen, Fred, and Glassie, Henry. "Building in Wood in the Eastern United States: A Time-Place Perspective." *Geographical Review* 56:1 (1966): 40–66.

Kolody, Annette. *The Lay of the Land: Metaphor As Experience and History in American Life and Letters.* Chapel Hill: U of North Carolina P, 1975.

Laskin, David. "Another Inscrutable House." *A Common Life. Four Generations of American Literary Friendship and Influence.* New York: Simon & Schuster, 1994: 334–344.

Lehman, David. *The Last Avant-Garde. The Making of the New York School of Poets.* New York: Doubleday, 1998.

Lentricchia, Frank. *Robert Frost. Modern Poetics and the Landscapes of the Self.* Durham: Duke UP, 1975.

Levinson, Marjorie. *Wordsworth's Great Period Poems: Four Essays.* New York: Cambridge UP, 1986.

Longenbach, James. "Elizabeth Bishop's Social Conscience." *ELH* 62:2 (1995): 467–486.

Lowell, Robert. *Collected Prose.* Ed. Robert Giroux. New York: Farrar, Straus and Giroux, 1987.

MacArthur, Marit. "Talking Points." Rev. of *The Notebooks of Robert Frost. The Yale Review* 95:4 (October 2007): 141–153.

Mathews, Jane De Hart. "Arts and the People: The New Deal Quest for Cultural Democracy." *The Journal of American History* 62:2 (September 1975) 316–339.

McCabe, Susan. *Elizabeth Bishop. Her Poetics of Loss.* University Park: Pennsylvania State UP, 1994.

McCannell, Dean. *The Tourist. A New Theory of the Leisure Class.* Berkeley: U of California P, 1999.

McElvaine, Robert S. *The Great Depression. America, 1929–1941.* New York: NY Times Books, 1984.

Mertins, Louis. *Robert Frost. Life and Talks-Walking.* Norman: U of Oklahoma P, 1965.

Meyers, Jeffrey. *Robert Frost: A Biography.* Boston: Houghton Mifflin, 1996.

Millier, Brett C. *Elizabeth Bishop. Life and the Memory of It.* Berkeley: U of California P, 1993.

Mullen, Richard. "Elizabeth Bishop's Surrealist Inheritance." *American Literature* 54:1 (1982): 663–680.

Nash, Roderick Frazier. *Wilderness and the American Mind.* 4th edition. New Haven: Yale UP, 2001.

Ogle, Maureen. *Key West. History of an Island of Dreams.* Gainesville: U of Florida P, 2003.

Pandiani, John A. "The Crime Control Corps: An Invisible New Deal Program." *The British Journal of Sociology*, 33:3 (September 1982): 348–358.

Parini, Jay. *Robert Frost. A Life.* New York: Henry Holt, 1999.

Parker, Blanford. "Frost and the Meditative Lyric." *The Cambridge Companion to Robert Frost.*

Paton, Priscilla. *Abandoned New England. Landscape in the Works of Homer, Frost, Hopper, Wyeth and Bishop.* Hanover: U Press of New England, 2003.

Perloff, Marjorie. *The Poetics of Indeterminancy: Rimbaud to Cage.* Princeton: Princeton UP, 1981.

Poirier, Richard. *Robert Frost. The Work of Knowing.* New York: Oxford UP, 1977.

Porter, Jeane. *Key West: Conch Smiles.* Tampa: Mancorp, 1999.

Quinn, Alice. An Interview with Meghan O'Rourke. *The Believer* (March 2006).

Richardson, Mark. "Frost and Poetic Choice." *The Cambridge Companion to Robert Frost.*

"Robert Frost Farm. Home of Robert Frost 1900–1911." National Historic Landmark. Route 28. Pamphlet. Derry, New Hampshire: New Hampshire State Parks, 1998.

Roman, Camille. *Elizabeth Bishop's World War II—Cold War View.* New York: Palgrave Macmillan, 2001.

Ross, Andrew. *The Failure of Modernism. Symptoms of American Poetry.* New York: Columbia UP, 1986.

Rotella, Guy. "'Synonymous with Kept': Frost and Economics." *The Cambridge Companion to Robert Frost.*

Sayer, Karen. *Country Cottages. A Cultural History.* New York: Manchester UP, 2000.

Schuyler, James. *Just the Thing. Selected Letters of James Schuyler. 1951–1991.* Ed. William Corbett. New York: Turtle Point, 2004.

Shetley, Vernon Lionel. *After the Death of Poetry: Poet and Audience in Contemporary America.* Durham: Duke UP, 1993.

Shoptaw, John. *On the Outside Looking Out: John Ashbery's Poetry.* Cambridge, MA: Harvard UP, 1994.

Steinshouer, Betty Jean. "Bishop and Place: Florida." Unpublished. Delivered at the American Literature Association Conference. May 24, 2006. San Francisco.

Stevenson, Anne. *Elizabeth Bishop.* New York: Twayne, 1966.

Szalay, Michael. *New Deal Modernism: American Literature and the Invention of the Welfare State.* Durham: Duke UP, 2001.

Thompson, Lawrance. *Robert Frost. The Early Years 1874–1915.* New York: Holt, Rinehart & Winston, 1966.

———. *Robert Frost. The Years of Triumph 1915–1938.* New York: Holt, Rinehart & Winston, 1970.

Thompson, Lawrance and Winnick, R.H. *Robert Frost. The Later Years. 1938–1963.* New York: Holt, Rinehart & Winston, 1976.

Thoreau, Henry David. *Walden and Civil Disobedience.* New York: Penguin, 1986.

Travisano, Thomas J. *Midcentury Quartet: Bishop, Lowell, Jarrell, Berryman, and the Making of a Postmodern Aesthetic.* Charlottesville: UP of Virginia, 1999.

Trilling, Lionel. "A Speech on Robert Frost: A Cultural Episode." *Partisan Review* 26 (1959): 445–452.

U.S. Census Bureau. *Report of the Population of the U.S. at the Eleventh Census, 1890.* Part I. Washington, DC: Government Printing Office, 1895.

———. *Seventh Census of the U.S. 1850*, Vol. I. Washington, DC: Robert Armstrong Public Printer, 1853.

———. *Statistics of the Population of the U.S., Tenth Census, 1880*, Vol. I. Washington, DC: Government Printing Office, 1883.

U.S. Census Bureau. "Urban and Rural, Table (4), United States Population: 1790–1990." Accessed April 16, 2003. <http://landview.census.gov/population/censusdata/table-4.pdf>

Vendler, Helen. "Domestication, Domesticity, and the Otherworldly." *Elizabeth Bishop. Modern Critical Views.* New York: Chelsea House, 1985: 83–96.

———. *Soul Says. On Recent Poetry.* Cambridge, MA: Belknap/Harvard UP, 1995.

———. "Understanding Ashbery." *John Ashbery. Modern Critical Views.* Ed. Harold Bloom. New York: Chelsea House, 1985: 179–194.

von Hallberg, Robert. *American Poetry and Culture 1945–1960.* Cambridge, MA: Harvard UP, 1985.

Walsh, John Evangelist. *Into My Own. The English Years of Robert Frost.* New York: Grove Weidenfeld, 1988.

Watson, Nicola J. *The Literary Tourist: Readers and Places in Romantic and Victorian Britain.* Basingstoke: Palgrave Macmillan, 2006.

Weber, Eugen. *The Hollow Years. France in the 1930s.* New York: W.W. Norton, 1994.

Westover, Jeff. "National Forgetting and Remembering in the Poetry of Robert Frost." *Texas Studies in Literature and Language* 46:2 (Summer 2004): 214–242.

White, Edmund. *My Lives. A Memoir.* New York: Harper Perennial, 2006.

Williamson, Alan. *Introspection and Contemporary Poetry.* Cambridge, MA: Harvard UP, 1984.

Wordsworth, William. *William Wordsworth. Selected Poetry.* Ed. Mark Van Doren. New York: Modern Library, 1950.

Yates, Timothy. Unpublished E-mail Communication. May 25, 2004.

Acknowledgments

Many people have encouraged and helped me with this book in various ways, great and small, since it began as a short paper on Frost in 2000. I am extremely grateful to Alan Williamson, David Simpson, Sandra M. Gilbert, Joanne Feit Diehl, Dave Cerf, Charles Altieri, Catherine Robson, Kari Lokke, John Ashbery, Ivy Schweitzer, my mother, Rachel Buxton, Ann Mikkelsen, Lisa Sperber, Michael Sperber, Bonnie Costello, Robert Faggen, Paul Muldoon, Alice Quinn, David Kermani, Michael Ziser, Claire Waters, Kacper Bartczak, Christa Wells, Terry Nugent, Melisa Stark and Megan Manning. I am also deeply in debt to biographical work on these poets, particularly Lawrance Thompson's *Robert Frost. The Early Years 1874–1915*, *Robert Frost. The Years of Triumph 1915–1938*, and *Robert Frost. The Later Years. 1938–1963;* to Jay Parini's *Robert Frost. A Life;* to Brett C. Millier's *Elizabeth Bishop. Life and the Memory of It*; and to David Lehman's *The Last Avant-Garde. The Making of the New York School of Poets.* In my research, I benefited from the assistance of Dean M. Rogers, Special Collections, Vassar College Library; the staff of the Houghton Library, Harvard University; and from humanities reference librarians Roberto Delgadillo and Diana King, Shields Library, the University of California, Davis. A Dissertation Quarter Fellowship and a Summer Research Fellowship from UC Davis, and grants from the Research Council of the University and the Teaching and Learning Center at California State University, Bakersfield, provided me with time and resources to travel, do research, present my work, revise the manuscript and employ research assistants. I would especially like to thank Linda Wagner-Martin for recommending the book for publication, and Farideh Koohi-Kamali, Julia Cohen, and Brigitte Shull at Palgrave Macmillan for guiding me through the production process. Finally, many thanks to my dear husband, Greg Miller, for his invaluable editing and immeasurable devotion and encouragement.

Reprinted by permission of Georges Borchardt, Inc., on behalf of John Ashbery:

Excerpts from John Ashbery, "Frederic Church at Olana. An Artist's Fantasy on the Hudson River," *Architectural Digest* (June 1997): 60–68;

Excerpts from "The Poet's Hudson River Restoration," *Architectural Digest* (June 1994): 36–44;

Excerpts from unpublished letters by John Ashbery to Elizabeth Bishop, Elizabeth Bishop Papers, Vassar College Library;

Excerpts from various interviews with John Ashbery.

Reprinted by permission of Georges Borchardt, Inc., and by Carcanet Press Limited, on behalf of John Ashbery:

Excerpts from *And the Stars Were Shining*, *As We Know*, *Can You Hear, Bird?*, *Chinese Whispers*, *The Double Dream of Spring*, *Flow Chart*, *Houseboat Days*, *Hotel Lautréamont*, *Rivers and Mountains*, *Some Trees*, *Three Poems*, *Wakefulness*, and *A Wave*, by John Ashbery. Copyright © 1994, 1979, 1995, 2002, 1966, 1970, 1997, 1991, 1975, 1977, 1992, 1962, 1966, 1997, 1956, 1997, 1970, 1971, 1972, 1997, 1988, 1999, 1984 by John Ashbery.

Excerpts from the John Ashbery Papers, ca. 1927–1987, AM 6, reprinted by permission of the Houghton Library, Harvard University, and by Georges Borchardt, Inc., on behalf of John Ashbery.

Excerpts from "As You Came from the Holy Land," copyright © 1973 by John Ashbery, "Farm," "The One Thing That Can Save America," copyright © 1975 by John Ashbery, "Voyage in the Blue," copyright © 1972 by John Ashbery, from *Self-Portrait in a Convex Mirror* by John Ashbery, copyright © 1972, 1973, 1974, 1975 by John Ashbery. Used by permission of Viking Penguin, a division of Penguin Group (USA) Inc., and by permission of Carcanet Press Limited.

Excerpts from *Selected Prose* by John Ashbery reprinted by permission of University of Michigan Press and by Georges Borchardt, Inc., on behalf of John Ashbery. Copyright © 2004 by John Ashbery.

Excerpt from "They Dream Only of America" in *The Tennis Court Oath* © 1962 by John Ashbery reprinted by permission of Wesleyan University Press.

Excerpts reprinted by permission of the publisher and Georges Borchardt, Inc., from *Other Traditions* by John Ashbery, pp. 11, 17, 35, Cambridge, Mass.: Harvard University Press, Copyright © 2000 by John Ashbery.

Excerpts from *Where Shall I Wander* Copyright © 2005 by John Ashbery reprinted by permission of HarperCollins and by Georges Borchardt, Inc., on behalf of the author.

Excerpts from unpublished manuscripts and letters by Elizabeth Bishop, Elizabeth Bishop Papers, Vassar College Library, reprinted by permission of Farrar Straus Giroux, LLC, on behalf of the Estate of Elizabeth Bishop. Copyright ® 2007 by Alice Helen Methfessel.

Reprinted by permission of Farrar, Straus and Giroux, LLC:

Excerpts from *The Complete Poems 1927–1979* by Elizabeth Bishop. Copyright © 1984 by Alice Helen Methfessel.

Excerpts from *Edgar Allan Poe & the Juke-Box. Uncollected Poems, Drafts and Fragments*, by Elizabeth Bishop, edited by Alice Quinn. Copyright © 2006 by Alice Methfessel.

Excerpts from *One Art* by Elizabeth Bishop, selected and edited by Robert Giroux. Copyright © 1984 by Alice Methfessel.

Reprinted by permission of The Estate of Elizabeth Bishop:

Excerpts from "Answers to Your Questions of March 6th," Elizabeth Bishop Papers, Washington University Libraries, Department of Special Collections.

Reprinted by permission of The Estate of Robert Lee Frost:

Excerpts from *The Letters of Robert Frost to Louis Untermeyer*; *The Selected Letters of Robert Frost*, Ed. Lawrance Thompson;

Excerpts from Lesley Lee Francis, *The Frost Family Adventure in Poetry. Sheer Morning Gladness at the Brim*. Copyright © 1963, 1964, 1994, The Estate of Robert Lee Frost and Copyright © 1967, 1970 by Lesley Frost Ballantine;

Excerpts from *Interviews with Robert Frost,* edited by Edward Connery Lathem. Copyright © 1966 by Lesley Frost Ballantine.

Excerpts reprinted by permission of the publisher and by The Estate of Robert Lee Frost from *The Notebooks of Robert Frost*, edited by Robert Faggen, pp. 324, 328, 393, Cambridge, MA: Belknap Press of Harvard University Press, Copyright © 2006 by The Estate of Robert Lee Frost.

Excerpts from "Directive," "The Gift Outright," "The Census-Taker," "The Need of Being Versed in Country Things," and "A Fountain, a Bottle, a Donkey's Ears and Some Books" from *The Poetry of Robert Frost* edited by Edward Connery Lathem. Copyright © 1923, 1947, 1969 by Henry Holt and Company, copyright © 1975 by Lesley Frost Ballantine, copyright © 1951 by Robert Frost. Reprinted by permission of Henry Holt and Company, LLC, and the Estate of Robert Lee Frost.

Excerpt from "Letter from Kenneth Koch to John Ashbery," undated, 1959, the John Ashbery Papers, ca. 1927–1987, AM 6, reprinted by permission of the Houghton Library, Harvard University and by permission of the Kenneth Koch Literary Estate.

A small portion of this work appeared originally in *The Yale Review* as "Talking Points," *The Yale Review* 95.4 (October 2007): 141–153.

Index

CPSIA information can be obtained at www.ICGtesting.com
Printed in the USA
LVOW10*2258230314

378541LV00008B/65/P